Lecture Notes in Computer Scie

T0237993

Commenced Publication in 1973
Founding and Former Series Editors:
Gerhard Goos, Juris Hartmanis, and Jan van Leeuwen

Dieter Hutter   Markus Ullmann (Eds.)

Security in Pervasive Computing

Second International Conference, SPC 2005
Boppard, Germany, April 6-8, 2005
Proceedings

Volume Editors

Dieter Hutter
German Research Center for Artificial Intelligence (DFKI GmbH)
Stuhlsatzenhausweg 3, 66123 Saarbrücken, Germany
E-mail: hutter@dfki.de

Markus Ullmann
Federal Office for Information Security (BSI)
Godesberger Allee 185-189, 53175 Bonn, Germany
E-mail: markus.ullmann@bsi.bund.de

Library of Congress Control Number: 2005922931

CR Subject Classification (1998): C.2, D.2, D.4.6, H.5, K.4.1, K.4.4, K.6.5, H.4

ISSN   0302-9743
ISBN-10   3-540-25521-4 Springer Berlin Heidelberg New York
ISBN-13   978-3-540-25521-5 Springer Berlin Heidelberg New York

Springer is a part of Springer Science+Business Media

springeronline.com

© Springer-Verlag Berlin Heidelberg 2005
Printed in Germany

Typesetting: Camera-ready by author, data conversion by Scientific Publishing Services, Chennai, India
Printed on acid-free paper   SPIN: 11414360   06/3142   5 4 3 2 1 0

Preface

This volume contains the papers presented at the 2nd International Conference on Security in Pervasive Computing (SPC 2005) held April 6–8, 2005 in Boppard, Germany. The objective of this second conference was to develop new security concepts for complex application scenarios based on systems like handhelds, phones, smartcards, RFID-chips and smart labels hand in hand with the emerging technology of ubiquitous and pervasive computing. In particular the conference focused on methods and technologies concerning the identification of risks, the definition of security policies, and the development of security and privacy measures, especially cryptographic protocols that are related to specific aspects of ubiquitous and pervasive computing like mobility, location-based services, ad hoc networking, resource allocation/restriction, invisibility, and secure hardware/software platforms.

We received 48 submissions. Each submission was reviewed by three independent reviewers and an electronic Program Committee meeting was held via the Internet. We are very grateful to the Program Committee members for their efficiency in processing the work and also for the quality of their reviews and discussions. Finally the Program Committee decided to accept 14 long papers and 3 short papers.

Apart from the Program Committee, we would like to thank also the other persons who contributed to the success of this conference: the additional referees for reviewing the papers, the authors for submitting the papers, and the local organizers, and in particular Hans-Peter Wagner, for the local organization of the conference in Boppard. SPC-2005 was hosted by the Bundesakademie für öffentliche Verwaltung of the Federal Ministry of the Interior, and was sponsored by the DFKI and BSI.

April 2005   Dieter Hutter and Markus Ullmann

Organization

SPC 2005 was organized by the German Research Center for Artificial Intelligence (DFKI GmbH) in Saarbrücken and the German Federal Office for Information Security (BSI) in Bonn.

Executive Committee

Program Co-chairs   Dieter Hutter (DFKI GmbH, Germany)
                                  Markus Ullmann (BSI, Germany)
Local Arrangements   Hans-Peter Wagner (BSI, Germany)

Program Committee

N. Asokan	Nokia Research
Michael Beigl	University of Karlsruhe, Germany
Sonja Buchegger	EPFL-IC-LCA, Switzerland
Dieter Hutter	DFKI Saarbrücken, Germany
Ari Juels	RSA Lab, USA
Paul Karger	IBM Center Watson Research T.J., USA
Dennis Kuegler	BSI, Bonn, Germany
Catherine Meadows	Naval Research Lab, USA
Takashi Moriyasu	Hitachi Ltd., Japan
Guenter Müller	University of Freiburg, Germany
Panos Papadimitratos	Cornell University, USA
Joachim Posegga	University of Hamburg, Germany
Yves Roudier	Institut Eurecom, France
Andrei Serjantov	The Free Haven Project, UK
Frank Stajano	Cambridge University, UK
Werner Stephan	DFKI Saarbrücken, Germany
Seiji Tomita	NTT Information Platform Laboratories, Japan
Markus Ullmann	BSI, Bonn, Germany

Invited Speakers

Lorenz M. Hilty	Swiss Federal Lab for Material Testing
Panos Papadimitratos	Cornell University, USA
Dennis Kuegler	BSI, Bonn, Germany
Frederic Thiesse	University of St. Gallen
Claudia Eckert	TH Darmstadt and FhG Darmstadt

Additional Referees

D. Balfanz	A. Hohl	G. Rock
L. Buttyan	H. Kelter	E. Rukzio
L. Cheikhrouhou	F. Koob	D. Schreckling
N. Courtois	R. Monroy	H. Schwigon
G. Durfee	A. Nonnengart	J. Seedorf
D. Forsberg	K. Nyberg	J. Suomalainen
M. Gilliot	C. Partridge	C. Wieschebrink
E. Gun Sirer	H.C. Poehls	S. Wohlgemuth

Sponsoring Institutions

Deutsches Forschungszentrum für Künstliche Intelligenz GmbH DFKI, Saarbrücken, Germany
Federal Office for Information Security, Germany.

Table of Contents

Session 6: Privacy and Anonymity

Session 7: Access Control and Information Flow

Pervasive Computing - A Case for the Precautionary Principle?

Lorenz M. Hilty

Technology and Society Laboratory,
Swiss Federal Laboratories for Materials Testing and Research, EMPA,
Lerchenfeldstrasse 5, CH-9014 St Gallen, Switzerland
`lorenz.hilty@empa.ch`

The Precautionary Principle aims to anticipate and minimize potentially serious or irreversible risks under conditions of uncertainty. It has been incorporated into many international treaties and pieces of national legislation for environmental protection and sustainable development. However the precautionary principle has not yet been applied systematically to novel Information and Communication Technologies (ICTs).

The results of EMPA's four-year research program "Sustainability in the Information Society" (`www.empa.ch/sis`), co-funded by the ETH board, suggest that precaution is necessary in the ICT field and show how the general principle of precaution can be put in concrete terms in the context of the information society. In particular, we advocate precautionary measures directed towards pervasive applications of ICTs (Pervasive Computing) because of their large potential impacts on society [3, 7].

Assessing a technological vision before it has materialized makes it necessary to deal with two types of uncertainty: first, the uncertainty of how fast and to which extent the technology will be taken up and how it will be used; second, the uncertainty of causal models connecting technology- related causes with potential social, health or environmental effects. Due to these uncertainties, *quantitative* methods to evaluate expected risks are inadequate. Instead, we developed a "risk filter" that makes it possible to rank risks according to a set of *qualitative* criteria based on the Precautionary Principle and on the principle of Sustainable Development [4].

The following potential negativ impacts of Pervasive Computing on society were identified: restriction of consumers' and patients' freedom of choice, stress caused by time-rebound effects and by unreliable technology, a 'dissipation' of responsibility in computer-controlled environments, and threats to ecological sustainability caused by a new type of electronic waste [6]. It is indisputable that ICT plays an necessary role in tackling the most difficult challenge facing global society today – Sustainable Development [1, 5]. In particular, Pervasive Computing offers great opportunities to society, but we will only be able to exploit this potential if we minimize the risks it brings about at an early stage of development. Since RFID technology is one of the forerunners of Pervasive Computing, and as such is expected to play an important role in daily life in the near future [2, 6], it will be used as an example to illustrate our approach.

D. Hutter and M. Ullmann (Eds.): SPC 2005, LNCS 3450, pp. 1–2, 2005.

References

1. Arnfalk, P.; Erdmann, L.; Goodman, J.; Hilty, L. M. (2004): The future impact of ICT on environmental sustainability. *EU-US Scientific Seminar on New Technology Foresight, Forecasting & Assessment Methods*, 13-14 May 2004, Seville, Spain
2. BSI (Hrsg., 2004): *Risiken und Chancen des Einsatzes von RFID-Systemen. Trends und Entwicklungen in Technologien, Anwendungen und Sicherheit.* Bonn: Bundesamt fr Sicherheit in der Informationstechnik.
3. Hilty, L. M.; Behrendt, S.; Binswanger, M.; Bruinink, A.; Erdmann, L.; Fröhlich, J.; Köhler, A.; Kuster, N.; Som, C; Würtenberger, F. (2003): *Das Vorsorgeprinzip in der Informationsgesellschaft – Auswirkungen des Pervasive Computing auf Gesundheit und Umwelt.* Herausgegeben vom Zentrum fr Technologiefolgen-Abschtzung (TA-SWISS), Bern (TA 46/2003).
4. Hilty, L. M.; Som, C.; Köhler, A. (2004): Assessing the Human, Social, and Environmental Risks of Pervasive Computing. *Human and Ecological Risk Assessment.* Vol. 10, No. 5, 853-874
5. Hilty, L. M.; Seifert, E.; Treibert, R. (eds., 2005): Information Systems for Sustainable Development. Hershey (PA): Idea Group Publishing
6. Kräuchi, P.; Eugster, M.; Grossmann, G.; Wäger, P.; Hilty, L. M. (2005): Impacts of Pervasive Computing: Are RFID Tags a Threat to Waste Management Processes? *IEEE Technology and Society Magazine.*
7. Som C., Hilty L. M.; Ruddy T. (2004): The Precautionary Principle in the Information Society. *Human and Ecological Risk Assessment.* Vol. 10, No. 5, 787-799

TENeT: A Framework for Distributed Smartcards

Masayuki Terada[1], Kensaku Mori[1], Kazuhiko Ishii[1], Sadayuki Hongo[1],
Tomonori Usaka[2], Noboru Koshizuka[3], and Ken Sakamura[4]

[1] Network Management Development Dept., NTT DoCoMo, Inc.
[2] University Museum, Univ. of Tokyo
[3] Information Technology Center, Univ. of Tokyo
[4] Interfaculty Initiative in Information Studies,
and Graduate School of Interdisciplinary Information Studies, Univ. of Tokyo

Abstract. This paper proposes a new architecture that allows
distributed smartcards to interact with one another as well as interacting with application programs on their hosts. Since these interactions are
handled distribution transparently through message dispatching agents
deployed on each host, the smartcards can autonomously conduct distributed protocols without turning to off-card application programs. The
proposed architecture thus reduces the complexity of application programs and makes it easier to develop smartcard-based services that offer
a high-level of functionality.

1 Introduction

Personal trusted devices, smartcards are the most typical example, are becoming
the preferred tool for realizing secure and convenient electronic commerce.

The early smartcards had limited computing power and were thus used as
data carriers with simple access control. Recent smartcards, however, are far
more powerful and can be treated as external secure computing devices rather
than mere secure memory devices[1]. Smartcards are now being used as auxiliary devices of regular computers (i.e. PCs), as well as trusted conductors of distributed protocols in several systems: e.g., trading electronic money and vouchers
among smartcards[2, 3]. Smartcards are no longer auxiliary devices in these systems, but rather their hosts can be considered as auxiliary devices which supply
I/O functionality to the smartcards.

One impediment is that the standard interface and architecture for interacting with smartcards, namely ISO7816-4, is rather classic and doesn't support
modern smartcard functionalities such as conducting distributed protocols. In
ISO7816-4, the data format named APDU (Application Protocol Data Unit)
depends too much on the original internal smartcard structure, interactions are
asymmetric, and smartcards must always be "passive" transponders; there is
no way of getting the smartcard to issue a command to its host. These drawbacks of ISO7816-4 make it unacceptable as a platform on which to develop

D. Hutter and M. Ullmann (Eds.): SPC 2005, LNCS 3450, pp. 3–17, 2005.

application programs for systems that want to fully utilize smartcards with high functionality.

Several approaches have been proposed to offer more sophisticated and abstracted interaction with smartcards, which can be accessed in similar ways to more abstracted and familiar devices such as filesystems, web servers and remote objects[4, 5, 6, 7]. These approaches reduce the cost of developing application programs since they conceal the internal detail data format of smartcards. Unfortunately, the architectures proposed so far are still asymmetric in which smartcards are considered as merely passive transponders, they cannot facilitate the development of systems that depend on smartcards conducting distributed protocols.

In this paper, we propose a framework named TENeT (Trusted Environment with Networking eTRON), which provides symmetric and distribution transparent interactions among smartcards and application programs in a distributed environment.

Every smartcard and application program (on hosts) in this architecture interacts with the others by distributed message passing. Since each message is delivered automatically according to its destination, a smartcard can (logically) interact with another smartcard autonomously. Since the interaction is concealed from the application program running on the host, there is no need for the program to parse or mediate messages between smartcards. Instead, the application program simply sends a message that asks the smartcard to start the protocol and waits to receive the result of the protocol.

The rest of the paper is organized as follows: Section 2 mentions the characteristics of smartcards and describes problems of ISO7816-4 which is commonly used as the specification for interacting with smartcards. Section 3 looks at the previous approaches related to the problems. We then introduce the structure of the proposed framework named TENeT in Sect. 4, and discuss the security aspect of the framework in Sect. 5.

2   Smartcards

A smartcard is a tamper-resistant device that prevents external entities from illegally accessing stored data and programs. Some low-end cards are not programmable and merely offer simple authorization using shared secret and read/write (or increment/decrement) access to its memory, but this paper assumes a programmable smartcard that has a micro-processor for executing programs.

Since a smartcard usually has no (long-life) battery or user interface, it cannot be used standalone. When using a smartcard, it is connected to another device that supplies power and I/O support. We refer to such a device as the "host" of the card. A personal computer that has a smartcard reader/writer and a mobile phone with a SIM or UICC slot are typical hosts.

Both a smartcard and its host have application programs which interact with each other. Those on the smartcard are called on-card application programs (on-card APs) and those on the host are called off-card application programs (off-card APs).

Smartcard–host interaction normally follows ISO7816[8] which specifies the protocol and the data format.

ISO7816 consists of several parts; i.e. ISO7816-1 (ISO7816 part 1) and 7816-2 specify the physical constraints, 7816-3 specifies the electrical characteristics and transmission protocols, and 7816-4 specifies the data format named APDU and some basic commands.

For contact-less smartcards, another standard named ISO14443 is specified, but the ISO7816-4 APDU is appropriated for command use. The ISO7816-4 APDU format is thus widely used as the specification for interaction between a smartcard and an off-card AP except for some smartcards that have their own proprietary format.

An ISO7816-4 smartcard behaves as a reactive transponder; the host sends a command (Command APDU) to the smartcard and the smartcard responds with the result of the command execution (Response APDU). The smartcard never sends any command to the host in this scheme.

This scheme works well for smartcards that provide only low-level functionalities such as read/write or simple sign/verify, however, it doesn't support the high-end functionalities of recent smartcards such as conducting distributed protocols. A description of the problems with ISO7816-4 is given below:

Lack of Abstraction. An off-card AP that wants to utilize a smartcard has to generate and parse APDUs, which is a low-level format that strongly depends on the smartcard's internal structure. This makes off-card APs complicated and requires their developers to have special knowledge of smartcards and APDU specifications.

Asymmetry of the Architecture. Since ISO7816-4 assumes that smartcards will not behave proactively, it is difficult for a smartcard to request or notify something to external entities; e.g., it is difficult to apply the Observer pattern[9], which is commonly used for notifying events in object-oriented designed systems. A series of APDUs can provide a roughly equivalent function, however, it makes both the on-card APs and off-card APs much more complicated.

No Support for Distribution. Since there is no support for a distributed environment in ISO7816-4, a smartcard cannot interact with remote entities such as smartcards on remote hosts and server programs on remote servers unless an off-card AP on its host intermediates the interactions. Because of the asymmetry of the architecture, intermediation procedures tend to become cumbersome and complicated.

3   Previous Works

Several approaches have been proposed to address the above problems in ISO7816-4 and to make it easier to develop smartcard-based application systems.

SCFS (Smart Card File System)[4] enables external entities to treat the (non-volatile) memory of smartcards as a filesystem; Users and off-card APs can read/write files from and to a smartcard as if it were a floppy disk. This approach can make utilizing "memory cards" simpler, but it cannot be extended to support other functions.

Webcard[6] and WebSIM[5] enable a smartcard to mimic an HTTP server, with which users and off-card APs can interact using the HTTP protocol; i.e., a user can access a smartcard using a web browser like Internet Explorer and Mozilla Navigator. This approach would be quite useful in certain applications wherein users would directly interact with their smartcards, however, smartcards in this approach are still passive transponders and so it is difficult to extend this approach to support smartcards that must conduct distributed protocols, in spite that they enables an off-card AP to access smartcards on remote hosts.

JASON[7] and JavaCard2.2[10] provide facilities similar to RMI (Remote Method Invocation), the facility for invoking methods on remote objects in Java, for invoking functions on smartcards. These facilities, which are called SMI (Secure Method Invocation) in JASON and JC-RMI (JavaCard RMI) in JavaCard2.2, enable off-card APs (written in Java) to interact with smartcards as if interacting with remote objects using RMI. Since the detailed format of the interactions is concealed from off-card APs, the developers don't need to be aware of the detailed format or indeed the protocol used in RMI.

However, neither SMI nor JC-RMI allows smartcards to invoke external entities; both facilitate only invoking functions on smartcards from off-card APs. They, therefore, cannot support smartcards that conduct distributed protocols.

To address to the disadvantages caused by asymmetric interactions between a smartcard and its host, there have been proposed several interaction schemes based on the Intelligent Adjuncts paradigm[11, 12], which enables a smartcard to have access to off-card resources of the host.

Proactive UICC[13, 14] provides mechanism for a smartcard to issue commands to its host; e.g., display some messages or fetch input from a user. In the initial state, an off-card AP issues a command to a smartcard and the smartcard responds to the command, alike usual ISO7816-4 smartcards. When the smartcard wants to issue a command to the off-card AP, it sends back a response that includes the special state code ("91 XX", where XX is the size of the command to be issued by the card) instead of the normal state code ("90 00"). The off-card AP then issues a FETCH command that requests the card to send back the command to be issued. The proactive UICC mechanism thus enables smartcards to inverse the command/response direction.

The card-centric framework[15] takes a similar but more aggressive approach, wherewith the roles of a smartcard and a host are completely swapped; a smartcard becomes proactive as soon as it is attached to the host.

The disadvantage of the proactive UICC approach is that the switching of the command/response direction requires an extra handshake cycle, which causes considerable performance overheads and complicates off-card AP design. The card-centric framework eliminates these overheads by considering only the case where a smartcard makes use of resources on the connected host, however, this approach consumes much more processing power of the smartcard and the im-

plementation result[15] shows that applying this approach is not feasible yet for
current smartcards.

4 Our Proposal

In order to solve the problems described in the previous sections, we propose
TENeT (Trusted Environment with Networking eTRON), which is a symmetric
and distribution transparent architecture and interaction scheme for smartcards
in a distributed environment.

4.1 Design Goals

The main design goals of TENeT are as follows:

Provide Efficient Symmetric Interactions. As mentioned in Sect. 2, an
asymmetric architecture makes mutual interactions among smartcards difficult
to implement. To facilitate the development of application systems that require
distributed smartcards to interact with one another, we need a symmetric architecture in which a smartcard can interact with another entity in coordination
with an off-card AP, and it should be implemented effciently.

Provide Distribution Transparency. To reduce the cost of creating an off-
card AP, it is important to provide distribution transparency, which enables a
smartcard to interact with remote entities without the off-card AP being aware of
the interactions; off-card APs can be liberated from intermediating interactions
between them.

Provide Security. Distribution transparency suggests that it is possible for
malicious remote entities to conduct illegal acts on a smartcard without tipping
off the off-card AP or its user. To avoid this situation, TENeT must prevent
such illegal acts on smartcards.

To achieve the above design goals, we took following approaches in designing
TENeT.

The most straightforward approach to provide symmetric interactions efficiently is to realize a "true" call/return mechanism which allows smartcards to
invoke external entities and vice versa, without external handshakes to switch
the direction. However, this approach requires a smartcard to preserve its execution context (i.e. the execution stack) until the invocation is returned from the
external entity. It is not easy for smartcards, which tend to be scarce of volatile
memory (i.e. RAM), to efficiently preserve execution contexts, especially considering the need to support nested (reentrant) invocations.

We therefore dropped the call/return approach and instead adopted the message passing approach, in which all interactions among smartcards and external
entities including off-card APs and remote servers are performed by exchanging
messages. This requires that off-card APs be executed in an event-driven manner instead of command/response or call/return manner, but we consider that

this is not a problem since the event-driven architecture is commonly used in the object-oriented programming area, especially when developing GUI applications.

To provide distribution transparency, each entity exchanging messages has its own identifier, and each message includes two identifiers: the source and the destination of the message. Messages are routed automatically according to the identifier of its destination. The details of the identifier are described in Sect. 4.2.

Security against malicious entities is provided by a filtering facility named Guard, which is detailed in Sect. 4.3.

4.2   Message Structure

The messages exchanged among entities in TENeT, including smartcards and off-card APs are named eTP messages.

Similar to IP packets in the Internet, An eTP message consists of a Header, which includes its source and destination, and a payload. For easier implementation of message parsers in smartcards, the header includes a code designating "message type", which determines the format of the payload; i.e., an eTP message is represented by the 4-tuple (`src`, `dst`, `mtype`, `param`): `src` and `dst` represent the sender and destination, respectively, `mtype` represents the code designating the format of the `param`, and `param` is a set of parameters described in the format designated by `mtype`.

To realize distribution transparent message passing, it is required that 1) identifiers of entities including smartcards and off-card APs are unique, and 2) it should be easy to route messages according to the identifier.

In TENeT, each smartcard has a 128bit identifier named uCode, which is a globally unique identifier assigned to smartcards and RF-ID tags by an organization named uID center[16].

Since it is not practical to similarly identify each off-card AP, which would require the assignment of an identifier per AP installation, an off-card AP in TENeT acquires its identifier from a smartcard on the same host; the 16byte (128bit) identifier is divided into 12+4 bytes. The 12byte set is called "domain" and the 4byte set is called "port".

Each smartcard is assigned its own domain from the center; let it be D. An off-card AP requests the smartcard on the same host to assign a port P, which is a unique number in the domain and is never reused. In case of successful assignment, the identifier of the application is $D|P$, where $x|y$ is the concatenation of x and y. $P = 0$ is reserved for the identifier of the smartcard itself and never assigned to APs; i.e. the identifier of a smartcard is $D|0$ (12byte domain D followed by 4bytes of 0's).

This dynamic identifier assignment scheme efficiently assures the uniqueness of identifiers as well as making message routing easier. Since a smartcard and all off-card APs on the same host have the same domain D, messages can be routed by managing pairs of domain and network address of the host instead of managing each identifier; this reduces the cost of address resolution for message routing.

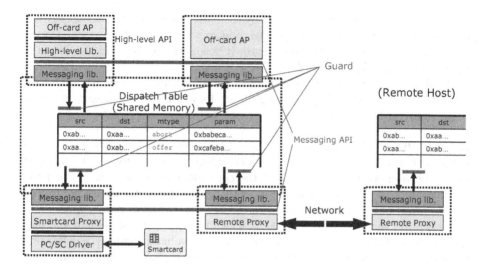

Fig. 1. Architecture of TENeT

4.3   Architecture of TENeT

To realize the symmetric and distribution transparent delivery of eTP messages, we adapt an architecture based upon distributed shared memory. Figure 1 depicts the modules forming TENeT. The roles of the modules are described below:

Dispatch Table. The dispatch table stores messages sent from smartcards and off-card APs until received by another entity. Every sent message is temporarily stored in this table. A message is sent by storing the message in the table via the messaging library, and received by reading the message. The dispatch table is implemented as shared memory in our current implementation.

Messaging Library. The messaging library provides a means of sending or receiving messages to or from off-card APs and proxies by providing access to the dispatch table; i.e., store a message in the table (sending a message), read a message from the table (receiving a message), and register a message handler which notifies of the storage of the specified message in the table (notification of a message).

High-level Library. The high-level library provides the functions needed to convert the data format used in off-card APs from and to that used in eTP messages. These functions are used as wrappers which construct and parse messages so as to conceal the detailed data format of messages from off-card APs.

Smartcard Proxy. The smartcard proxy provides a means to send and receive messages in place of a smartcard. This proxy is an independent process that accesses the messages using the messaging library; i.e., when notified of the arrival of a message for the smartcard by the handler registered to the messaging library, this proxy receives the message and forwards it to the card, and upon receiving a message from the smartcard, it stores the message in the dispatch table via the messaging library.

To detect the arrival of messages for the smartcard, the smartcard proxy registers a handler with the messaging library for any message whose destination is the smartcard.

Remote Proxy. The remote proxy provides a means to route messages from/to remote entities. This proxy is also an independent process; it forwards a message to another remote proxy located on the corresponding remote host when the destination of the message is a remote entity. Upon receiving a message from a remote proxy of another host, it stores the message in the dispatch table.

This proxy manages a routing table, which includes pairs of domain and network address of the host (cf. Sect. 4.2) and registers a handler with the messaging library for any message whose destination matches any managed domain.

Guard. Guard filters messages according to the conditions provided by off-card APs to prevent malicious remote messages from being forwarded to a smartcard.

Guard consists of sets of conditions and a message handler registered by off-card APs. The corresponding handler is invoked when a suspicious message that matches any of the provided conditions arrives at the dispatch table. When invoked, the handler inspects the message in detail and discards the message if it is considered harmful for the application; an off-card AP can thus provide the logic of inspection that suits to securing its application.

4.4   Example Message Flows

The following examples illustrate message flows among smartcards and off-card APs in TENeT.

In this example, an off-card AP P_A on host A sends a message to another off-card AP P_B on remote host B, through a secure channel established by smartcards S_A and S_B, which are located on host A and B, respectively. To simplify the example, it is assumed that S_A and S_B have a pre-shared secret key k, and the remote proxy on host A knows the pair (D_B, B) where D_B is the domain of entities on host B.

1. At first, P_A creates an eTP message m_1 whose destination is S_A using the high-level library, then P_A stores m_1 in the dispatch table using the messaging library (i.e. sends message m_1).
2. The smartcard proxy of S_A is notified of the storage of m_1 from the low-level library. The proxy then receives m_1 and forwards it to S_A. In our current implementation, every message exchanged between a smartcard and its proxy is wrapped in an ISO7816-4 compliant APDU envelope.
3. S_A receives m_1 and creates and sends the next message m_2 to S_B. The contents of m_2 are encrypted by k.
4. The proxy of S_A receives m_2 and stores it in the dispatch table.

5. Since m_2 is addressed to a remote entity on host B (i.e. S_B), the remote proxy on host A is notified of m_2 and picks it up. m_2 is then forwarded to the remote proxy on host B.

6. m_2 is stored in the dispatch table on host B and is forwarded to S_B by its proxy in a similar way to the proxy of S_A.

7. S_B receives m_2, decrypts it by k, and sends the last message m_3 to P_B. The proxy of S_B stores it in the dispatch table.

8. P_B is notified of m_3 and decodes it to obtain m using the high-level library.

The proposed framework thus enables smartcards to exchange messages autonomously without the help of off-card APs. This example initially seems to require a number of steps to forward a message, however, what off-card APs have to do are: 1) P_A creating and storing m_1 using the high-level/messaging libraries, and 2) P_B decoding m_3 to obtain the message.

Furthermore, this framework can provide better modularity of the system. Since interactions between smartcards can be completely concealed from off-card APs, it is quite easy to alter the encryption scheme used by the smartcards; e.g., when using the Diffie-Hellman key exchange scheme for sharing the encryption key instead of using a pre-shared secret key, there would be little impact on off-card APs because they don't have to be aware of the additional interactions needed for the key exchange between smartcards. For off-card APs, the protocols performed among smartcards can be treated as "pluggable" black boxes.

5   Implementation Result

5.1   Optimistic Fair Exchange Protocol for Trading Electronic Vouchers

We applied this approach to implement a prototype fair voucher trading system, which enables users to trade electronic vouchers stored in their smartcard fairly among the smartcards, using the optimistic fair exchange protocol proposed in [3]. This protocol exchanges vouchers v_1 and v_2 each of which stored in smartcards S_A and S_B respectively as follows[1], where Table 1 gives the definitions of the symbols used in describing the protocol:

1. P_A orders S_A to start the exchange of v_1 stored in S_A and v_2 stored in S_B.
2. S_A sends S_B offer message m_1: $\{v_1, v_2, n_1\}$, which means an offer to exchange v_1 and v_2.
3. S_B deletes v_2 and sends S_A agreement message m_2: $\{(h(v_1|v_2|n_1)|h(n_2))_{PkB},$ $Cert_B\}$ iff offer m_1 is acceptable.
4. S_A deletes v_1 and sends S_B confirmation message m_3: $\{(h(n_2))_{PkA}, Cert_A\}$ iff agreement m_2 is successfully verified.

---

[1] To simplify the explanation, the details of the verification procedure and management of n_1 and n_2 are omitted in this paper.

Table 1. Definition of the symbols used in the protocol description

S_A, S_B	smartcards located on hosts A and B, respectively
P_A, P_B	(off-card) wallet application programs that manage S_A and S_B
v_1, v_2	vouchers initially stored in S_A and S_B
v_1, v_2	identifiers of v_1 and v_2
n_1, n_2	random numbers generated by S_A and S_B
h()	a secure hash function (e.g. SHA1)
PkX	a public key of asymmetric cryptography
$(m)_{PkX}$	a signed message that consists of m and a signature verifiable by PkX
$Cert_X$	a public key certificate of PkX

5. S_B stores v_1 and sends S_A commitment message m_4: n_2 iff confirmation m_3 is successfully verified; or else, S_B runs the abort subprotocol.
6. S_A stores v_2[^2] iff commitment m_4 is successfully verified; or else, S_A runs the resolve subprotocol.

When the protocol above is interrupted due to network errors or other reasons, a user can be fallen into an unfair condition, wherein the smartcard of the user has deleted its voucher without storing the voucher to be received. In this case, both P_A and P_B can recover fairness by performing a resolve subprotocol and an abort subprotocol, respectively, with a trusted third-party T.

The resolve subprotocol is performed as follows:

1. P_A orders S_A to start the resolve subprotocol.
2. S_A sends T resolve request message m_{r1}: $\{(resolve|h(n_2))_{PkA}, Cert_A\}$, where n_2 is used as the identifier of the exchange to be resolved or aborted.
3. T sends S_A resolve admission m_{r2}: $\{(resolve|h(n_2))_{PkT}, Cert_T\}$ iff m_{r1} is successfully verified and the exchange identified by n_2 has not been aborted yet; or else, sends abort admission m_{a2}: $\{(abort|h(n_2))_{PkT}, Cert_T\}$ iff m_{r1} is successfully verified and the exchange has already aborted by S_B.
4. S_A stores v_2 iff received resolve admission m_{r2} and it is successfully verified, or (re-)stores v_1 iff received abort admission m_{a2} and it is successfully verified.

The abort subprotocol is performed in a similar way:

1. P_B orders S_B to start the abort subprotocol.
2. S_B sends T abort request message m_{a1}: $\{(abort|h(n_2))_{PkB}, Cert_B\}$.
3. T sends S_B abort admission m_{a2} iff m_{a1} is successfully verified and the exchange has not been resolved yet; or else, sends resolve admission m_{r2} iff m_{a1} is successfully verified and the exchange has already resolved by S_A.
4. S_B (re-)stores v_2 iff received abort admission m_{a2} and it is successfully verified, or stores v_2 iff received resolve admission m_{r2} and it is successfully verified.

[^2]: v_2 is assumed to be generatable (i.e. can be stored) from v_2 by S_A.

Note 1. In [3], n_1 is used as the identifier of an exchange in the resolve and abort subprotocols, however, n_2 must be used instead in order to prevent illegal abort requests; when using n_1 as the identifier, the (malicious) user of S_B can force S_A to abort the exchange that S_B has already completed, by replaying m_1 followed by an abort request.

5.2   Implementation

The protocol can be quite easily implemented using the proposed framework; each message m_i can be 1-to-1 mapped into an eTP message. Most of these messages can be exchanged between smartcards S_A and S_B autonomously, so the off-card wallet APs have nearly nothing to do with running the protocol, except: 1) wallet P_A sends a message to start the exchange, and 2) wallet P_B should confirm whether offer m_1 is acceptable or not to its user.

The former also can be mapped into an eTP message obviously, and the latter can be implemented in the following ways: 2a) use Guard, which prompts the user if the offer is accepted and discards the offer when the user rejects it; or 2b) change the destination of offer m_1 to P_B instead of S_B, and insert an additional message m_1', which means the acceptance of the offer, sent from P_B to S_B. Both approaches should work well, but we took approach 2b) for our prototype implementation.

The protocol thus can be implemented using the proposed framework as follows, where pa, pb, sa, and sb are the identifiers of P_A, P_B, S_A, and S_B, respectively.

1. P_A sends S_A (pa, sa, start-exchange, $\{v_1, v_2, pb\}$).
2. S_A sends P_B (sa, pb, offer, m_1).
3. P_B examines m_1 in the received message, and sends S_B (pb, sb, accept, m_1) iff m_1 is considered acceptable.
4. S_B deletes v_2 and sends S_A (sb, sa, agreement, m_2).
5. S_A deletes v_1 and sends S_B (sa, sb, confirmation, m_3) iff m_2 is successfully verified.
6. S_B stores v_1 and sends S_A (sb, sa, commitment, m_4) iff m_3 is successfully verified; or else, S_B runs the abort subprotocol.
7. S_A stores v_2 iff m_4 is successfully verified; or else, S_A runs the resolve subprotocol.

The resolve and abort subprotocols can be implemented in a similar way.

The number of messages handled by the smartcards is exactly the same as in the original protocol[3]; the proposed framework doesn't demand any extra interactions to implement the protocol. In addition, implementation of off-card APs is quite simple; what they have to do is to trigger the start the exchange (for P_A) and to confirm the offer of the exchange (for P_B).

---

[3] The accept message is an addition, however, the number of the messages the smartcards handle doesn't change since S_B doesn't need to handle the offer message.

Table 2. Time to process message

Message type	CPU (ms)	I/O (ms)	Total (ms)
start-excg.	50	129	179
accept (m_1)	191	153	344
agreement (m_2)	553	153	706
confirmation (m_3)	402	91	493
commitment (m_4)	24	42	66
Whole exchange	1,220	568	1,788

Table 3. Specifications of the system

Smartcard	Infenion SLE66CLX320P
CPU clock	15 MHz
Card R/W	Gemplus GemPC Twin
Interface speed	38.4 kbps (Card–R/W), 12 Mbps (R/W–Host)
EEPROM	32 KB
RAM	5 KB
To generate a signature	125 ms (ECDSA, 163bit)
To verify a signature	185 ms (ECDSA, 163bit)

Although it doesn't appear explicitly in the above message flow, either wallet P_A or P_B can check the progress of the exchange if needed, by hooking messages exchanged between smartcards using handlers registered with the messaging library (cf. Sect. 4.3); this also can be achieved without involving any additional messages.

5.3   Performance Result

Table 2 shows a performance result of the implementation described above, and Table 3 gives the specification of the system used for the measurement.

In Table 2, the columns show (from left to right) message type, CPU time consumed by the smartcard (and crypto co-processor), that for I/O interaction (including time to send the next message), and the sum of the two. The last row lists the time taken to process all messages. We can see that it takes only about 1.8 sec. to complete an exchange among the smartcards. These figures don't include the time needed for networking or message handling in the host, however, message handling cost is negligible when compared to the time consumed by smartcards, and networking cost is not so large because only 2-round communication is needed in an exchange.

As Table 3 shows, it takes about 125 ms to sign a message and 185 ms to verify a signature by the smartcard used in the system, and the implemented fair exchange protocol needs two signatures (to generate m_2 and m_3) and 4 signature verifications (verifying m_2 and m_3, as well as verifying the 2 certificates $\mathrm{Cert_A}$

and $Cert_B$). It accordingly takes 990 ms for cryptography and the remaining 230 ms is consumed by pure processing in the smartcards. No considerable performance penalty caused by applying the proposed framework can be observed in this prototype implementation.

6   Security Discussions

6.1   Preventing Malicious Remote Messages

In previous smartcard systems, a smartcard can be protected from malicious messages from remote entities by an off-card AP since the off-card AP, which has to intermediate every message to the smartcard, can check the messages. However, since a smartcard in TENeT can directly interact with remote entities without the help of an off-card AP, we need a way of protecting smartcards from malicious messages.

As described in Sect. 4.3, Guard prevents such malicious messages from arriving at a smartcard. It inspects messages from remote entities in place of off-card APs, according to the logic provided by off-card APs. If the message is considered harmful, it is discarded without exception.

Guard can do more than just inspect messages. It can also protect the smartcards from suspicious programs, for example, running downloaded Java applets in a sandbox.

Guard thus prevents illegal access to smartcards and provides security which is not less than that of previous smartcard systems, while it offers better modularity and more flexibility of inspection.

6.2   Providing Confidentiality and Integrity

While most previous systems that offer remote access to smartcards make an effort to provide confidentiality and integrity of the accesses, messages in (our current implementation of) TENeT are not encrypted, nor do they follow MAC. This is one of our design decisions.

These schemes require a key exchange in advance of message exchange unless we can assume pre-shared secret keys shared by all entities exchanging messages. Performing key exchange protocols, however, is too "heavy" for smartcards, whose I/O performance is quite limited, to apply at the beginning of every interaction.

Most cryptographic application protocols utilizing smartcards, e.g. transfer protocols for electronic money or vouchers, are designed without the assumption of secure channels among entities; each message which has to be assured of confidentiality or integrity is already protected by adequate cryptographic techniques like encryption or digital signatures. Applying them in the message transport layer would be redundant and should be avoided to ease performance concerns.

If it is required to secure messages from third parties for privacy, providing a secure connection between remote proxies using SSL or IPSec would be enough and much faster than providing secure channels between smartcards. Encrypting messages in smartcards should also be avoided in this case considering the performance disadvantage.

When applying the proposed framework to embedded systems, smartcards would often have higher performance than their hosts, especially with regard to cryptographic processing. For such systems, it is also possible to provide secure communication channels as per the example described in Sect. 4.4. Note that it is also not necessary to provide security in the message transport layer in this case.

7   Conclusion

In this paper, we proposed a new framework for a distributed smartcard environment, named TENeT, which provides message based symmetrical interactions among smartcards and application programs. Since this framework enables smartcards to directly interact with one another, application programs that utilize smartcards can be much simpler and better modularized than those in previous systems.

Although the proposed framework offers flexible interactions among smartcards and application programs, its feasibility and efficiency are not compromised; it can be efficiently implemented using current smartcards since nested smartcard invocations are avoided by adopting the message passing approach and security overhead is minimized by avoiding the redundant application of cryptography.

The feasibility and efficiency of this approach has been confirmed by implementing a prototype fair voucher trading system that enables users to trade electronic vouchers fairly among the distributed smartcards, using an optimistic fair exchange protocol[3]. The implementation result shows that such a system utilizing distributed smartcards can be quite easily implemented using the framework, without incurring any performance overheads that spoil feasibility of the system.

References

1. Rankl, W., Effing, W.: Smart Card Handbook. 2nd edn. John Wiley & Sons (2001)
2. Terada, M., Kuno, H., Hanadate, M., Fujimura, K.: Copy prevention scheme for rights trading infrastructure. In: Proc. the 4th Working Conference on Smart Card Research and Advanced Applications (CARDIS), IFIP (2000) 51–70
3. Terada, M., Iguchi, M., Hanadate, M., Fujimura, K.: An optimistic fair exchange protocol for trading electronic rights. In: Proc. the 6th Working Conference on Smart Card Research and Advanced Applications (CARDIS 2004), IFIP (2004) 255–270
4. Itoi, N., Honeyman, P., Rees, J.: SCFS: A UNIX filesystem for smartcards. In: Proc. USENIX Workshop on Smartcard Technology, USENIX (1999)
5. Guthery, S., Kehr, R., Posegga, J.: How to turn a GSM SIM into a web server. In: Proc. the 4th Working Conference on Smart Card Research and Advanced Applications (CARDIS 2000), IFIP (2000) 209–222

6. Rees, J., Honeyman, P.: Webcard: a java card web server. In: Proc. the 4th Working Conference on Smart Card Research and Advanced Applications (CARDIS 2000), IFIP (2000) 197–208

7. Brinkman, R., Hoepman, J.H.: Secure method invocation in JASON. In: Proc. the 5th Working Conference on Smart Card Research and Advanced Applications (CARDIS 2002), USENIX/IFIP (2002)

8. ISO/IEC: Integrated circuit(s) cards with contacts — Part 4: Interindustry commands for interchange. (1995) ISO/IEC 7816-4:1995(E).

9. Gamma, E., Helm, R., Johnson, R., Vlissides, J.: Design Patterns. Addison Wesley Longman (1995)

10. Sun Microsystems: Java Card Specification 2.2.1 Final Release. (2003)

11. Balacheff, B., Wilder, B.V., Chan, D.: Smartcards - from security tokens to intelligent adjuncts. In: Proc. the 3rd Working Conference on Smart Card Research and Advanced Applications (CARDIS 1998), IFIP (1998) 71–84

12. Balacheff, B., Chan, D., Chen, L., Pearson, S., Proudler, G.: Securing intelligent adjuncts using trusted computing platform technology. In: Proc. the 4th Working Conference on Smart Card Research and Advanced Applications (CARDIS 2000), IFIP (2000) 177–195

13. European Telecommunications Standards Institute (ETSI): ETSI TS 102 223: Card Application Toolkit (CAT) (Release 6). (2004)

14. 3rd Generation Partnership Project (3GPP): 3GPP TS 31.111: USIM Application Toolkit (USAT) (Release 6). (2004)

15. Chan, P.K., Choy, C.S., Chan, C.F., Pun, K.P.: Card-centric framework - providing I/O resources for smart cards. In: Proc. the 6th Working Conference on Smart Card Research and Advanced Applications (CARDIS 2004), IFIP (2004) 225–240

16. Sakamura, K., Koshizuka, N.: Business of the ubiquitous id center. Barcode **16** (2003) 15–20 (in Japanese).

P2P Digital Value Fair Trading System Using Smart Cards

Masayuki Hanadate[1], Masayuki Terada[3], Shinji Nagao[1],
Toshiyuki Miyazawa[1], Yukiko Yosuke[1], Seiji Tomita[2],
and Ko Fujimura[1]

[1] NTT Information Sharing Platform Laboratories
[2] NTT Cyber Space Laboratories,
1-1 Hikari-no-oka, Yokosuka, Kanagawa, Japan
[3] NTT DoCoMo Network Management Development Department,
3-5 Hikari-no-oka, Yokosuka, Kanagawa, Japan

Abstract. This paper proposes an extension of the Digital Value Exchange Protocol that enables fair exchange of digital values, e.g., electronic money and digital tickets, over a P2P system without requiring the use of an external negotiation facility. The digital values stored in the partners' smart cards are exchanged through the network using 4 message exchanges based on the Optimistic Fair Exchange Protocol; digital values are directly exchanged between a pair of users; the Trusted Third Party(TTP) is accessed to resolve the conflict only if this exchange is interrupted. Traditionally, the partners and the exchanged digital values are determined by external negotiation before the exchange. Our proposed protocol dispenses with the external negotiation facility while sticking to the same 4 message exchange. We also implement a smart card application that can generate the messages for the proposed protocol within 1 second and examine its feasibility.

1 Introduction

When Alice and Bob exchange their digital values, e.g., electronic money and digital tickets, through the network, Alice may not get Bob's digital value even though she sent hers; Bob fails to send his digital value after getting Alice's. The TIHF Protocol[8] can prevent such problems when exchanging digital values over the network since it uses the Optimistic Fair Exchange Protocol[1, 2, 3]. Digital values used in the TIHF Protocol are stored in tamper-resistant devices(e.g. smart cards) to prevent illegal acts such as the copying, reproduction, or alteration of the digital values. According to the TIHF Protocol, just 4 message exchanges are needed if the Trusted Third Party(TTP) is not accessed. These messages are generated by tamper-resistant devices. The TTP redresses the loss of the digital value in the interrupted exchange regardless of whether the interruption was due to network trouble or malicious message termination.

In the Optimistic Fair Exchange Protocol, various digital items (e.g. digital documents, digital signatures, and digital values) are exchanged without the

D. Hutter and M. Ullmann (Eds.): SPC 2005, LNCS 3450, pp. 18–30, 2005.

TTP. The TTP resolves the conflict between the parties only if the exchange is interrupted. Existing protocols based on this Optimistic Fair Exchange Protocol [3, 4, 5] as well as the TIHF Protocol make it possible to exchange digital values stored in smart cards. However, prior to the exchange, the parties must agree on what digital values are to be exchanged; an external negotiation facility is most often assumed to be used for this purpose. The use of this facility raises the problem of ensuring that the results of the negotiation are accurately reflected in the exchange process.

In this paper, we extend the TIHF Protocol to dispense with this external negotiation facility. This protocol folds negotiation into the process. Therefore, the results of the negotiation are always reflected in the exchange process.

In the extended TIHF Protocol, one user sends a proposal to many other users that details her digital value but exchanges values with only one as follows. First, the first user selects as her partner the user whose digital value is the most desirable from among the many users who replied to her message. This constitutes part of the exchange of digital values.

Once Alice selects Bob as her partner, the exchange process with all other users is terminated. These users turn to the TTP to resolve the problem of the termination of their digital value exchange. If there are many unselected users and only one TTP, the TTP will be overwhelmed. Against this we envisage multiple TTPs.

This paper is structured as follows: In Section 2, we explain the requirement for smart cards used to store digital values and overview the TIHF Protocol. We also describe our motivation in proposing the extended TIHF Protocol. In Section 3, we describe some problems with the extend TIHF Protocol and their solutions. Section 4 describes a smart card application that can generate the messages for the extended TIHF Protocol and we show its processing time. The results confirm the feasibility of the extended TIHF Protocol. Finally, we discuss the security and TTP efficiency in the extended TIHF Protocol.

2   TIHF Protocol

A digital value is information representing a value, e.g., money or a ticket. Digital values must be protected from illegal acts such as copying, alteration, and reproduction, a difficult task since they are transferred across public networks. The token transfer protocol proposed in [9] can prevent those illegal acts. In this protocol, an information *token* is used to manage the ownership of digital values. A token represents the genuineness of a digital value and consists of some information, e.g., the identity of its content, the identity of its issuer and the amount of value. For example, consider an airline ticket for the Tokyo to Berlin flight on 5th January, 2005 and issued by the Japan Airline Company. The corresponding token consists of the content ID, the SHA-1 hash value of this ticket description, the issuer ID of Japan airline company, and the number of the ticket. Tokens are stored in secure devices, e.g., smart cards, and transferred securely from one secure device to another.

Considering the exchange of tokens between Alice and Bob across the network, it is impossible to transfer both tokens at the same time. Tokens are transferred in turns as follows: First, Alice transfers her token to Bob. Next, Bob transfers his token to Alice. In this case, Bob is able to receive Alice's token and then refuse to send his token. To avoid such unfair states, one solution is to use the "TIHF Protocol[8]", in which tokens stored in secure devices are fairlly exchanged through the network using the Optimistic Fair Exchange Protocol[1, 2, 3]. In this section, we define notations used in this paper and explain the requirements placed on secure devices as well as overviewing the TIHF Protocol.

2.1   Notation

The notations used in this paper are defined as follow: A key pair used in a public key encryption system is represented by (S_k, P_k), where S_k is a secret key and P_k is the corresponding public key. $(m)_{P_k}$ represents a message consisting of the plain text m and its digital signature generated using S_k corresponding to P_k. $boolean = V_{P_k}(s)$ represents the function to verify $s = (m)_{P_k}$, where $boolean$ represents binary values, i.e., $true$ or $false$. $digest = H(m)$ represents the hash function $H(\cdot)$, e.g., SHA-1, used to generate the message digest of the plain text m. Sentence $P?X : Y$ represents the process X if the result of process P is $true$, or else Y. ϕ represents NULL.

2.2   Smart Card

In the TIHF Protocol, secure devices, e.g., smart cards, are used for storing tokens in order to avoid illegal acts. Since smart cards are used as the most secure, compact and widespread device for implementing these secure devices, in this paper, we implement an application on a smart card to check feasibility of the TIHF Protocol. In this section, we explain the requirements placed on the smart cards by the TIHF Protocol. A smart card has a CPU and a coprocessor as well as memories, e.g., EEPROM, RAM. The smart card can execute various programs, e.g., to generate a message or to calculate a digital signature. A smart card application consists of programs and data areas allocated in memory. An application can communicate with external equipment, e.g., mobile phones and PCs, receive a command message $(command\ name, parameter)$, execute a program corresponding to $command\ name$ using $parameter$ and send $response$ as the result of this process.

We must presume that the smart card fulfills the following requirements:

Tamper-Resistance. Smart cards have to be protected so that it is impossible for any external equipment to read out or change secret data and programs stored in the smart card.

Atomicity. All smart card programs have to correctly process all tasks or do nothing.

Secure Issuance. Only an issuer trusted by all smart card holders is able to construct and load a smart card application.

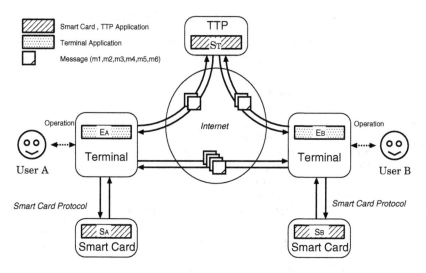

Fig. 1. System Model

If an application for the TIHF Protocol is executed on a smart card that meets all these requirements, it will be possible to generate and verify signatures, or store and remove tokens securely.

We note that existing smart cards have relative few computational resources, e.g., CPU power, communication speed, memory size compared to PC's. For example, CPU clock speed is about 10MHz, EEPROM size is a few tens of Kbytes, RAM size is a few Kbytes, and the communication speed with external equipment ranges from a few Kbps to a few 100Kbps. Thus, to implement a smart card application, we must consider these computational resource limits.

2.3   Protocol Overview

In this section, we explain how the TIHF Protocol exchanges tokens stored in smart cards across a network. Figure 1 shows the system model considered here. Each user has a smart card and a terminal. The TTP is the third party trusted by all users and provides the service of resolving the conflict of interrupted exchanges. These smart cards, terminals, and TTP run an application for the TIHF Protocol.

We assume that user A and B exchange tokens. $U(\in \{A, B\})$ represents the symbol that identifies the users who exchange tokens using the TIHF Protocol. $\tilde{U}$ represents the partner who exchanges tokens with U. U has the smart card application S_U and the terminal application E_U. S_T is the TTP application. S_U and S_T generate messages according to the TIHF Protocol. E_U is the following application process: message generation using S_U, message transmission to $E_{\tilde{U}}$, message reception from $E_{\tilde{U}}$, and confirmation of the received or sent messages for U. S_U has $\{U, (Sk_U, Pk_U), C_U, Pk_X, Pk_T\}$. S_T has $\{(Sk_T, Pk_T), Pk_X\}$. (Sk_U, Pk_U) is the key pair of S_U. (Sk_T, Pk_T) is the key pair of S_T. C_U is the public key certificate issued by CA(Certificate Authority) who has the key pair

Table 1. Processing Flow of the TIHF Protocol

		Main Protocol
Step1	S_A	generate r_A
	$S_A \to S_B$	$m1$ $(= (f))$
Step2	S_B	remove i_B
	$S_B \to S_A$	$m2$ $(= ((g)_{Pk_B}, C_B))$
Step3	S_A	$(V_{Pk_X}(C_B)$ & $V_{Pk_B}((g)_{Pk_B}))$?:exit
		remove i_A
	$S_A \to S_B$	$m3$ $(= ((g)_{Pk_A}, C_A))$
Step4	S_B	$(V_{Pk_X}(C_A)$ & $V_{Pk_A}((g)_{Pk_A}))$?:exit
		store i_A
	$S_B \to S_A$	$m4$ $(= (r_B))$
Step5	S_A	$H(r_B(\in m4)) = H(r_B)(\in g)$?:exit
		store i_B
		Resolve Protocol $(U \in \{A, B\})$
Step6	S_U	hold g
	$S_U \to S_T$	$m5$ $(= ((e, g)_{Pk_U}, C_U))$
Step7	S_T	$(V_{Pk_X}(C_U)$ & $V_{Pk_U}((e, g)_{Pk_U}))$? :exit
		$d = search(g, \sigma)$
	$S_T \to U$	$m6$ $(= ((d, g)_{Pk_T})$
Step8	S_U	$V_{Pk_T}((d, g)_{Pk_T})$? :exit
		resolve g $(d =' Abort'$? store i_U:store $i_{\tilde{U}})$

(Sk_X, Pk_X), where $C_U = ((Pk_U)_{Pk_X})$. S_U has Pk_X to verify $C_{\tilde{U}}$ and has Pk_T to verify $((d, g)_{Pk_T})$. S_T has Pk_X to verify C_U.

The TIHF Protocol is composed of the Main Protocol and the Resolve Protocol. The Main Protocol is used to exchange tokens stored in smart cards. The Resolve Protocol is to resolve any conflict that arises. Table 1 shows the processing flow of these protocols. r_U represents the random number generated by U so as to make the exchange transaction unique. $f = (A, B, i_A, i_B, r_A)$ represents the offer which involves token i_A and i_B by A. $g = (A, i_A, B, i_B, r_A, H(r_B))$ represents the agreement on the exchange. Flag e represents the following role of the user: '*Originator*' represents the user who begins the exchange, i.e., generates the offer. '*Recipient*' represents the partner of '*Originator*'. Flag d represents the result output by TTP in resolving the conflict: '*Commit*' represents the fulfillment of the exchange. '*Abort*' represents the cancellation of the exchange.

The **Main Protocol** is described below:

(Step1) S_A generates r_A and stores $f(generate\ r_A)$. S_A sends $m1$ to S_B.

(Step2) S_B generates r_B, makes i_B unavailable, and stores (g, r_B) (*remove* i_B). S_B sends $m2$ to S_A. It is impossible to calculate r_B from $H(r_B)$.

(Step3) S_A makes i_A unavailable and stores $g(remove\ i_A)$, where $f \in g$. S_A sends $m3$ to S_B.

(Step4) S_B stores i_A and removes $(g, r_B)(store\ i_A)$, where $g \in m3$. S_B sends $m4(= r_B)$ to S_A.

(Step5) S_A stores i_B and removes $g(store\ i_B)$, where $(H(r_B)(\in g)) = H(r_B(\in m4))$.

The **Resolve Protocol** is described below:

(Step6) When the exchange using g is interrupted, S_U makes g unavailable (*hold* g) so as to prevent the reproduction of tokens after restarting the interrupted exchange. S_U sends $m5$ to S_T.

(Step7) S_T decides the value of d according to the following rules $(d = search(g, \sigma))$.

If g is received from the recipient earlier than the originator, $d = Abort$.

If g is received from the originator earlier than the recipient, $d = Commit$.

S_T sends $m6$ to S_U.

(Step8) S_U stores the token according to d and removes the unavailable $g(resolve\ g)$.

If $d = Abort$, S_U stores i_U.

If $d = Commit$, S_U stores $i_{\tilde{U}}$.

The function $search(g, \sigma)$ computes d according to the following algorithm using g and the historical data σ :

$$search(g, \sigma)\{\ If\ (d, g)\ including\ the\ element\ g\ is\ found\ in\ \sigma$$
$$d0\ is\ equal\ to\ the\ element\ d\ of\ the\ found\ (d, g).$$
$$else$$
$$(e = Originator)?d0 = Commit : d0 = Abort$$
$$store\ (d0, g)\ into\ \sigma$$
$$return\ d0;$$
$$\}$$

2.4   Motivation

It is necessary for the partners to complete their negotiation before commencing the exchange[6, 7] as follows: In the negotiation, a user finds the partner whose token is most desirable to the user. Once agreement is reached, the partners enter the exchange phase. As one example, consider the Trading Framework proposed in [7]. The Trading Framework is a generic exchange framework that cooperates with an external negotiation facility.

Tokens used in the Trading Framework are exchanged indirectly through an intermediate TTP. In case of the TIHF Protocol, tokens are exchanged directly between the partners without recourse to the intermediate TTP. The TTP in TIHF Protocol is accessed only for conflict resolution. Since most exchanges can be assumed to conclude successfully, the TIHF Protocol is cheaper.

In the TIHF Protocol, the extended negotiation facility is not assumed to cooperate with the exchange protocol, although users must use the message $m1$ that is equal to the result of the negotiation. They may make a mistake and use a different message from the result of the negotiation. If the TIHF Protocol could allow negotiation to become part of the exchange process, the transaction between the negotiation and the exchange, which is to commence the exchange using the negotiation result, is easily guaranteed since tokens are always exchanged in combination with the negotiation in the unique sequence established by the TIHF Protocol. For example, we assume that a user sends an e-mail message proposing an exchange, e.g., $m1$, to many users and selects as her partner the user whose token is the most desirable, e.g., $m2$. In this case, the messages can be sent and received via a regular e-mail application. In this paper, we propose an extended TIHF Protocol that allows the external negotiation facility to be eliminated in order to ensure the validity of the trade.

3   Approach

This section describes the extended TIHF Protocol.

3.1   TIHF Protocol Extension

We assume that user A and N users $B_k(k = 1...N)$ exchange tokens. $\upsilon = \{A, B_k|k = 1...N\}$ is the set of these users. U is a member of υ. In this case, the Main Protocol in the extended TIHF Protocol proceeds as follows:

A generates f and stores it in smart card S_A. f contains no description of partner B and his token i_B. A sends $m1$ to multiple users who check $m1$ sent from A. B_k who wants to get i_A described in f makes his own token i_{B_k} unavailable. B_k sends $m2_k$. A receives N $m2_k$ and checks them. A selects as the best user B whose token is the most desirable. A sends $m3$ to B. A and B continue the remaining steps from (Step4).

In this process, when U receives $m1$ or $m2_k$, U checks them as follows:(1) U checks whether the token described in f or in g_k is desirable for U. (2) U checks the validity of $\tilde{U}$ using the public key certificate $C_{\tilde{U}}$. Therefore, $m1$ used in the extended TIHF Protocol includes C_A.

Tokens in this extended TIHF Protocol are determined using $m1$ or $m2_k$, not the external negotiation facility. Therefore, the following instances can intentionally interrupt the Main Protocol during the negotiation process:

(a) A receives no agreement g_k because token i_A is not desirable to any user.
(b) A cannot select the best partner although A receives g_k because no token described in g_k is desirable for A.

These represent *failure of the negotiation*. In both cases, A simply removes f stored in S_A since i_A now becomes available. In case (a), B_k does nothing since B_k only read the message. However, in case (b), i_{B_k} is left unavailable because B_k doesn't receive $m3$ from A but has already made i_{B_k} unavailable in sending $m2_k$. B_k makes i_{B_k} available again by following the same Resolve Protocol as used by the original TIHF Protocol.

We assume that the TTP in the extended TIHF Protocol provides the following service: **Cancel** is provided to all unselected users. **Redress** is provided to a pair of users, i.e., A and B, who commenced an exchange that was later interrupted.

If only one TTP is used, it would be overwhelmed by the many unselected users. To avoid this problem, we consider that multiple TTPs are used for **Cancel**. If multiple TTPs are used, however, a pair of users can illegally reproduce tokens by accessing different TTPs. We assume that $A(originator)$, who received $m2_k$, uses $TTP1$ and $B(recipient)$, who received $m3$, uses $TTP2$. $TTP1$ says 'Commit' to A , $TTP2$ says 'Abort' to B. As a result, token i_A disappears and token i_B doubles.

To prevent this malicious behavior, only one TTP should support **Redress** while multiple TTPs can offer cancellation. Thus we add the following step: T is one of multiple TTPs. CA issues the public key certificates C_T for S_T.

(a) To prevent a conflict from being resolved by two TTPs, T is described in g_k by B_k. T is registered with smart card S_U in advance. The TTP verifies that T described in g_k is equal T in the Resolve Protocol.
(b) To prevent a conflict from being resolved by an uncertified TTP, S_U verifies C_T issued by CA in the Resolve Protocol.

3.2   The Summary of the Protocol Flow

We provide a summary of the extended TIHF Protocol. We assume that user A and N users $B_k(k = 1...N)$ exchange tokens following the extended TIHF Protocol. $v = \{A, B_k | k = 1...N\}$ is the set of these users. U is a member of v. $\tau = \{T_k | k = 1...M\}$ is the set of M TTPs. T is a member of τ. CA has two key pairs (Sk_X, Pk_X) and (Sk_Y, Pk_Y). CA issues the public key certificates $C_U = ((Pk_U)_{Pk_X})$ for S_U and $C_T = ((Pk_T)_{Pk_Y})$ for S_T. S_U has $\{U, (Sk_U, Pk_U), C_U, Pk_X, (T, Pk_Y)\}$, where T is the symbol to identify S_T used in the Resolve Protocol and Pk_Y is the public key needed to verify C_T. S_T has $\{T, (Sk_T, Pk_T), C_T, Pk_X\}$. Pk_X is the public key needed to verify C_U.

Table 2 shows the sequence of the extended TIHF Protocol. The following messages are used in this flow: $f = (A, i_A, r_A)$, $g_k = (T, A, i_A, B_k, i_{B_k}, r_A, H(r_{B_k}))$, where $T(\in g_k)$ is the symbol identifying S_T used in the Resolve Protocol.

The sequence of the **Main Protocol** is described as follows:

(Step1) S_A generates r_A and stores $f(generate\ r_A)$. S_A sends $m1 = (f, C_A)$ to B_k, where $m1$ contains C_A.
(Step1') B_k checks i_A and A with C_A verified by S_{B_k}. If B_k doesn't want to get i_A, then B_k does nothing.
(Step2) S_{B_k} generates r_{B_k}, makes i_{B_k} unavailable and stores (g_k, r_{B_k}) $(remove\ i_{B_k})$. S_{B_k} sends $m2_k = ((g_k)_{Pk_{B_k}}, C_{B_k})$ to S_A. $m3$ includes T used in Resolve Protocol.
(Step2') A checks i_{B_k} and B_k with C_{B_k} verified by S_A. If A cannot find the best partner within N users B_k whose token i_{B_k} is desirable for A, then A removes f.
(Step3) S_A makes i_A unavailable and stores $g_k(remove\ i_A)$, where $f \in g_k$. S_A sends $m3$ to S_{B_k}.
(Step4) S_{B_k} stores i_A, removes $(g_k, r_{B_k})(store\ i_A)$, where $g \in m3$. S_{B_k} sends $m4(= r_{B_k})$ to S_A.

Table 2. DVES processing flow

		Main Protocol
Step1		(A enters i_A.)
	S_A	generate r_A
	$S_A \rightarrow S_{B_k}$	$m1 \ (= (A, i_A, r_A, C_A))$
Step1'	S_{B_k}	$V_{Pk_X}(C_A)$?:exit
		(B_k checks C_A & i_A. If NG, exit.)
Step2		(B_k enters i_{B_k}.)
	S_B	remove i_{B_k}
	$S_{B_k} \rightarrow S_A$	$m2_k \ (= ((g_k)_{Pk_{B_k}}, C_{B_k}))$
Step2'	S_A	$V_{Pk_X}(C_{B_k})$?:exit
		(A checks C_{B_k} & i_{B_k}. If NG, exit.)
Step3	S_A	$V_{Pk_B}((g_k)_{Pk_B})$?:exit
		remove i_A
	$S_A \rightarrow S_{B_k}$	$m3 \ (= ((g_k)_{Pk_A}))$
Step4	S_{B_k}	$V_{Pk_A}((g_k)_{Pk_A})$?:exit
		store i_A
	$S_{B_k} \rightarrow S_A$	$m4 \ (= (r_{B_k}))$
Step5	S_A	$H(r_{B_k}(\in m4)) = H(r_{B_k})(\in g_k)$?:exit
		store i_{B_k}
		Resolve Protocol
Step6		(U enters g_k.)
	S_U	hold g_k
	$S_U \rightarrow S_T$	$m5 \ (= ((e, g_k)_{Pk_U}, C_U))$
Step7	S_T	$(V_{Pk_X}(C_U)$ & $V_{Pk_U}((e, g_k)_{Pk_U})))$?: exit
		$d = search(g_k, \sigma)$
	$S_T \rightarrow S_U$	$m6 \ (= ((d, g_k)_{Pk_T}, C_T))$
Step8	S_U	$V_{Pk_Y}(C_T)$?: exit
		(U checks C_T. If NG, exit.)
	S_U	$V_{Pk_T}((d, g_k)_{Pk_T}))$?: exit
		resolve g_k

(Step5) S_A stores i_{B_k} and removes $g(store \ i_{B_k})$, where $H(r_{B_k}(\in m4)) = H(r_{B_k})(\in g_k)$.

The sequence of the **Resolve Protocol** is as follows:

(Step6) S_U makes g_k unavailable($hold \ g_k$). And S_U sends $m5$ to S_T described in g_k.

(Step7) S_T calculates $d(= search(g_k, \sigma)$ and sends $m6$ to S_U.

(Step8) S_U stores tokens according the following rules and removes the unavailable g_k.

If d='Commit', S_U stores $i_{\tilde{U}}$.

If d='Abort', S_U stores i_U.

4   Implementation

We implemented a smart card application for the extended TIHF Protocol and measured its processing time in order to examine its performance and the feasibility of the extended TIHF Protocol. We start by describing the specification of the smart card application. Table 3 shows the system environment for the smart card application.

The smart card application has ISO/IEC 7816-compliant files to store data used in the extended TIHF Protocol. To access these files, it has ISO/IEC 7816-4-compliant basic commands, e.g., Select File, Read Record, and additional commands for the extended TIHF Protocol. To implement these additional commands, we consider the following points:

(1) To reduce program size, we designed two generic commands that are used in (Step1), (Step2), and (Step8), which is to verify a public key certificate and to get a public key certificate of the smart card.
(2) To reduce the communication time between the smart card and the terminal, their messages are composed of minimum data without loss of security.
(3) To prevent irregular command sequences in case multiple commands are executed in regular sequence, each command checks the status of smart card application on RAM upon receipt of the message or sets it to RAM before sending the message.

As the processing time, we used the period from when the terminal application sent the message to this smart card application to when the application's reply was received. Table 4 shows the processing time in each steps. The results confirm that it is possible to build all commands into one smart card and each step in the extended TIHF Protocol are executed within 1 second using this smart card.

5   Discussion

In [8], the original TIHF Protocol is shown to achieve security and efficiency as follows: This security means preventing illegal acts, e.g., token copying, to-

Table 3. The system environment for the smart card application

IC Chip	μ-P	Infineon SLE66CLX320P (15MHz)
	RAM/ROM/EEPROM	1280 bytes / 128kbytes / 32kbytes
	Crypto	ECDSA($GF(2^m)$), SHA-1
R/W		Gemplus GemPC430
	Card side I/F	ISO/IEC 7816 T=1 9600bps
	PC side I/F	USB1.1(Hi)
User Client	CPU	Intel Pentium3 866MHz
	OS	Windows XP
	R/W Driver API	PC/SC v1.0

Table 4. Smart card processes and times taken

	Main Protocol	Time (ms)
Step1	generate r_A	355
Step1'	$V_{Pk_X}(C_A)$?:exit	593
Step2	remove i_{B_k}	628
Step2'	$V_{Pk_X}(C_{B_k})$?:exit	593
Step3	$V_{Pk_B}((g_k)_{Pk_B})$?:exit, remove i_A	742
Step4	$V_{Pk_A}((g_k)_{Pk_A})$?:exit, store i_A	674
Step5	$H(r_{B_k}(\in m4)) = H(r_{B_k})(\in g_k)$?:exit, store i_{B_k}	102
	Resolve Protocol	
Step6	hold g_k	378
Step8	$V_{Pk_Y}(C_T)$?: exit	593
	$V_{Pk_T}((d, g_k)_{Pk_T}))$?: exit, resolve g_k	561

ken alteration, and token reproduction, and to exchange tokens without losing fairness. Its efficiency is because the TTP is used only to resolve the conflicts caused by exchange interruptions. The extended TIHF Protocol must offer equal security and efficiency.

First we discuss the security of the extended TIHF Protocol. As described in (Step1), the originator broadcasts a message containing her token, i.e., i_A, to other. The following steps from (Step2) are the same as in the original TIHF Protocol. Thus we discuss the impact on security of this extension.

B_k is able to confirm C_A verified by S_{B_k} upon receipt of $m1$ in order to prevent an exchange with A who has an invalid public key certificate, e.g., the Term-of-validity has expired. However, a malicious user A', can send $m1' = ((A, i_{A'}, r_{A'}), C_A)$ since everyone can obtain any public key certificates. Upon receiving $m1'$, B_k thinks that A' is A since he can verify C_A in $m1'$, and sends $m2_k$ to A'. It is impossible for A' to generate $m3$ and $m5$ corresponding to $m1'$ because A' does not know A's secret-key Sk_A. B_k finds this out and enters the cancel phase. While this spoofing attack cannot be prevented in the proposed protocol, it does not weaken the security of the extended TIHF Protocol which equals that of the original protocol. Note that the extended TIHF Protocol has no problem in guaranteeing that the result of the negotiation is accurately reflected in the exchange process.

We next turn to efficiency. The Main Protocol of the extended TIHF Protocol is interrupted by negotiation failure in addition to the accidents possible in the TIHF Protocol. Negotiation failure is caused inevitable when multiple parties reply to the first message, while exchange interruption is caused only occasionally. Multiple TTPs are needed to provide the cancel service to unselected users. As a result, the extended TIHF Protocol has decreased efficiency in terms of the number of TTPs in comparison with the original TIHF Protocol.

To resolve this problem, our idea is that unselected users B_ks cancel the exchange using the cancel message sent from A at Step 4 instead of using the TTP. If this cancel message is not received from A, B_ks cancels the exchange using the TTP. This greatly reduces the frequency with which TTP is used. For example, B_k receives $m3$ from A at Step 4 and stores her own token i_{B_k} upon satisfying the following conditions:

(1) the signature $(g_k)_{Pk_A}$ of $m3$ is verified successfully,
(2) $f = (A, i_A, r1)$ of $m1$ received at Step 2 is equal to $(A, i_A, r1)$ of $m3$,
(3) her user ID B_k is not equal to (B) of $m3$.

Message $m3$ acts as the guarantee of the cancellation for unselected users as well as the agreement of the exchange for the pair of selected users. As a result, we can realize the extended TIHF Protocol which offers high efficiency.

6 Conclusion

In this paper, we proposed the extended TIHF Protocol with the goal of combining negotiation with the token exchange. We also wrote a smart card application that realized the extended TIHF Protocol and measured its processing time on a regular smart card. We confirmed the feasibility of the extended TIHF Protocol since the smart card application was able to generate each message used in the extended TIHF Protocol within 1 second.

In the proposed protocol, a user broadcasts an offer and selects as her partner the user with the best response. Since their message constitute part of the token exchange process, only 4 message exchanges are needed to conclude the exchange, the same as in the original TIHF protocol. Note that no external negotiation facility is needed. Since only one of the responders while be accepted, there may be many rejected suitors, all of whom must initiate the cancel process with the TTP. We offset the overhead by assuming the use of multiple TTPs for this purpose.

In this paper, we did not describe how to select the best partner and a future goal is to realize a system for selecting the best user. We will also consider P2P auction protocols to exchange digital values using the extended TIHF Protocol.

References

1. Zhou, J.: Non-repudiation in Electronic Commerce, Artech House, Inc. (2001).
2. Pagnia, H., Vogt, H. and Gärtner, C.: Fair Exchange, *The Computer Journal*, Vol.46, No.1,pp.55-75 (2003).
3. Asokan, N., Shoup, V. and Waidner, M.: Asynchronous protocols for optimistic fair exchange, *In Proceedings of the IEEE Symposium on Research in Security and Privacy*, IEEE Computer Society Press, pp.88-99 (1998).
4. Vogt, H., Pagnia, H., and Gärtner, C.: Using smart cards for fair exchange, *Electronic Commerce - WELCOM 2001*, Heidelberg, 16-17 Nov., LNCS 2232, pp.101-113, Springer-Verlag, Berlin.
5. Vogt, H., Gärtner, C., and Pagnia, H.: Supporting Fair Exchange in Mobile Environments, *Mobile Networks and Applications*, 8, pp. 127-136, Kluwer Academics Publishers(2003).
6. Lacoste, G., Pfitzmann, B., Steiner, M., Waidner, M.: SEMPER - Secure Electronic Marketplace for Europe, LNCS vol. 1854, Springer-Verlag, Berlin (2000).

7. Iguchi, M., Terada, M., Nakamura, Y. and Fujimura, K.: A Voucher-Integrated Trading Model for C2B and C2C E-Commerce System Development, *2nd IFIP Conference on e-Commerce, e-Business, and e-Government (IFIP I3E 2002)* (2002).

8. Terada, M., Iguchi, M., Hanadate, M. and Fujimura, K.: An Optimistic Fair Exchange Protocol for Trading Electronic Rights, *6th Smart Card Research and Advanced Application IFIP Conference(Cardis2004)* (2004).

9. Terada, M., Iguchi, M., Hanadate, M. and Fujimura, K.: Copy prevention scheme for rights trading infrastructure, *4th Smart Card Research and Advanced Application IFIP Conference(Cardis2000)* (2000).

"Devices Are People Too"
Using Process Patterns to Elicit Security Requirements in Novel Domains: A Ubiquitous Healthcare Example

Yang Liu, John A. Clark, and Susan Stepney

Department of Computer Science, University of York, UK

Abstract. We present a set of process patterns that can be used to as a systematic way of analysing security requirements in a novel domain, taking ubiquitous healthcare as an example.

Keywords: Ubiquitous systems, security requirements, process patterns.

1 Background

Conventional computer technology designed for office use is inadequate for use in a hospital setting. Characteristics of medical work are fundamentally different from those of typical office work [Bardram 2003]: extreme mobility, *ad hoc* collaboration, interruptions, high degree of communication, etc. In a hospital setting, pervasive computing elements will be embedded in things such as instruments, tablet blister packs, bottles, wheelchairs, badges and staff uniforms. Security is a difficult issue in current healthcare systems, e.g. [Anderson 1996a, Anderson 1996b, Vaclav 1998], and traditional security models are very hard to apply to the new kinds of pervasive systems. Worse, for pervasive healthcare systems it is not yet clear what the security requirements even are.

When such systems become established we will be faced with all the old problems of traditional IT systems, plus many more due to the characteristics of ubiquitous computing (pervasive access, wireless communications, significant mobility, etc). What should the security requirements be for such systems? How should a healthcare system designer go about determining such requirements? We do not know: there is no systematic approach or guidelines to tackle the pressing concerns for healthcare systems incorporating pervasive technologies.

We propose the use of **process patterns** to guide the elicitation of new security requirements of novel pervasive computing application domains. We have developed useful patterns and anti-patterns that characterise issues, problems and some policy strategies, in a manner inspired by software engineering patterns work. Several such patterns are presented in this paper.

2 A Way Forward - Process Patterns

Patterns [Alexander *et al.* 1977] capture expert knowledge about commonly occurring problems and situations, and their solutions, expressed in ways that (should) assist

D. Hutter and M. Ullmann (Eds.): SPC 2005, LNCS 3450, pp. 31–45, 2005.

less experienced users to solve problems. As such, individual patterns may sometimes appear relatively banal, especially to those expert users. However, the purpose of patterns is to codify good engineering experience, and the cumulative effect of a whole Pattern Language can exceed the sum of its individual patterns.

Patterns are used in software engineering to document and promote best practice, and to share expertise. Existing patterns cover a range of issues, from coding standards [Beck 1997], through program design [Gamma *et al.* 1995], to domain analysis [Fowler 1997] and formal specification [Stepney *et al*, 2003], and meta-concerns such as team structures and project management [Coplien 1995]. The pattern concept has been extended with antipatterns, illustrating developmental pitfalls and their avoidance or recovery [Brown et al. 1998].

Our eventual goal here is the creation of a catalogue of specific policy requirement patterns for ubiquitous systems. System developers would browse such a catalogue to determine which patterns were suited to their particular needs. Suitable patterns could then simply be incorporated into security policies. The catalogue could be viewed as an analogue of the security patterns catalogue from the Open Group [Open Group 2002], but addressing higher level (policy) concerns.

However, much work is needed before such a catalogue of specific patterns can even be started. There are no available patterns for security *requirements*, and little in the way of security requirements for ubiquitous healthcare systems. The state of practice is that we do not yet know what the regularly occurring problems are, let alone their solutions. A catalogue today could provide patterns that are only provisional solutions (at a policy/requirements level) to problems we *believe* will occur. Also, whatever security catalogue becomes available, new systems will inevitably raise concerns that are not covered by it. What then should developers do? Can we help them to create new requirements and requirements patterns? What is needed now is a process for *creating* the catalogue in the first instance: *process patterns* for eliciting novel requirements.

We have developed an initial version of such a process pattern catalogue. The patterns it includes should be useful not only in the ubiquitous healthcare domain, but in a wider set of novel application domains. Indeed, the generation of this catalogue itself is a novel domain, and the patterns can be used at a meta-level: we applied the patterns we were developing to their own development.

Here we present an outline of some of the patterns in our catalogue that are most specific to ubiquitous healthcare, and how we applied them, both to get more specific patterns, and in the generation of the process patterns themselves. The full catalogue can be found in [Liu 2004].

3 Structure of the Patterns

Each pattern given in the text below is presented in a common four-part structure:

- **Name**. This provides an easily remembered and intuitive name for the pattern.
- **Intent**. A summary of what the pattern provides, what task it aims to facilitate.
- **Motivation**. A brief rationale for why the pattern is needed.
- **Solution**. This provides a description of how the intent of the pattern can be realised. There may be several such solutions.

In the text below each major pattern is presented in a section on its own, with the name of the pattern indicated in the section header in quotes. The first such pattern is the "Getting Started" Pattern.

4 "Getting Started" Pattern

Intent
To get started in an unfamiliar domain, where requirements are not fully understood.

Motivation
Security is a difficult issue in current healthcare systems; the security issues emerging from pervasive computing will be even more complicated and unpredictable. We have no *systematic* approach or guidelines to tackle the such systems. However, we do have some generic requirements elicitation techniques at our disposal that should be part of any requirements elicitation process.

Solution1: Literature review. Get up to speed by reading the existing literature.

Solution2: Stakeholder interview.   Use the classic requirements elicitation technique of identifying and interviewing all the relevant stakeholders.

Solution3: Security experts. Discuss requirements with general security experts, to get overall requirements for secure systems, in order to adapt them to the specific domain.

Solution 4: Brainstorms.   This potentially very useful technique can help to highlight big issues and requirements arising from the earlier reviews and discussions. It can also identify issues missed or not in the scope of other techniques.

Solution 5: Scenarios are an important classic technique, and form a specific process pattern of their own (see later).

Origin and Application of the "Getting Started" Pattern

Literature review.   The current literature highlights ubiquitous healthcare environments comprising a mixture of participants, including people, devices, other infrastructure etc. The distinction between people and devices is somewhat blurred, with some similarities between device and personal concepts. This suggests that a deliberate blurring of the two could provide inspiration for pattern generation operated by equating analogous concepts between the two domains. If we have a requirement for one this immediately suggests a possible requirement for the other. This eventually led to formulation of the "**Devices are People too**" pattern.

Stakeholder interviews. We interviewed two senior Hospital staff responsible for security issues of the current IT systems. Various security issues were raised during this meeting. Of particular note was the "erroneous mapping" issue between the virtual (computer) model of the system and what is actually happening in the real physical world. This led us to consider a much more general issue of mapping between the two worlds, and to the "**Model out of sync**" antipattern.

Security issues of portable devices is another point exposed by this interview. The security requirements of the mixture of participants involved in ubiquitous healthcare environment are major concerns, especially embedded devices with sensors that may exchange information with other agents (people or devices). The security requirements of devices need to be considered as analogous to those of people, incorporated into "**Devices are People too**".

Security expert discussions. For this research, two of the authors who had extensive experience of industrial security (Clark and Stepney) acted as the security experts. The literature survey highlighted the importance of privacy as an issue. Agents in ubiquitous systems require privacy, but also want services to be provided. There are obvious conflicts to be addressed. We chose to consider conflicting goals of a service requester and those of a service provider under a variety of different scenarios (not discussed further in this paper; see [Liu 2004] for details).

Brainstorms. We know that all stakeholders should be able to "buy in" to ubiquitous system policies and should be treated appropriately. So we considered some specific requirements, and asked what would happen if we replaced the stakeholder subject to it by another. We used this to help generate "**Substitution**" as a means of generating new requirements from old. In those cases where substitution does produce a further acceptable requirement, then the old and new requirements can be regarded as specific instances of a higher level one. We used this to help generate "**Generalisation**", to create a more widely applicable or abstract version of a specific requirement.

5 "Build Scenario" Pattern

Intent
To systematically identify the situations an agent will find itself in and consider the security issues that apply.

Motivation
Determining requirements is hard. Often important requirements are missed or are inaccurate. It is very easy to miss subtleties that apply to specific circumstances (or even appreciate what special circumstances there are – see "**Consider Modes**")

Experience is a great educator: one of the best ways to appreciate a need is to be faced with that need. We need to pre-empt the experience we will have when the system is built.

In normal requirements engineering, a *scenario* can be used to capture a particular transaction in a concrete way (and then be abstracted to a more general Use Case [Cockburn 2001] [Adolph *et al* 2003], for example). Traditional Use Case scenarios tend to focus on functionality, but scenarios are also excellent ways to focus attention on non-functional issues, such as security [19]. Scenarios allow us to 'walk through' situations that an agent may encounter, at early stages in the requirements process.

On walking through situations, we can see what encounters are generated, and so can consider what we need to do in those circumstances.

For many agents in the system we can develop a scenario of the whole of their activity over time, not just a single transaction. Thus, the working life of a person is a scenario, with an entry point (a nurse joins the hospital), a middle (a series of working days which may involve significant repetition) and an end (the nurse leaves the hospital). And if a nurse has a lifetime-scenario, then so does a scalpel, or a broom, or indeed any other device. The scenario allows us to consider the circumstances agents will find themselves in over various timescales.

This pattern prompts the security analyst to systematically consider situations otherwise neglected. The lifetime of an agent can be viewed as a series of internal actions and interactions with other agents. Interactions take place via protocols. By exploring the life of an agent through a scenario we are prompted to consider the agents it comes into contact with, and in which contexts, and to consider the security issues that arise.

Solution
Build scenarios by tracing through the activities of an agent over time. The scenarios represent the operational contexts for an agent. Use the scenarios as prompts to discover the situations an agent will encounter, and so increase the chances of completeness in requirements.

Step 1. Simple scenario. Identify a feasible series of actions over an appropriate timescale. This may be the steps in a procedure, or the whole lifetime of an agent. Identify the agents one encounters, together with any possible interactions between those agents and the agent in question. Identify any locations entered and boundaries that are crossed and consider any security issues that arise.

Step 2. Fully moded scenario. Using "**Consider Modes**", produce a whole lifecycle of an agent (person or device), and generate various modes that happen in each stage.

Step 3. Analogous scenarios. Using the various "**Analogy**" patterns ("Analogy", "Substitution", "Generalisation", "Specialisation", "Devices are People too"), form other related scenarios to generate further requirements, by considering analogous lifecycle events of any device or any person.

Origin and Application of the "Scenario" Pattern

After brainstorming, we chose to apply the Scenario pattern to "A day in the life of a SmartBroom" – a mundane device that might be used in new ways once made "smart", and hence lead to new security requirements.

Step 1. Simple scenario
A broom starts its day in the cupboard, is taken out, is used to sweep a variety of floors, is cleaned at some point, and is eventually returned to the cupboard to await use again. Its locations are restricted (a ward broom should not be used to sweep the garden, or an operating theatre, to avoid spread of material and infectious agents). Tracing the location of a device as it proceeds through its day is useful.

For safety reasons, access control is an important issue (this SmartBroom is an expensive and powerful device): we must guarantee that a broom can be accessed only by legitimate users. Identification, Authorisation and Authentication need to be considered: who is participating in this scenario (e.g. cleaners, brooms, other staff, devices nearby, cupboards/storerooms, rooms/corridors)? Who may open a cupboard and take a broom out? When can it be taken out? And what protocols are needed?

The broom must be used only in places authorised by the security policy. The policy should cover aspects such as: where this broom is allowed to clean; how the broom is allowed to move from one place to another; what it is allowed to remember of the places it is near or passes through; and whether it is allowed to tell other agents (people or devices) where it is or has been, etc. We may wish to restrict the places a broom may be used: a general ward broom should not be used to sweep the garden, or a sterile operating theatre. Thus, there needs to be an enforceable policy of restricted use. We must be careful in how we partition space in the hospital and what restrictions we impose. There is little point in authorising a broom for use in a particular room, but denying it access to the corridors by which that room is reached from the storage cupboard!

We might specify whatever policy we might wish to hold, but this will need to be enforced. In some cases there may be a direct and clear implementation of policy: if a cleaner is not authorised to access a storeroom, then the room may simply remain electronically locked. In others, some rectifying action must be taken. A broom will generally be unable to prevent itself being moved by a cleaner through an unauthorised corridor. In such circumstances we might require some notification be generated, with an expectation of action. For example, a talking broom might inform its user that a security breach has occurred, or the environment might detect the breach and sound an alarm. Such considerations lead to the development of the more general "**Alarms and Emergencies**"; other considerations during this phase of the scenario lead to input to "**Conflict Resolution**" (Liu 2004).

What happens to the internal state of a broom when it is returned to storage. Should its current working memory be erased? It may be appropriate to break any association established earlier with a particular cleaner, but what happens to the history of its day? The latter question was sparked by use of "**Devices are People too**": memory is one of the concepts subject to that analogy. It reminded us that there are potential "device privacy" implications from day-to-day historical information. Issues of memory must be considered when brooms and other items of equipment are disposed of, leading into the "fully moded scenario".

Step 2. Fully moded scenario
A device may have many modes: maintenance mode, emergency mode, work/stand by mode, normal/abnormal mode, etc. A patient may have chronic disease/acute disease mode, in hospital/at home mode, etc. A doctor may have work/holiday mode, day/night mode, weekday/weekend/bank holiday mode, full-time/part-time/retired mode etc.

Scenarios occurring in the hospital exhibit various timescales. Some situations happen over a lifetime (e.g. the lifetime of devices or patients). Some situations happen in a day (e.g. family visitors coming to visit patients, emergency circumstance). Even so, we can discover common features. For example, we may find many situations that are *repeated* (e.g. multiple entries of a patient to hospital, a broom repeatedly taken out to clean the floor and taken back after use). These patterns give us clues to help build up a suite of temporal modes for all agents.

Step 3. Analogous scenarios
By analogy to devices, nurses, doctors, patients might be tracked over time. What does a nurse do during the day? Where do they visit? Thus, a nurse will come into the hospital, change into uniform, look through patients' records, prepare tablets and injections for patients, go to see patients in the wards, and routinely record what things happen. If a general device is attached to a nurse, should it be allowed to announce its location? In the extreme circumstance, if a nurse is attending a sensitive patient (e.g. a famous patient or an HIV patient), devices attached to them might be required not to announce location, except to specific requestors. The lifecycle of a nurse can be "Substituted" by the lifecycle of a consultant to see what happens, and what new requirements emerge.

Such considerations helped us to develop "**Analogy**" and its raft of specialisations.

6 "Consider Modes" Pattern

Intent
To systematically generate and consider relevant modes of system use.

Motivation
It would be convenient if our security requirements were simple and our systems obeyed a one-size-fits-all philosophy. However, circumstances change, and our requirements may change with them, subtly, or in major ways. For example, we may prohibit the use of fire exits in normal usage, but certainly wish to allow their use in times of fire. Similarly, night-time operations may have different requirements from day-time operations. Once such varying circumstances and qualifiers have been identified, we can consider whether policy refinements are needed in their context. However, identifying such circumstances is not easy. Moding has been found to be a useful concept in the safety domain. This pattern provides a process to prompt us to systematically generate and consider relevant circumstances.

Solution
Four classes of abstract qualifier are particularly useful: **time-scale** mode, **spatial** mode, **event/circumstance** mode, and **attributes** mode.

- When a requirement is generated for one component of a mode (usually "normal operation", such as "daytime" or "on ward"), systematically ask questions of all the other mode components.
- When a new mode is discovered, generate all the mode components for it, and add them to this Consider Modes catalogue

Time–scale mode. A variety of temporal modes can be determined by calendar perspective, people perspective, and devices perspective.

- Calendar perspective: day (day/night, morning/afternoon/evening/night), week (weekday/weekend, specific days of week), month, season, calendar year, financial year (special last month of financial year), other kinds of years (tax, academic etc.)
- People perspective: (a) staff: on-shift/off-shift/break, holiday/at work, healthy/off sick, full-time/part-time/retired; (b) patients: short-term/long-term stay, etc.
- Devices perspective: (**Analogise** the people perspective) time modes for devices might be include shutdown/hibernation/at work/stand by, normal operation/abnormal operation, maintenance/upgrade/emergency, and full-time/part-time/disposed.

Spatial mode. A hospital can be partitioned by location in a variety of ways: partition by location type (such as cupboard, operating theatre, wards or corridors); partition by floor (basement, ground, first floor etc.); inside the hospital building, outside the hospital buildings (in the grounds) etc.

Event/circumstance mode. This mode relates to operational events/circumstances. Thus, we may identify a normal mode of operation. This reflects perhaps the most common set of circumstances. (In Use Cases normal operation would be reflected in the normal flow of events.) However, sometimes things deviate from such normality. For example, we can identify two sorts of emergency. There may be an externally generated emergency, such a major rail accident; such circumstances are fortunately not normal, but hospitals must nevertheless be prepared for their occurrence. An internally generated emergency would be a fire in the hospital. These two different classes of emergency must obviously be dealt with in different ways, and give rise to different security requirements.

Furthermore, circumstances can be considered on a loading axis: very busy (e.g. train accident), busy (e.g. regular peak time loading), not so busy (e.g. normal operation) etc.

Attributes mode. Different system components and stakeholders need to be treated in different ways according to particular attributes they possess. Requirements may be partitioned according to the attributes of each agent.

The most obvious attribute is role. Medical staff will be able to access data that patients should not. More generally, the actual role played by stakeholder will determine the rights and constraints that should be applied to them.

Other attributes might be used for making distinctions. A device may be mobile or immobile. It may be easy to casually steal a mobile device (such as a PDA), but stealing a scanning machine weighing several tonnes and fixed to the floor is a different prospect. One might wish to permit free communication (e.g. with respect to giving away location information) with immobile devices on account of this.

Different values of scalar attributes of a system may act as a cause for discrimination. Thus, we might consider agents with different physical attributes (such as size, weight or shape) differently. Non-physical attributes such as cost of replacement may also be relevant.

Origin and Application of the "Consider Modes" Pattern

The recognition of the modal nature of the "in cupboard/in use" part of the SmartBroom scenario sparked a **Generalisation**, which led us to develop the "**Consider Modes**" pattern, and many of its examples, in parallel with developing the Scenario pattern instance. This led us to generalise the scenario pattern to include a "fully moded scenario" step.

7 "Analogise" Pattern

Intent

To elicit and derive requirements for some agents and circumstances by analogy with requirements for other, analogous, agents and circumstances.

Motivation

Analogy has been found to be a great tool in the history of thinking [18]. The process is not generally subject to automation and so requires imagination. Thus, revisiting some security requirements elements but choosing to 'wear a different hat' forces the analyst to consider whether analogous concepts exist. This is a generally applicable pattern. We can apply it to specific technical requirements patterns for the system or to patterns for generating patterns etc.

Ubiquitous healthcare environments will comprise a mixture of agents. These may be people, infrastructure or mobile devices. We explicitly construct a variety of analogies between these classes of agents.

Solution

The solution can be at a very high level of abstraction. It reduces to taking a concept from one area of investigation and reinterpreting it in another situation.

In practice, more specific instances of this pattern are used, where we draw analogies between various classes of people and devices, taking characteristics of one and interpreting them for the other. We do not expect *every* application of the pattern to result in new requirements – some analogies simply do not hold – but we do expect the systematic application to throw up new and unexpected considerations in many cases.

"**Substitute X with Y**" systematically reinterprets requirements when one class of agent is substituted for another (for example, "consultant" for "nurse"). "**Specialise**" is an example of "Substitute", where Y is more specific than X, to check that a general requirement makes sense in specific cases. ("All devices shall announce their location when queried; specialise "device" to "dangerous drug bottle" and reanalyse.) "**Generalise**" is an example of Substitute, where Y is more general than X , to investigate if a more generic requirement can be formulated. And if X corresponds to people, and Y to devices, we get "**Devices are People too**", expanded below.

Origin and Application of the "Analogise" Pattern and Its Specialisations

We formulated "**Analogise**" very early on, since analogy is such a useful tool, then developed the particular specialisations subsequently. These patterns formed an important part of the process of deriving the other process patterns, by deliberately applying them to the patterns themselves. For example, "**Consider Modes**" was generated by application of "**Generalise**" to the modes discovered in the SmartBroom "**Scenario**" instance.

8 "Devices Are People Too" Pattern

Intent
Apply "**Substitution**", with X =people, Y = devices.

Motivation
In ubiquitous healthcare systems the distinction between people and devices is blurred (for example, we may often take the presence of one as indication of the presence of the other). We may be able to take advantage of this. We have well-established notions of what people want to maintain in terms of their personal well-being, but we have far less idea of what should be the well-being of a device or infrastructure component. If the distinction between people and computational facilities/devices is becoming blurred, perhaps we should consider how requirements established for one apply to the other.

For example, a requirement for a person to undergo a health check can translate to a requirement for a device to undergo a maintenance check (e.g. to calibrate an instrument). Although this may seem a little odd at first sight, it can have useful consequences. For example, we might not otherwise consider aspects such as the 'privacy' of a device, which has interesting interpretations.

By analogy with people, security issues can be identified for devices (e.g. trays, brushes, scalpels, tablets) in various situations. The application of such analogy patterns allows the early generation of ideas and requirements. The earlier such ideas/requirements are generated the better. (Some such ideas can also be generated by the application of other patterns.)

Solution
Starting with an assertion such as "Devices are people too" or "People are devices too", we define requirements for one, and then reinterpret these for the other. Some analogies may be more natural than others. The analyst is free to reject any that seem inappropriate. We simply wish to generate ideas for consideration.

In daily life, people have basic needs (e.g. food, sleep, privacy, health etc.). Using the analogy "Devices are people too" we can consider the corresponding needs of devices (e.g. power, maintenance, upgrade, security policy, privacy, input or output, communication with people etc.).

The table below captures some analogous concepts between people and devices. Some concepts have direct interpretations, e.g., memory (though it is perhaps easier to upgrade a devices memory!). Others are clear with re-interpretation, e.g. sleeping and standby operations (some devices are even described as being in sleep or power saving mode). There is also a clear analogy between training/retraining and maintenance upgrades. One can also generate analogies between the various forms of audit activities, e.g. health checks.

Person	Device
Food	Energy
Sleep	Stand-by
Training	Upgrade/maintenance
Holiday	Shutdown/hibernation
Audit	Audit
Communication	Communication
Privacy	Privacy
Well-being	Health

When applying analogy, we must think about what the devices really need, what happens if devices go wrong, what kinds of granularity are appropriate, what would happen if we upgrade the device to a new version, or we reconfigure the devices, or whatever. For example, at intervals, medical staff need to be retrained; by analogy, we might consider that it is essential to update or upgrade the devices.

Origin and Application of the "Devices Are People Too" Pattern

We are used to considering security issues such as confidentiality for patients, but is there a corresponding notion for devices? By analogy with patient privacy, we look for some privacy policy for devices (e.g. trays, rooms, brooms, tablets). Suppose a SmartBroom is to be used only to sweep an HIV patient's room. If this broom is tracked by other things (people or devices) without legitimate privilege, its 'privacy' would be leaked, and it might be possible to link it with other things (e.g. location, room number and patient in that room). Thus, by considering the need for privacy of a broom, we have helped maintain the privacy of a person. The usefulness of an analogy is determined by the eventual results of generating it. People might say that the whole concept of device privacy is nonsense; this is in fact a minor concern. However, by simply considering the analogy we have generated new concerns that must be dealt with. The analogy can serve a purpose simply by prompting new questions.

Take another security requirement such as "The location of nurses shall be determinable only by agents with appropriate authority." What about devices? Should access to device location be similarly constrained? We could ask 'What is the reason for the requirement?' There may appear to be good personal safety reasons why nurses would not wish to disclose their location in various circumstances. Are there circumstances where devices should be similarly 'concerned' for their own 'safety'? Drug addicts might have designs on dangerous drugs bottles. More generally, if a device has high value then thieves might wish to obtain its precise location in order to steal it. So here we see how a reinterpretation of the concept of 'personal safety' for devices sparks considerations from which new requirements inevitably occur.

Here we might also investigate the privacy angle? If we are constrained in our ability to track a nurse but have free access to where their Personal Digital Assistant is, then (for many hours of the day at least) we do in fact know where they are. Thus we are prompted to consider the privacy aspects of devices and people together.

"**Devices are People too**" arose early in "**Brainstorming**", and was later formalised as a pattern. Concepts of device privacy led to several of the more specific patterns such as "**Conflict Resolution**" (Liu 2004).

9 "Model Out of Sync" Anti-pattern

Intent

To investigate the link between the computer model and reality by applying the notion of "**Devices are People too**" and "**Consider Modes**".

"Devices are people too" leads to consideration of incorrect links between the physical device and its model. "Consider modes" leads to consideration of the times of establishing and breaking the links.

Problem

A real world agent (person or device) is generally represented in the computer by some model of that agent, and the model is updated by sensing attributes of the real-world agent (possibly indirectly by sensing some attached *tagging* device). It is possible for the real world and the model to get out of synchronisation, for a variety of reasons. (See also [Jackson 2001, chapter 7]). This can potentially lead to severe problems.

We might evaluate the model status of a tag in order to deduce the real world status of an agent. We want the location of the person; we measure the location of their tag; we assume these are strongly linked, that we can take the tag to be a *proxy* for the person. If the link between tag and agent is broken (e.g. sensor removal), or the mapping between real world and model is wrong, then we get a mistaken view of the status of the real world.

Causes of Real World out of Sync with Model

Erroneous Linking Assumption

The link between what is measured in the real world and what is deduced about the real world from that measurement might be incorrect.

The location of an agent is not necessarily equal to the location of its tag. A person might accidentally mislay their badge, or deliberately remove it because they do not want anybody know where they are. The assumption "real world location of X's tag equals real world location of X" does not necessarily hold.

This is a particular example of a more general problem. Consider the example of monitoring the tablets a patient takes by tagging each strip of tablets so that the removal of a tablet can be sensed. If a tablet is removed from the strip, we might assume that the tablet is consumed by the patient. However, a patient might remove the tablet, but then throw it away, or give it to another patient to consume. The assumption "tablets removed from X's strip" does not necessarily imply "tablets consumed by X".

Erroneous Mapping

What is measured in the real world might be incorrect. Even if the modelling assumptions are correct, it is possible for software or physical problems to cause the mapping between the model and the real world to drift out of sync. For example, a sensor might not sense its location correctly, due to low power, a software glitch, or communications interference. So we get the erroneous mapping between the sensor and the real world. The assumption "reported location of X equals real world location of X" does not necessarily hold.

Solution

There are several ways to bring the model and the real world back in synch.

Step 1: Identify linking assumptions

Identify the linking assumptions and the reasons for these linkings. Often it is not possible to guarantee these assumptions (how would you guarantee a member of staff did not remove their tag?), and so techniques to resync the model in the case of the identified assumptions not holding need to be designed.

Step 2: Analyse how links might break

In order to design a suitable resyncing strategy, we need to know how likely the link breakage is to occur, and what the consequences of such a break are. Infrequent low-consequence occurrences will have different recovery mechanisms from high-frequency high-consequence ones. For example, we might have information concerning how often tablets are removed but not consumed, whether this happens accidentally or deliberately, and what the consequences are if it happens.

Step 3a: Choose Calibration and Testing

While the model is running, it can be tested and calibrated it in order to find problems (e.g. wrong data, erroneous mapping). The "**Consider Modes**" pattern suggests use of the maintenance mode to ensure the normal status and keep the system workable. If we test or calibrate the model frequently, it is much easier to find the mismatching or the wrong mapping between the model and the real world. Step 2 gives input to how frequently this needs to be done in each case.

Step 3b: Chose Redundancy

Redundant sensing (multiple sensors) can be used to make the links stronger, and reduce the possibility of errors. In the tablets example, for high-consequence cases, it would be reasonable for a nurse to watch the patient taking tablets rather than leave the patient alone, to ensure that the tablets are consumed, and hence ensure the link is not broken. Again, Step 2 gives input to how much redundancy is appropriate in each case

Origin and Application of the "Model Out of Sync" Anti-pattern

In our discussions with the Health officials, it became clear that their current major concern is the difficulty of keeping the computer-based patient records up-to-date, since the current state of the art data entry is nowhere near as immediate as pen and paper note taking. We formalised this into a pattern, then applied "**People are Devices too**" and "**Consider Modes**" to generate the "**Model out of sync**" pattern.

10 Meta-patterns

One of the most interesting parts of this work was how it was possible to apply these process patterns to the process of generating the patterns themselves. This has convinced us that the patterns are more widely applicable that just to pervasive healthcare, or even just to the pervasive computing domain.

11 Discussion and Conclusion

We have provided an account of several *process patterns* for eliciting security requirements in novel domains, and of how the actual patterns were developed. Some of the patterns are very abstract and so find wide applicability. Thus, "**Generalisation**" and "**Specialisation**" are two crucial, but very general, thinking tools. One might argue that we should not be surprised that such patterns can be applied. However, we find that the deliberate application of such patterns brings useful results.

An informal appreciation of the blurring in healthcare systems (and pervasive system generally) of the distinction between devices and people led directly to "**People are Devices too**". Applying "**Generalisation**" to this allowed it to be seen as a particular instance of "**Analogy**". Applying "**Analogy**" and its specialisations to requirements can be a useful way of generating new particular requirements, and also a good way of 'sanity checking' requirements of supposed general applicability.

The "Day in the life of a SmartBroom" work provided valuable insights in itself, and when subject to "**Generalisation**" led to the creation of "**Build Scenario**", which is highly flexible and can be instantiated as required. (Of course, we have simultaneously generalised away from broom, to device, to agent).

We believe "**Consider Modes**" and "**Devices are People too**" to be the patterns most valuable for ubiquitous systems. This work demonstrates that applying process patterns to generate new requirements patterns has considerable promise.

Acknowledgements

We thank Ian Sutcliffe (Director of Communications & Information) and Andy Moore (Head of IT) from Harrogate Healthcare NHS Trust, UK, for very helpful discussions in the early stages of this work.

References

[1] S. Adolph, P. Bramble, A. Cockburn, A. Pols. *Patterns for Effective Use Cases.* Addison-Wesley, 2003.

[2] C. Alexander, et al. A Pattern Language: towns, buildings, construction. OUP, 1977

[3] R. J. Anderson. Security in Clinical Information Systems. *British Medical Association*, Jan 1996.

[4] R. J. Anderson. *An Update on the BMA Security Policy.* (1996). Available from http://www.cl.cam.ac.uk/users/rja14/bmaupdate/bmaupdate.html

[5] J. E. Bardram. Hospitals of the Future – ubiquitous computing support for medical work in hospitals. In *Proc. Second Ubiquitous Healthcare Computing*, 2003

[6] K. Beck. *Smalltalk Best Practice Patterns*. Prentice Hall, 1997

[7] J. Bohn, F. Gartner, H. Vogt. Dependability Issues of Pervasive Computing in a Healthcare Environment. In *Proc. First International Security in Pervasive Computing*, 2003

[8] W. J. Brown *et al*. *AntiPatterns*. Wiley, 1998

[9] A. Cockburn. *Writing Effective Use Cases*. Addison Wesley, 2001

[10] J. O. Coplien. A generative development-process pattern language. In J. O. Coplien, D. C. Schmidt, eds, *Pattern Languages of Program Design*. Addison-Wesley, 1995.

[11] M. Fowler. *Analysis Patterns*. Addison-Wesley, 1997

[12] E. Gamma *et al*. *Design Patterns*. Addison Wesley, 1995

[13] Michael Jackson. *Problem Frames*. Addison Wesley, 2001

[14] Yang Liu. *Security in Ubiquitous Healthcare Systems*. MSc thesis, Dept Computer Science, University of York, UK. 2004

[15] The Open Group. *Guide to Security Patterns*, Draft 1. April 2002

[16] S. Stepney, F. Polack, I. Toyn. An Outline Pattern Language for Z. In D. Bert *et al*, eds. *ZB2003: Third International Conference of B and Z Users, Turku, Finland, June 2003*. LNCS vol 2651, pp 2–19. Springer, 2003

[17] J. M. Vaclav. Protecting Doctors' Identity in Drug Prescription Analysis. *Health Informatics Journal*, December 1998.

[18] Medieval Theories of Analogy. Entry in Stanford Encyclopedia of Philosophy. http://plato.stanford.edu/entries/analogy-medieval/#3

[19] Effective Security Requirements Analysis: HAZOPs and Use Cases. Jill Srivatanakul, John A Clark and Fiona Polack. Proceedings of Information Security, 7th International Conference, ISC 2004. Lecture Notes in Computer Science, Vol. 3225, pp 416-427.

[20] Challenging Formal Specifications with Mutation: A CSP Security Example. Jill Srivratanakul, John Clark, Fiona Polack and Susan Stepney. Proceedings of the 12th IEEE Asia Pacific Software Engineering Conference (APSEC) 2003.

Securing Ad Hoc Networks

Panos Papadimitratos

The Bradley Department of Electrical and Computer Engineering,
Virginia Polytechnic Institute and State University
papadp@vt.edu

Securing the operation of ad hoc networking protocols is a multifaceted and complex problem that poses new and unique challenges. All network nodes constitute a self-organizing infrastructure, while operating in an inherently unreliable and insecure environment. The boundaries of an ad hoc network are blurred, if not inexistent, and its membership may frequently change. Without security measures, attackers have ample opportunity to control, disrupt, and degrade the services or even disable communications of other users. As a result, applications based on the ad hoc networking technology cannot proliferate, unless such vulnerabilities are eradicated. For example, search-and-rescue, law enforcement, or battlefield networks must guarantee secure and reliable communication, even if a significant fraction of the network nodes are disabled or controlled by an adversary. Similarly, users will not enable their portable devices to join and form ad hoc networks, unless access to the sought services is protected from compromise. This talk discusses threats and security measures, focusing on a comprehensive solution for secure and fault-tolerant communication in ad hoc networks. We discuss our design of a protocol suite that addresses the security of the route discovery and the security of the data transmission in ad hoc networks. The presented material reflects on-going research, as well as research conducted over the past four years at Cornell University under the supervision of Prof. Z. J. Haas.

The security of the route discovery ensures desired properties for the discovered routes, which must be up-to-date and reflect factual network connectivity in spite of active adversarial disruptions. The Secure Routing Protocol (SRP) is a reactive routing protocol suitable for a broad range of MANETs, operating in an end-to-end manner without restrictive assumptions on network trust and security associations. Low route discovery delay with low network and processing overhead can be achieved, even when a significant fraction of the network nodes disrupt the route discovery. To broaden the scope of secure routing, two alternative secure routing protocols were designed: SRP-DV, which performs a secure distance-vector-like discovery, and SRP-QoS, which ensures the accuracy of the metric(s) provided by a Quality-of-Service (QoS) aware route discovery.

The above-mentioned reactive secure routing protocols interoperate the Neighbor Lookup Protocol (NLP), which provides localized neighbor discovery and authentication. In addition, the Secure Link State Protocol (SLSP), a proactive secure routing protocol, can discover the network connectivity within an extended, multi-hop neighborhood. SLSP can be a stand-alone protocol with a network-wide scope, or it can be combined with a secure reactive protocol in a hybrid secure routing scheme.

D. Hutter and M. Ullmann (Eds.): SPC 2005, LNCS 3450, pp. 46–47, 2005.

However, the security of the route discovery does not ensure undisrupted data delivery, because an up-to-date route cannot be considered free of adversaries. In fact, an intelligent adversary can first become part of a route, for example, by fully complying with the employed routing protocol, and then tamper with in-transit data. Worse even, the adversary can hide its malicious behavior for long periods of time, and strike at the least expected time, or when the attack would have the highest impact.

The Secure Message Transmission (SMT) and the Secure Single Path (SSP) protocols were designed to thwart such malicious behavior and secure the data transmission, operating on top of a secure routing protocol. Among the salient features of the SMT and SSP protocols is their ability to operate solely in an end-to-end manner and without restrictive assumptions on the network trust and security associations. As a result, SMT and SSP are applicable to a wide range of network architectures. They can sustain highly reliable communication with low delay and delay variability, even when a substantial portion of the network nodes disrupt communication. This is so independently of the attack pattern, with adversaries that may corrupt and discard traffic systematically, randomly, or selectively, in an attempt to conceal the attack and avoid detection. The protocols robustly detect malicious and benign transmission faults, and continuously configure their operation. This way, they avoid compromised and failing routes, tolerate data loss, and ensure the availability of communication. This is achieved at the expense of moderate transmission and routing overhead, which can be traded off for delay. Overall, our secure communication protocol suite enables fast and reliable data transport even in highly adverse network environments.

Secure Identity Management for Pseudo-Anonymous Service Access

Michael Hitchens[1], Judy Kay[2], Bob Kummerfeld[2], and Ajay Brar[2]

[1] Department of Computing, Macquarie University,
Sydney Australia 2109
`michaelh@ics.mq.edu.au`
[2] School of Information Technologies,
University of Sydney, Australia 2006
`{judy,bob, abrar1}@it.usyd.edu.au`

Abstract. In this paper, we propose an architecture to enable service providers personalise services in a pervasive environment, while minimising risks to users' privacy. We describe the design of two critical parts of such systems: a mechanism forr defining authenticated personas that can be pseudonymous; and mechanisms for users to share such personas with service providers. A trust-based approach supports decisions about accepting personas. We describe a prototype implementation and performance evaluations.

1 Introduction

Pervasive computing has the potential to offer improved personalised services if service providers have access to some information about the user. For example, staff at a help desk may be more effective if they know the client's knowledge and background, or service providers may grant selective access to services. Essentially, we see the potential for improved services service providers can have access to information about users and can verify its accuracy and authenticity.

Conversely, customers may wish to limit the amount of information available to a service provider. For example, a person purchasing alcohol may wish to prove their age without revealing their name or address. Such situations obviously involve considerations of privacy/and or anonymity. At the same time, service providers may want that partial information authenticated.

Current research into privacy in pervasive systems has focussed primarily on location [1,2,3] or sensors information [4] rather than the issues of managing broad collections of user information and selective subsets of it. This has had some attention in relation to the world wide web [5].

We propose an architecture that can aid service providers in giving their users enhanced levels of service while minimising the risks to the users' privacy. In Section 2 we introduce the area of user models, linked to anonymity. Section 3 outlines the aims of our system. Section 4 presents our architecture while Section 5 describes an implementation of our design. Section 6 presents our conclusions and future plans.

D. Hutter and M. Ullmann (Eds.): SPC 2005, LNCS 3450, pp. 48–55, 2005.

2   User Models and Anonymity

This work draws on two other research areas, user modelling and anonymity. The former provides a flexible mechanism for structuring, storing and communicating the information about the users. The latter provides the necessary privacy for the users.

A user model has been defined [12, 13] as a system's set of beliefs about a user. This drives personalization. The importance of privacy and security of user models and personal information in ubiquitous computing is reflected in emerging principles [14,] and research towards implementing support for them, such as [15].

We define a **persona** as a subset of a user model. We want to enable users to define personas with *minimal effort*. Then the ubiquitous computing environment must correctly interpret the user models: applications in that environment must share the vocabulary used to define the user models. These are important, yet neglected research areas that must be designed with security in mind from the ground up.

Anonymity has been a research topic for some time, in relation to the World Wide Web [5], the internet [6,9], as a study in itself [7] and in relation to location privacy in pervasive computing [8]. In general terms "the *nymity* of a transaction can be defined to be the amount of information about the identity of the participants that is revealed" [6]. For more discussion on the definitions involved see [16].

Most research into anonymity has been directed at protecting the identity of the originator of a message – such as an e-mail message, http request or internet packet. The explicit aim has been to minimise the information in a message to reduce the risk of inadvertent identity disclosure. The reasoning is that a hostile entity is more likely to deduce identity from message contents as the amount of information in the message increases [9]. However, in a pervasive environment, the user population is so large that such means of identification become progressively difficult. The advantages of personalisation may be seen to outweigh such dangers. This leads to our proposal, where the user deliberately provides certain information about themselves, but in a way that should preserve the privacy of their identity. The pseudonymous identity then becomes not just a trusted, but sterile, identity, but one that has some guaranteed characteristics. The challenge becomes one of how to provide this information in a secure manner while still protecting the user's "true" identity.

3   Aims

Our design goal is to allow users to provide some information about themselves, while reducing risks to their privacy. Our aims can be summarised as:

1.   Allow users to provide subsets of information (ie personas) concerning themselves, in a form the service providers will understand.
2.   Allow the creation of personas with minimal user effort
3.   Ensure that the provision of information in the form of personas has minimal chance of breaching the user's privacy, especially in terms of their identity.
4.   Provide a flexible and extensible means of storing and communicating personas.

5. Provide a basis on which the service providers can have at least some level of trust in the accuracy of the provided information.

The personas that a user has available are held in their PSD (Personal Server Device). A service provider needs to be aware of **persona templates** to make sense of information released about the user. A **persona template** (or simply template) is a definition of the structure of a persona. Identification of the appropriate template is included within a persona. A persona is certified by some entity (normally a third party). In our design, this certification takes the form of a signature on the persona and the provision of public key pair for the persona. The key pair allows the entity associated with the persona to prove their right to use the persona. For anonymity we need to support multiple personas for each user, with no easy means linking personas to each other or to an underlying identity.

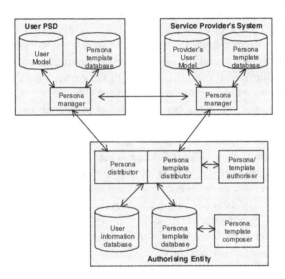

Fig. 1. Architectural Overview

4 System Architecture

Figure 1 is an overview of the architecture to provide controlled levels of anonymity in situations such as those mentioned above. It consists of users, service providers and authorising entities. Detailed descriptions of interactions between the components can be found in [17].

An authorising entity provides a service to users by defining a range of authorised templates for its users and by guaranteeing the veracity of information that will be used in constructing actual personas. The authorising entity needs to create the authorised personas it will supply to users and the authorised persona templates it will give to service providers so that they will be able to interpret the personas of users. The *Persona Template Composer* allows authorised individuals to construct new templates, modify or delete existing templates and to define which users are to be given personas adhering to a template. The template structure may be defined in some structured language, such as XML, or in manner specified by the user modelling software. Once defined, persona templates are added to the authorising entity's *Persona Template Database*.

The *Persona Template Distributor* uses the *Persona/template Authoriser* to create authenticated versions that are released to providers and users. The *Persona/template Authoriser* does this by signing the template structure using the private key of the authorising entity. Service provider systems need the templates to decide which ones they will request and accept from users. Users' PSDs need the templates to be able to understand such requests. The *Persona Managers* of users and service providers place the persona templates in their system's *Persona Template Database*.

When an authorising entity needs to provide a user with an authenticated persona, the *Persona Distributor* selects the appropriate template from the *Persona Template Database* and then consults the *User Information Database* to construct the partial user model for that person (ie, fill in the template to create an instance persona). The authorising entity authenticates the persona and the *Persona Distributor* delivers it to the user's PSD. Authentication takes the form of creating an asymmetric key pair for the information, and signing the information and public key of the pair. Obviously grouping information together will improve efficiency, as there will be fewer keys to manage and less computation will be required to authenticate a complete persona. On the other hand using a finer granularity of authentication will provide more flexibility to the user in creating further personas from the individual pieces of information.

The authorising entity may also, in the same way, provide a persona to a service provider's system. The main differences between service providers and users are:

- The systems of service providers will typically be more powerful and have more storage, not being personal wireless devices.
- Service providers will probably be less interested in anonymity. If the service provider has a physical presence – such as a shop front – anonymity has little appeal to them.
- Service providers will normally advertise their existence by some form of service discovery protocol, thus initiating the exchange between user and service provider.

These differences make it useful to distinguish the two classes of system. The personas of the service providers can be sent to the PSD's of users to authenticate the service provider. This could either be as part of a broadcast by the service provider or in response to an explicit request from a user's PSD. This gives an obvious symmetry of roles to the users and service providers (beyond the question of who initiates the communication). User-to-user communication within our architecture is thus possible as long as one PSD takes responsibility for initiating the communication.

On receipt of a persona the *Persona Manager* of the user (or service provider) first ensures that a copy of the appropriate template is available. If it is not, it is obtained from the authorising entity. The authenticated persona is then added to the *User Model*. It can now be supplied to service providers or other users. The information contained within it can also be used to create additional, **un**authenticated, personas.

The user's *Persona Manager* enables the user to obtain new personas and templates from the authorising entity and handles interaction with the service providers. In user modelling terms, the persona information obtained from the authorising entities, provides evidence for the user's own user model. The *Persona Manager* enables the user to use either signed personas or to create new personas. Note that such personas will not be signed by an authorising entity. The service provider may choose to place less trust in such information in such personas.

At this point, the service provider has details of the persona templates defining what user model personas it can expect from users. Correspondingly, a user carries their PSD, containing their user model. When a user enters the vicinity of a service provider, communication is established between the PSD and service provider's system. The service provider sends the list of names of accepted persona templates. The PSD, possibly after interaction with the user (via the Persona Manager), selects a persona for release to the service provider. The service provider may now, possibly after authentication of the persona, begin application-level communication with the user (ie actual service provision).

5 Implementation

We have implemented a prototype (see figure 2) based on the architecture described in this paper. This prototype was implemented in Python and comprises the following components: a Web component for creating and distributing personas and persona templates, a privacy proxy for evaluating privacy policies against user preferences, a simulated service provider, and a user agent implemented on the user mobile device that provides functions for verifying downloaded personas, managing the user model and allowing the automated exchange of personas with service providers.

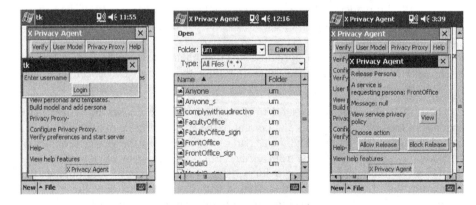

Fig. 2. Screenshots of Implementation

The Web component is implemented as CGI scripts running on an Apache web server. The component provides an administrator interface for creating and modifying personas (encoded in XML) and persona templates and assigning them to users. The user interface allows users to log in and download personas and persona templates assigned to them along with their corresponding RSA signatures. The simulated service provider comprises a service beacon (a Python script) that broadcasts messages advertising the URI to the service provider's privacy policy and the requested persona along with the address of the service provider's server. The service provider server listens for SSL connections, receives and displays personas.

The user agent was implemented on a Toshiba Pocket PC e740 running Pocket PC 2002. The user agent comprises the following components: a *verify* component that connects to the Certification Authority (currently simulated) to verify downloaded signed personas and templates; the PersonisLite [10] user modeling server; a *persona manager* which interacts with PersonisLite and builds and manages the user model, a UDP server that listens for service provider beacon messages, and a *privacy agent* which retrieves the information in the beacon and passes the policy URI along with user preferences to the remote privacy proxy.

We have conducted some performance tests on the prototype to gain some indication of its usability in real world situations. The tests were conducted on a Pentium 4 3GHz 512 MB RAM PC running Windows XP operating system. The facilities on the PDA available to us did not allow these tests to be carried out on it. However, the known processing power of both systems allows relative comparisons to be made. Figure 3 displays a comparison when each component of the persona is signed and verified individually. While the times are significant the verification times (a fraction of a second) are still within likely user tolerances.

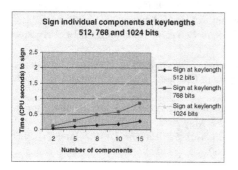 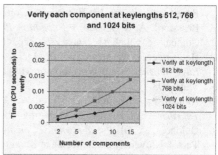

Fig. 3. Signing vs. Verifying various key lengths keys

The test code was written using Python 2.3.4 and sign/verify operations were performed using the RSA implementation in the Python Cryptography Toolkit (http://www.amk.ca/python/code/crypto.html). The time was profiled using the Python 'profile' module and represents the actual time taken to perform the set of instructions. Unfortunately space prevents us fully reporting these results and we include here only a representative sample. See [18] for more detail.

6   Conclusion

We have presented an architecture that allows users to provide information to service providers in such a way that users do not have to reveal their identity and service providers can establish a level of trust in the information. The service providers can then use the information to provide personalised service.

The architecture presented meets our aims as stated in Section 3. The employment of user modeling techniques to handle the personas that encapsulate the information gives a high degree of flexibility to the management of personas. This minimizes the risk to the user's privacy and hence protects their identity. The use of authorising entities to sign the information allows the service providers to establish trust in the information. We have implemented a prototype of the system and conducted performance measurements upon it. The results of these tests indicate that the system would be usable in real world situations.

A persona may consist of information authenticated by a number of entities. A service provider would require some means of evaluating such a persona. We mentioned the possibility of using a heuristic trust model, but more work would need to be done to determine which mechanism would be most suitable.

References

1. Jiang, X. & Landay, J.A., *Modeling Privacy Control in Context-Aware Systems*, IEEE Pervasive Computing, vol. 1, #3, July 2002, p. 59-63
2. Myles, G., Friday, A. & Davies, N., *Preserving Privacy in Environments with Location-Based Applications*, IEEE Pervasive Computing, vol. 2, #1, January 2003, p. 56-64
3. Beresford, A. & Stajano, F., *Location Privacy in Pervasive Computing*, IEEE Pervasive Computing, vol. 2, #1, January 2003, p. 46-55
4. Hengartner, U. & Steenkiste, P., *Access Control to Information in Pervasive Computing Environments*, Ninth Workshop on Hot Topics in Operating Systems (HotOS IX), ACM, May 2003
5. Ishitani, I., Almedia, V. & Meira, W., *Masks: Bringing Anonymity and Personalisation Together*, IEEE Pervasive Computing, vol. 2, #2, May 2003, p.18-23.
6. Goldberg, A., *A Pseudonymous Communications Infrastructure for the Internet*, PhD Thesis, University of California at Berkely, 2000.
7. Vinge, V., *True Names*, Dell Books, 1981
8. Campbell, R., Al-Muhtadi, J., Naldurg, P., Sampemane, G. & Mickunas, M.D., *Towards Security and Privacy for Pervasive Computing*, "Software Security -- Theories and Systems." Springer LNCS Volume 2609, 2003.
9. Rao, J. & Rohatgi, P., *Can Pseudonymity Really Guarantee Privacy?*, 9th USENIX Security Symposium, Denver, USA, August 2000, p.85-96.
10. Kay, J, R J Kummerfeld and P Lauder, (2002) Personis: a server for user models, De Bra, P, P Brusilovsky, R Conejo (eds), *Proceedings of AH'2002, Adaptive Hypertext 2002*, Springer, 203 -- 212.
11. Kobsa, A. and J. Schreck (2003): Privacy through Pseudonymity in User-Adaptive Systems. *ACM Transactions on Internet Technology* 3 (2), 149-183 .

12. Kobsa, A. (1989): A Taxonomy of Beliefs and Goals for User Models in Dialog Systems. In: A. Kobsa and W. Wahlster, eds.: User Models in Dialog Systems. New York etc: Springer Symbolic Computation.

13. A. Kobsa (2001): Generic User Modeling Systems. *User Modeling and User-Adapted Interaction* 11(1-2), 49-63.

14. Langheinrich, M. A Privacy Awareness System for Ubiquitous Computing Environments. Gaetano Borriello, Lars Erik Holmquist (Eds.): *UbiComp 2002: Ubiquitous Computing*, 4th International Conference, Göteborg, Sweden, September 29 - October 1, 2002, Proceedings. Lecture Notes in Computer Science 2498 Springer, 237-245.

15. Myles, G., A Friday and N Davies. (2003) Preserving privacy in environments with location-based applications. *IEEE Pervasive Computing*, 2(1):56-64.

16. Pfitzmann, A and Hansen, M., Anonymity, Unobservability, Pseudonymity and Identity Management – A Proposal for Terminology. http://www.freehaven.net/anonbib/cache/terminology.pdf

17. Hitchens, M., Kay, J. and Kummerfeld, R.J. School of Information Technologies, Secure identity management for pseudo-anonymous service access. *TR 546* School of Information Technologies, University of Sydney, June 2004.

18. Brar, A. and Kay, J.: Privacy and Security in Ubiquitous Personalized Applications. *TR 561*. School of Information Technologies, University of Sydney, November 2004.

Security Issues for Pervasive Personalized Communication Systems

Bertin Klein, Tristan Miller, and Sandra Zilles

DFKI GmbH, Erwin-Schrödinger-Straße 57, 67663 Kaiserslautern, Germany
{Bertin.Klein, Tristan.Miller, Sandra.Zilles}@dfki.de

Abstract. Technological progress allows us to equip any mobile phone
with new functionalities, such as storing personalized information about
its owner and using the corresponding personal profile for enabling communication to persons whose mobile phones represent similar profiles.
However, this raises very specific security issues, in particular relating to
the use of Bluetooth technology. Herein we consider such scenarios and
related problems in privacy and security matters. We analyze in which
respect certain design approaches may fail or succeed at solving these
problems. We concentrate on methods for designing the user-related part
of the communication service appropriately in order to enhance confidentiality.

1 Introduction

Ubiquitous or pervasive computing is so commonplace today that few are aware
of its origins—namely, Weiser and his seminal work [11]. Discount chains like
Aldi sell ever more portable and smaller computers, which will soon be nothing
but "mobile phone computers". Eventually everybody will carry their computer
around in their pocket and use it also to do phone calls. Recently, we envisioned
that the content of people's writing desks will also be transferred to the virtual
world and manipulated with such devices [6]. Already today has much of this
vision been realized.

We are currently designing prototypes for TINKERBELL, a social networking
application run on Bluetooth-enabled mobile phone computers (also known as
mobile digital assistants, or MDAs). The original idea behind TINKERBELL was
to obviate the need of some pretext for initiating and enjoying contact with
other people. However, we soon discovered that, through the incorporation of
knowledge-based technology, the potential applications for such a system would
be legion. By intelligently and efficiently observing, managing, and sharing information about their owners, TINKERBELLs could become something like mirrors
of or proxies for their owners. It is obvious, then, that privacy and security
concerns will play an important role in the development of such systems.

This paper introduces TINKERBELL's communication model and discusses the
privacy and security issues arising therefrom. Researchers and developers have
long recognized privacy and security as central concerns in the development and

D. Hutter and M. Ullmann (Eds.): SPC 2005, LNCS 3450, pp. 56–62, 2005.

deployment of ubiquitous systems [10, 8]. We believe that these concerns will be at the forefront of consumers' purchasing decisions once they are in a position to choose between competing systems. Seemingly small details could then tip the scales and have great consequences.

2   Tinkerbell's Communication Model

Since people socialize based mainly on their similarities to one another—i.e., shared properties or shared opinions—a basic TINKERBELL can be rather simple. It need only host some information that is representative of its owner and check with other TINKERBELLs for similarities with the information about their owners. Our current prototypes encode and exchange personal information using an information scheme (an ontology) which represents concepts like the town where one lives and hobby descriptions. However, TINKERBELL also makes use of information from other users in the vicinity, creating an interesting flavor of context and locality.

The information that a TINKERBELL carries is initially a simple set of preconfigured information items. However, it is constantly provided with new data from its "small-talk" with other TINKERBELLs or from interactions with its owner—perhaps in a Tamagotchi-game-like manner, or by new addressbook entries, or by learning semantic fingerprints of recent papers read by its owner, or perhaps by qualitative feedback about the matches it has made. And, knowing the current state of knowledge technology, it is not so far-fetched to conceive of TINKERBELL as becoming more and more a personalized counterpart to its owner (though certainly not further than the owner wishes).

In general TINKERBELL is designed to require neither central services nor prior knowledge of access/address information. (This is probably why we call it pervasive.) TINKERBELLs which come into proximity with each other will automatically swap information (some of which may be encoded with one-way hashing functions). When a TINKERBELL learns that its owner has a certain number of contacts, hobbies, or other characteristics in common with someone else, it will immediately notify its owner. The owner can then take the appropriate action, which might range from a simple hello to engaging in personal or business-related dialogue with the second party.

With this architecture, TINKERBELL is near being able to offer to its owner all the six categories for pervasive context-aware services [1]:

1. proactive triggering of events (if it records past events)
2. streamlining interaction (because it is involved in its owners interaction)
3. memory for past events (it can at least record its interactions)
4. reminders for future events (this is already a feature of current MDAs)
5. optimizing patterns of behavior (e.g., when passers-by are identified as not interesting)
6. sharing experience (that is one of the ideas behind the notion of small-talk)

3   Security and Privacy Issues

For applications like TINKERBELL, in order to survive on a market or in a society, it is crucial to invest in some thought on system vulnerability and possible countermeasures to misuse or attack. Of course no system can be "secure" in an absolute sense; it can be secure only to some degree or level of confidence. However, human culture is by now, for the most part, well acquainted with this state of affairs. Security is rightly seen as a trade-off between risk and reward [10].

Security has a highly social dimension. That is, we should always be cognizant of the sometimes-overlooked fact that the security of any system involving humans crucially depends on human behaviour. Consequently our philosophy of security and privacy for TINKERBELL is based on how to minimize the security risks associated with human oversight. Our first task is therefore to systematically generate a plan to identify such risks. The last step to be taken is to ensure that these risks are addressed with the appropriate technology—technology which people will actually use. Unfortunately, however, establishing the security of a system is almost impossible to fully accomplish during the design stages. Absence of security in unlikely places is often discovered only later, after people have already experienced losses.

According to Robinson & Beigl [9], most security issues in pervasive computing arise from the difficulty of coordinating the symbiosis of physical and virtual entities. We can therefore identify two main sources of security issues of pervasive applications like TINKERBELL:

1. **Transfer of real to virtual.** The transfer of processes from the real to the virtual blurs human understanding and attention. Security issues arise where new technologies create new virtual spaces which are not covered by state-of-the-art security procedures and conventions.
2. **Access of computational power to data.** When information is stored on electronic devices and is accessible to computational processes, there are new possibilities created to use the data, and thus also to do security-compromising things.

Note that when considering an application like TINKERBELL which is thought of as a service to be sold to private users, it is important not only to provide actual security, but also to provide the user with a *feeling* of security. The user's perception of security often includes that he himself is involved in the security mechanisms and thus has a certain amount of control. But this may also make a system susceptible to certain threats. For example, the user can be confused or persuaded into corruptive actions by hackers manipulating information. This subject, known as social engineering, is studied in detail by Cybenko et al. [2].

3.1   Specific Security Issues

Security in the specific context of TINKERBELL is considered with respect to the following four criteria:

- *Confidentiality* is the guarantee that information is shared only between a user and the entities the user is willing to communicate the information to.
- *Authenticity* is the assurance that the mobile phone in a Bluetooth connection has the claimed identity and has subscribed to the TINKERBELL service.
- *Integrity* means the correctness of stored and communicated personal (and annotation) data in the sense that only the corresponding person (the author or a responsible moderator) can alter them.
- *Availability* means that the TINKERBELL service is accessible and usable for subscribed persons using appropriate mobile devices.

Confidentiality. First of all, it is worth noting that the design of the TINKER-BELL service should allow the user to prioritize the confidentiality of his data. That is, he should be able to declare which of his data are absolutely or first-grade confidential (i.e., no one should be allowed to read them), second-grade confidential (only members of certain TINKERBELL user groups should be allowed to read them), third-grade confidential, and so on down to the nth-grade confidential, where access in granted to every other TINKERBELL user regardless of identity.

This somehow reflects a quite discrete notion of the idea of a so-called *digital aura*, a thought model for spontaneous interaction between moving objects defined by Ferscha et al. [3]. A digital aura reflects the "aura" of an object (person or thing) in the context of wireless communication. As soon as two objects are located near each other, they start comparing profile data (which would be nth-grade confidential data in our scenario); further communication and data exchange is enabled only in case the profiles of the two objects are sufficiently similar. (Here the notion of "similarity" has to be defined appropriately on a context-by-context basis.) This concept of digital auras has also successfully been implemented into a software framework enhancing the development of context-aware peer-to-peer applications [4].

Given our discrete notion of digital auras, the central question is how the user can declare which grade of his personal data may be provided to which persons/mobile devices.

A first and simple possibility might be to introduce blacklists with names or device IDs of persons for which access should be denied. Similarly, whitelists ("friend lists") can name people or mobile devices for which access is permitted. This of course in turn requires methods for assuring a certain grade of confidentiality and integrity of the blacklist (and whitelist) data. A disadvantage of blacklists is that the user can define them only if the contact to some inconvenient discussion partner has been established at least once. (Otherwise the user wouldn't know the partner is undesirable.)

A second possibility, aiming at denying contact to inconvenient persons in advance, would be to annotate persons/device IDs. The registration process alone is a first step in this direction. Of course, here an additional security aspect concerns the annotation data, which need to be stored on a server. Not only the usual considerations apply here, but we also see a difference in trust into a system when it hosts such personal data, with the potential for police and comparable agencies to be empowered to access these data immediately on short notice.

Privacy aspects are of particular importance when annotating data on persons. In case someone knows one of the user's secrets, he can publish this secret in the user's annotations—a massive privacy attack! Even if the policy of the annotation service allows for removing annotations of a particular personal kind, there is the risk that third parties will become aware of the annotations (and thus of the user's secret) before the user himself notices and removes them. Of course, in the first step, third parties will not be able to assign any person to the negative annotations, because they stick to a device ID. But in case contact is built up, the secret can be associated to the corresponding person. Even more simple, the attacker can place its victim's name into the annotation.

Because of these risks, there is a moral barrier which may get in the way of acceptance of annotating persons. A method preventing too big a misuse of the annotation idea is to trace back the attacker via his or her device ID, which could be stored for the author of each annotation.

A third possibility would be to preselect possible contact partners by their profiles. Here some part of the user's nth-grade confidential data could be used to form a profile which is matched with the corresponding profiles of other TIN-KERBELL users. A conceivable policy might be to establish a contact only to those whose profiles have a similarity with the concerned user's profile above some certain threshold. In order to keep even these profile data confidential in case of a mismatch, a good policy might be to use one-way functions to encode the profile data and then execute the matching algorithm on the encoded data, which cannot be decoded (cf. [7]). In case the threshold is not reached, further access is denied and both parties don't even know each other's profiles used for matching.

Authenticity. Regarding authentication, one small remark can be made in advance: even if authentication is provided, the user can never be sure that the authenticated partner behaves as desired. In other words, authentication does not establish trust. But this is of course a problem in our scenario which cannot be solved, because no one can prevent the owner of the authenticated device from misusing the data exchanged.

Perhaps TINKERBELL will provide a chance to systematically use the idea of disclosing differently "watermarked" information to other parties. People sometimes do this when filling out forms, such introducing intentional misspellings into their name, like "Jonn" instead of "John". When John later receives unwanted advertisements addressed to "Jonn", he has feedback on his information disclosure behavior and can learn to adapt and/or report the unscrupulous communication partner to a consumer protection agency. In many ways TINKERBELL could easily support such strategies.

Keeping the social aspect of TINKERBELL in mind, one guideline for authentication may be to approximate the human way of judging and talking to unknown or newly encountered people. People can make up their mind in a conversation with somebody rather unknown to disclose rather private information or they can decide very quickly that they don't want to. TINKERBELL extends the possibilities here. In case your TINKERBELL rings you up and tells you that a partner you encounter matches a profile you are looking for, but the real-life counterpart does not give you the same impression, you might become suspicious.

TINKERBELL, viewing it as a mirror of its owner, can store or be used as a substitute for biometric information of its owner. This could be used to identify the user to his TINKERBELL or to other users. It is further conceivable that a TINKERBELL, like government identification and credit cards, might host a picture of its owner, which in many cases can ease authentication.

Integrity. We are aware of the notion of "Bluetooth snarfing"—the access and deletion of the stored data on mobile phones via Bluetooth. However, we realize that on the deeper levels of hacking systems, to a large degree we need to rely on third party efforts. TINKERBELL will probably allow users to institute a policy of completely denying acceptance of any executable code. Further, encryption and signing of information stored on TINKERBELLs could be feasible to some degree (cf. [7]).

Availability. To achieve availability, several points have to be taken into consideration. First, and trivially, the server used must be prevented from breaking down. Moreover, it might be helpful to have as little data and as few modules as possible within the responsibility of the server. Second, also trivially, one has to take care of enabling Bluetooth communication whenever it is demanded. Additionally, denial of service attacks have to be prevented. These may include, for instance, spamming.

4   Conclusions

We have introduced TINKERBELL, an application for MDAs (mobile digital assistants, state-of-the-art mobile phone computers) which we consider to be a pervasive computing application. TINKERBELLs contact other TINKERBELLs in the vicinity (distance of Bluetooth reach), engage in small-talks, and give away a configurable amount of information about their owners, in order to instigate or facilitate social interaction.

A crucial area of concern with this technology is that the transfer of small-talk to the virtual world invites mismatches of the human feeling/assessment for the situation. In the real world, humans do give away their phone numbers, even to people they haven't known for long, but not to everybody. It needs to be ensured that (users instruct) their TINKERBELLs (to) behave in a comparable way so that unwanted surprises do not happen.

TINKERBELLs disclose and send information to others; they act in the name of a person and host information about their owners. Thus, it is clear that they are vulnerable in principle and that the security issues of how to assure confidentiality, authenticity, and integrity need to be taken care of.

TINKERBELLs and their owners will typically have a one-to-one relationship, with reach into the real world. (Mainly they appear together, even if TINKER-

BELLs can be given away or be stolen.) They are perhaps comparable to the ownership of cars—to a degree they open up the possibility to trace the activity of a person and/or his TINKERBELL. With a limited disclosure of information about all the individuals, this is enough to open up the chance for new (socially motivated and socially grounded) security applications.

Acknowledgments. The authors would like to thank Steffen Lange for helpful discussions.

References

1. Peter Brown, Winslow Burleson, Mik Lamming, Odd-Wiking Rahlff, Guy Romano, Jean Scholtz, and Dave Snowdon. Context-awareness: some compelling applications. In *Proceedings of the 2nd International Symposium on Handheld and Ubiquitous Computing*, 2000.
2. George Cybenko, Annarita Giani, and Paul Thompson. Cognitive hacking: A battle for the mind. *IEEE Computer*, 35(8):50–56, 2002.
3. Alois Ferscha, Manfred Hechinger, Rene Mayrhofer, Marcos dos Santos Rocha, Marquart Franz, and Roy Oberhauser. Digital aura. In *Proceedings of the 2nd International Conference on Pervasive Computing*. Springer-Verlag, 2004.
4. Alois Ferscha, Manfred Hechinger, Rene Mayrhofer, and Roy Oberhauser. A lightweight component model for peer-to-peer applications. In *Proceedings of the 24th International Conference on Distributed Computing Systems Workshops*, pages 520–527. IEEE Computer Society, 2004.
5. Dieter Hutter, Günter Müller, Werner Stephan, and Markus Ullmann, editors. *Proceedings of the 1st International Conference on Security in Pervasive Computing (revised papers)*, volume 2802 of *Lecture Notes in Computer Science*. Springer-Verlag, 2004.
6. Bertin Klein, Stevan Agne, Achim Ebert, and Michael Bender. Enabling flow: A paradigm for document-centered personal information spaces. In *Proceedings of the 8th IASTED International Conference on Artificial Intelligence and Soft Computing*, 2004.
7. Håkan Kvarnström, Hans Hedbom, and Erland Jonsson. Protecting security policies in ubiquitous environments using one-way functions. In Hutter et al. [5], pages 71–85.
8. PAMPAS consortium and constituency. Deliverable D04: Final roadmap (extended version). Technical Report IST-201-37763, PAMPAS consortium, 2004.
9. Philip Robinson and Michael Beigl. Trust context spaces: An infrastructure for pervasive security in context-aware environments. In Hutter et al. [5], pages 157–172.
10. Ian Smith, Anthony LaMarca, Sunny Consolvo, and Paul Dourish. A social approach to privacy in location-enhanced computing. In *Proceedings of the Workshop on Security and Privacy in Pervasive Computing*, 2004.
11. Mark Weiser, Rich Gold, and John Seely Brown. The origins of ubiquitous computing research at PARC in the late 1980s. *IBM Systems Journal*, 38(4):693–696, 1999.

Safeguards in a World of Ambient Intelligence*

Outline of a Research Agenda on the European Level

Michael Friedewald

Fraunhofer Institute Systems and Innovation Research, Breslauer Straße 48,
D-76139 Karlsruhe, Germany
m.friedewald@isi.fraunhofer.de

Abstract. Ambient Intelligence is a vision of the future information society stemming from the convergence of ubiquitous computing, ubiquitous communication and intelligent user-friendly interfaces. Beyond the possible benefits that are associated with this vision, it also requires a proper balance of a complex diversity of interests and values. The paper gives an outline of the various risks and vulnerabilities associated with Ambient Intelligence and argues why the design of safeguards and privacy enhancing mechanisms is a central task of European policy.

1 The Brave New World of Ambient Intelligence – Promises and Fears

Ambient Intelligence (AmI) has been described and characterised in a variety of ways and using a variety of terminologies. Pervasive computing, ubiquitous computing, embedded intelligence, invisible computing, seamless intelligence are just a few of the terms that have been used synonymously with Ambient Intelligence. Some have described the capabilities of AmI by the construction of scenarios and created roadmaps to indicate how we can arrive at such scenarios and the multi-faceted benefits that are expected to arise from the deployment of Ambient Intelligence [1, 2].

While the European Commission has supported and continues to support many projects that will help society reach this wondrous new world, in fact, the construction of the Ambient Intelligence environment has already begun. Sensors and actuators, key AmI technologies, have been in use for decades as a result of the exponential increase in electronic capabilities. However, the dramatic reduction in the cost of computing and communications and the rise of the Internet have facilitated the exchange of information among these early AmI devices and have contributed to laying the foundations for the scenarios envisaged for the future. Above all, the networking of the proliferating devices in recent years demonstrates that the future, despite the still remaining formidable technological challenges, is not so far off.

While the technologists have been at work concerns relating to privacy, security, identity, social inclusion and other issues are beginning to get more attention. The fears

---

* This paper outlines the objectives of the Project "Safeguards in a World of AMbient Intelligence (SWAMI), funded by the European Commission under Priority 8.1 (Policy Oriented Research) of the Sixth Framework Programme.

D. Hutter and M. Ullmann (Eds.): SPC 2005, LNCS 3450, pp. 63–69, 2005.

conjured up by the impact of an Orwellian Big Brother only complicate the apparent lack of trust, which hinders the full flowering of the Internet for e-commerce, e-government, e-health and much else. In November 2003, some 30 privacy advocacy groups joined together to produce a position paper calling for a halt to the deployment of radio frequency identification tags (RFIDs) until certain public policy issues are resolved [3]. After a fashion, their concerns reflect a few of the more numerous and even more complex issues raised by the IST Advisory Group (ISTAG) in their June 2002 paper entitled *Trust, dependability, security and privacy for IST in FP6* [4].

2   Challenges for European Policy

AmI should be seen as a set of artefacts requiring a proper balance which takes into account a complex diversity of interests and values related to access to information, protection of the individual sphere, trust, security, protection against discrimination, protection of identity, free speech, protection against intrusions and so on. Such a balance demands an approach which is not only driven by one or two actual, emotional, economic or social signals or events, but which proceeds by a rational mobilisation of the many possible relevant perceptions and definitions of the issues at stake. Such a balancing exercise raises a number of issues that need to be taken into account, e. g.,

- the increasing concern for security after 11 September 2001;
- technological innovation, its dissemination and consequences, only some of which can be foreseen (the invisibility of networked "intelligent" devices, ubiquity of computer communications, anonymity and privacy impacts, user friendliness, price, accessibility, etc.);
- a tendency toward privatisation of governance (the weakening of public power to control and steer the evolutions as a result of the increasing power of private actors both at local and global level).

Every one of us goes through life playing many different roles, which in essence could be reduced to three main ones that of the private individual, the professional and the public participant.

Private individuals are mindful of their pursuits and/or responsibilities as parents or members of a family or on their own who from time to time have concerns about their health or modes of entertainment and leisure activity or shopping or whatever. Living in a world of Ambient Intelligence should reduce the time it takes to pursue these things and increase the richness of daily experience [5]. Similarly, the professionals ability to communicate with his/her peers, either in the same office or on the other side of the world, to have an infinite world of information and intelligence at a fingertip to facilitate decision-making, will expand with Ambient Intelligence. In their public role, citizens will participate in social and political activities, perhaps lobbying for or supporting this or that cause. In each of these roles, the citizens level of trust and confidence in supporting technology and in those with whom (s)he might be in contact will vary.

Citizens demands for security, privacy, confidentiality, anonymity will also vary according to the situation, and the situations may be very fluid, changing many times in the course of a day. In some of their roles, they will place demands on others, in others, they must place demands on themselves or accept certain responsibilities. In some roles and at some times, they will provide consent to others, at other times, they will seek consent (access) and at still other times, they may be unaware of the computing, monitoring, networking going on around them. At all times, they must be alert to the possibility of social engineering and threats to their space, to their digital, if not their physical well-being. They need verifiable assurances that they can perform their roles according to the level of security, trust, confidentiality and anonymity that they dictate.

Therefore research is needed on the responsibilities and ethics related to the new technologies and on the social, economic, legal and technological aspects of AmI, in particular addressing:

- issues such as privacy, anonymity, manipulation and control, intellectual property rights, human identity, discrimination and environmental concerns;
- new societal and policy options including responsibilities and ethics of digital behaviour;
- protection of rights for all citizens in all their roles (private and professional) in the Information Society;
- safeguards and privacy enhancing mechanisms needed to ensure user control, user acceptance and enforceability of policy in an accessible manner;
- equal rights and opportunities of accessibility to the Information Society and its Ambient Intelligence environment.

However policy-makers are not the only constituency challenged by these issues. Many in industry are already sensitised to the emerging social and policy challenges inherent in the deployment of Ambient Intelligence technologies. ISTAG itself comprises leading manufacturers, software developers, and service providers and has produced some very good reports and recommendations. Similarly, many European enterprises participate in standards-setting bodies, which deal with privacy and security aspects. They should also profit from the early definition of possibilities to reach a certain level of security, trust and confidentiality.

3   Ambient Intelligence Issues in the EU Policy Framework

Reaching these objectives is seen as urgent for further development of Ambient Intelligence in Europe. Moreover, they are in line with those of the IST Priority and the broader Framework Programme 6 (FP6) objectives as well as related objectives stated by the Commission, the Council and others. The Framework Programme emphasises the importance of taking the human dimension into account in Ambient Intelligence. In doing so, it echoes the eEurope 2005 Action Plan that says Europe should have a secure information infrastructure and, to that end, it identifies FP6 priorities as including trustworthy network and information infrastructures with an emphasis on emerging technologies like Ambient Intelligence. Research activities, are expected to take into account the 'human factor' in security [6, p. 16]. The IST 2003 report puts it even more succinctly: Instead of making people adapt to technology, we have to design technologies for people [7, p. 10].

Taking the human factor into account is crucial in the construction of safeguards in a world of Ambient Intelligence. The success of AmI will depend on how secure its use can be made, how privacy and other rights of individuals can be protected and, how individuals can come to trust the intelligent world which surrounds them and through which they move. The European Commission has acknowledged and emphasised this dependency between technology and trustworthiness on numerous occasions.

The issues raised in the context of Ambient Intelligence affect all five key areas on which current IST research is focussed [7]: The first area includes research addressing solutions for trust and confidence. The second area includes basic technologies for Ambient Intelligence, namely communication and network technologies, embedded systems, and software technologies and distributed systems. Accordingly, they need to be considered in order to determine what mechanisms, what policy options are needed to ensure trust and confidence. The third IST area deals with components and microsystems and must be considered in the context of how they further the goals of Ambient Intelligence. The same applies to the fourth area – i.e., knowledge and interface technologies, especially knowledge technologies, digital content, intelligent interfaces and surfaces, and to the fifth area, IST future and emerging technologies.

Across the IST Priority, special emphasis must be placed on, inter alia, measures to strengthen international co-operation. Such co-operation has already been initiated within the context of Ambient Intelligence, notably with the United States [7, p. 117]. It is therefore necessary to formulate options for the Commission and other policy-making bodies with further regard to international co-operation. In a networked world, best symbolised by the Internet, in which communications and computing capabilities know no borders, international co-operation is a must if the privacy and rights of individuals are to be protected. Many risks and vulnerabilities to Europeans emanate beyond our borders, hence social and policy options must include a global outlook. The Cybercrime Convention is an important step in this direction since its 34 signatories include more than just the Unions Member States. In addition, representatives from the Commission, Member States and industry participate in many standards-setting bodies concerned with cyber security with a global perspective. Nevertheless, more initiatives are needed in that direction [4, p. 10].

The provenance of the term Ambient Intelligence is recent, although it has its precursors in the notions of pervasive computing, ubiquitous computing, and so on. As Erkki Liikanen, former Commissioner for Information Society, stated, FP5 provided important foundations for the vision of Ambient Intelligence, upon which the work in FP6 is being built [7, p. 3.]. Therefore it is high time to investigate if the research policy of recent years has produced lacunae with regard to policy development and if the scientific and industrial community has developed a hidden research agenda with priorities that are different from those considered important by policy.

The definition of safeguards for the world of Ambient Intelligence is relevant to the European policy, but its global relevance is also obvious. For example, a roundtable of security experts in 2001 identified the top ten security priorities for the next decade, with the first priority related to the "EverNet", which was their way of labelling AmI. The experts were concerned that billions of devices that are always on and always connected increase the complexity of our systems to the point where it is not possible to comprehend all of what we are using. We need to resolve issues of identity and authority when these devices conduct activities for people without human intervention, when no one is around to notice [8]. Thus, the experts were urging fast action to resolve these issues.

4   The Need of Safeguards for a World of Ambient Intelligence

The definition of safeguards for a world of Ambient Intelligence will make important contributions to scientific, technical, wider societal and policy objectives of IST Policy on the European level.

It is urgent to consider Ambient Intelligence technologies and developments and how the rights of individuals can best be protected and to formulate adequate social and policy options. This can contribute to the European policy development. Indirectly this can also contribute to scientific and technical development projects by highlighting the policy implications of the work. It is already obvious that realising the vision of Ambient Intelligence will require more than just technology and, as has happened throughout history, especially in the last decade or so, significant technological advances almost always raise policy issues.

The new regulatory framework aims for a more secure environment for e-commerce transactions and to ensure an adequate level of consumer protection. Here it is necessary to examine the adequacy of the new framework in the context of the emerging technologies, capabilities and properties that are embedded in Ambient Intelligence. This can contribute to the strengthening of the three pillars upon which the European Union's policy for the Information Society is based and, in particular, the second pillar which is the new regulatory framework covering all services or networks that transmit communications electronically [7, Forward by Erkki Liikanen].

While the world of Ambient Intelligence will bring many benefits, trust and security should be designed into the applications rather than inserted as an afterthought into an already constructed world of smart spaces. The success will depend on the acceptability by citizens and by taking steps to minimise their concerns with regard to how it might lead to further encroachments upon their privacy, safety and security.

So far, there are some bad omens, even though embedded technology is not new. What is new is that such devices are being networked and their numbers are set to increase by orders of magnitude. That has alarmed major privacy advocacy groups who recently made a joint statement calling for a halt in the use of RFIDs until key issues are resolved. Meanwhile, companies such as Wal-Mart in the US, the Metro Group in Germany and others are proceeding with their plans for a massive increase in the use of RFIDs, even before some standards issues have been resolved.

Similarly, location aware services have prompted concerns, even though they also offer many benefits. The increasing use of GPS in mobile phones in the United States in conjunction with services such as uLocate and Wherify Wireless enables those with mobile phones to be tracked wherever they go. While helping parents to know where their children are, the risks of unwanted and unwarranted surveillance have been highlighted by privacy advocates and others. These and similar examples highlight the need for urgent research in regard to the emerging world of Ambient Intelligence and, in particular, matters of privacy, security, trust, identity and so on.

The lack of consumer trust is often cited as the reason why e-commerce (and e-health and e-government) via the Internet is far from realising its potential. Attacks via the Internet are no longer confined to big name targets such as the military or credit card companies. Even individual users' home computers are being attacked or used as the staging platform for distributed denial of service attacks. Attacks are not only becoming more numerous, they are becoming much more sophisticated. The software security firm Symantec observed that, in July 2001, Code Red spread to 250,000 systems within six hours and the worldwide economic impact of the worm was estimated to be $2.62 billion. Code Reds spread was fast enough to foil immediate human intervention and the ramifications were huge. In the future, experts see the emergence of hypothesized threats that use advanced scanning techniques to infect all vulnerable servers on the Internet in a matter of minutes or even seconds [9]. Such predictions undermine trust and confidence.

Addressing security issues is crucial to stimulating demand for new electronic communications services, as the Commission said in its recent Communication "Electronic Communications: the Road to the Knowledge Economy" [10, p. 13]. This will be one of the principal tasks of the new European Network and Information Security Agency (ENISA), which is expected to become a centre of excellence for cyber security matters. ENISA's creation is a welcome development, especially to the extent that its purview includes Ambient Intelligence. In its 6 June 2001 Communication on ENISA, the Commission said one of the challenges to be faced will be to avoid unacceptable vulnerabilities and integrate security into the Ambient Intelligence architectures [11, Sect. 2.3]. The definition of safeguards for Ambient Intelligence is necessary for ENISA's activities in this area.

Security must be regarded as an enabler for the development of new markets, not an inhibitor, which is a point stressed by the ISTAG reports on Ambient Intelligence. As an example of where security contributes to market development, one needs look no further than the cars that we drive or the homes in which we live. Automobile manufacturers promote their products' various security features in marketing campaigns. Similarly, the insurance premiums we pay on our homes are diminished if we have installed security devices. In the electronic commerce area, some forms of business activities require or are facilitated by a particular level of trustworthiness. As an example, the availability of secure socket layer (SSL) encryption for Web traffic has caused consumers to feel more comfortable about sending credit card numbers across the Internet.

There are many good points in the aforementioned ISTAG paper on "Trust, dependability, security and privacy for IST in FP6" [4]. Of particular relevance is the ISTAG proposition that "security policies in this [AmI] environment must evolve, adapting in accordance with our experiences. Such approaches may be very different from present approaches to computational security policies, but may better embody our approaches to real-world person-to-person trust policies. This is the main new feature of the new paradigm for security in AmI Space." In the future AmI world new approaches to security, trust, privacy, etc., will be required and it is urgent that such new approaches will be considered before AmI becomes a reality, otherwise we, as a society, will be faced with a future akin to trying to squeeze toothpaste back into the tube [12]. It will be difficult to embed retroactively new security and trust paradigms in AmI when those technologies have been deployed. The early definition of safeguards can contribute to the development of such new approaches.

The definition of AmI safeguards also contributes to the four lines around which the eEurope 2005 Action Plan is structured [6, p. 9ff.], which are, firstly, policy measures to review and adapt legislation at national and European level; secondly, implementation of policy measures supported by the development, analysis and dissemination of good practices; thirdly, policy measures will be monitored and better focussed by benchmarking of the progress made in achieving the objectives and of the policies in support of the objectives; fourthly, an overall co-ordination of existing policies will bring out synergies between proposed actions.

References

[1] IST Advisory Group, Ducatel, K., Bogdanovicz, M., Scapolo, F., Leijten, J., Burgelman, J.C.: Scenarios for ambient intelligence in 2010. Institute for Prospective Technological Studies (IPTS), Seville (2001)

[2] Friedewald, M., Da Costa, O., eds.: Science and technology roadmapping: Ambient intelligence in everyday life (AmI@Life). Working paper, Institute for Prospective Technological Studies (IPTS), Seville (2003)

[3] Consumers against Supermarket Privacy Invasion and Numbering (CASPIAN): Position Statement on the Use of RFID on Consumer Products. (2003) http://www.privacyrights.org/ar/RFIDposition.htm.

[4] IST Advisory Group: Trust, dependability, security and privacy for IST in FP6. Office for Official Publications of the European Communities, Luxembourg (2002)

[5] Friedewald, M., Da Costa, O., Punie, Y., Alahuhta, P., Heinonen, S.: Perspectives of ambient intelligence in the home environment. Telematics and Informatics **22** (2005): Forthcoming.

[6] European Commission: eEurope 2005: An information society for all. An Action Plan to be presented in view of the Sevilla European Council, 21/22 June 2002. COM (2002) 263 final, Brussels (2002)

[7] European Commission: IST 2003 – The Opportunities Ahead. Office for Official Publications of the European Communities, Luxembourg (2003)

[8] Center for Education and Research in Information Assurance and Security, Purdue University West Lafayette, IN: CERIAS Security Visionary Roundtable: Call to Action. (2001)

[9] Schwarz, J.: Statement of John Schwarz, President, Symantec Corporation to the House Government Reform Subcommittee on Technology, Information Policy, Intergovernmental Relations and the Census, Hearing on Worms, Viruses and Securing Our NationÕs ComputersÓ. http://reform.house.gov/UploadedFiles/Schwarz-v5.pdf (2003)

[10] European Commission: Electronic Communications: The Road to the Knowledge Economy. COM (2003) 65 final, Brussels (2003)

[11] European Commission: Network and Information Security: Proposal for a European Policy Approach. COM (2001) 298 final, Brussels (2001)

[12] Beslay, L., Hakala, H.: Digital territory: Bubbles. In Wejchert, J., ed.: The Vision Book, Brussel (2005)

Challenge-Response Based RFID Authentication Protocol for Distributed Database Environment*

Keunwoo Rhee[1], Jin Kwak[1], Seungjoo Kim[2], and Dongho Won[1]

[1] Information and Communication Security Lab,
School of Information and Communication Engineering,
Sungkyunkwan University, 300 Cheoncheon-dong, Jangan-gu,
Suwon-si, Gyeonggi-do, 440-746, Korea
{kwrhee, jkwak, dhwon}@dosan.skku.ac.kr
http://dosan.skku.ac.kr
[2] Information Security and Cryptology Lab,
School of Information and Communication Engineering,
Sungkyunkwan University, 300 Cheoncheon-dong,
Jangan-gu, Suwon-si, Gyeonggi-do, 440-746, Korea
skim@ece.skku.ac.kr
http://www.isac.re.kr

Abstract. Recently, RFID system is a main technology to realize ubiquitous computing environments, but the feature of the RFID system may bring about various privacy problems. So, many kinds of protocols to resolve these problems have been researched. In this paper, we analyze the privacy problems of the previous protocols and propose more secure and effective authentication protocol to protect user's privacy. Then we analyze the security and effectiveness of the proposed protocol comparing with the previous protocols. The proposed protocol is based on Challenge-Response using one-way hash function and random number. The proposed protocol is secure against the replay the attack, spoofing attack and so on. In addition, the proposed protocol is fitted for distributed database environment.

Keywords: RFID system, authentication, Challenge-Response.

1   Introduction

RFID (Radio Frequency IDentification) system that is an automatic identification technology using radio frequency is a system to read and write the data of the entity [8]. Although over 5 billion bar codes are scanned daily [5], the bar codes are scanned only one time during the life of the product [22]. However not only automatic identification but also continuous service is possible if the RFID system is used. Therefore many companies are interested in RFID system to reduce supply chain management and inventory control cost.

---

* This work was supported by the University IT Research Center Project funded by the Korean Ministry of Information and Communication.

D. Hutter and M. Ullmann (Eds.): SPC 2005, LNCS 3450, pp. 70–84, 2005.

However, an automatic identification technology using RFID can suffer from the privacy problems such as tracking without user's recognition [1, 4]. Up to date, many kinds of protocols have been proposed to resolve these privacy problems. For example, the 'Kill command' approach [22], the hash-lock protocol [18, 19, 21, 22], the randomized hash-lock protocol [21, 22], the external re-encryption protocol [10], the 'Blocker tag' approach [11], the hash-chain protocol [14], and the hash-based ID variation protocol [9] are representative. However the previous protocols don't resolve privacy problems since the previous protocols can't reuse tag or the previous protocols are vulnerable to replay and spoofing attacks, and tag can be tracked.

In this paper, we analyze the problems of the previous protocols. Then we propose RFID authentication protocol that can protect privacy problems by an attacker using the hash function and the random number in order to change data which tag transmits to reader and is suitable for ubiquitous environment such that databases, readers, and tags are in anywhere. Moreover, we analyze the security and effectiveness of the proposed protocol comparing with the previous protocols. Section 2 gives an introduction to composition of the RFID system and security requirements. Section 3 analyzes problems of the previous RFID system security techniques. Section 4 explains proposed RFID authentication protocol and then shows that the proposed protocol is secure and effective as we compare the proposed protocol with the previous protocols. Then Section 5 gives a conclusion.

2   RFID System

2.1   Composition of the RFID System

Generally, RFID system is composed of tags, readers, and back-end databases. The details of each element are written in the next. Fig. 1 shows the composition of the RFID system.

(1) Tag

When the reader queries, the tag also called transponder transmits data of the things, animals and human beings and so on. Tag is composed of a coupling element for wireless communication and a micro chip to compute and store data. Tag is divided into active and passive tag by the method to be powered.

- *Active tag*: An active tag is powered by on-board battery. So it can transmit data far away. However the tag is high cost because of on-board battery. In addition, the active tag has a drawback that tag's life span is dependent on on-board battery's life span. An active tag is usually used of a sensing system to check pressure of the tires, a patient management system and so on.
- *Passive tag*: A passive tag is inductively powered via an RF signal from the reader. The passive tag is usually used to transmit data to a short distance because tag's power is relatively lower than reader's power. The passive tag is

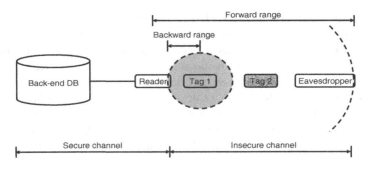

Fig. 1. RFID system

low cost and its life span is permanent as the passive tag doesn't include on-board battery. So it is generally used of supply chain management, inventory control.

(2) Reader

A reader, the device collects identification data from tags, is often called transceiver. A Reader emits a RF signal to the tags to supply power and transmit data which is received from back-end database. Besides the reader can read and write the data of the tags.

(3) Back-end database

A back-end database stores data received from reader and computes complex computation instead of the tags or the readers since their computing abilities are low. In addition back-end database discriminates between right and wrong of the data collected by readers since back-end database stores the information to identify the tags.

In Fig. 1, forward range is the area that readers can transmit a RF signal to the tags and backward range is the area that the tags can transmit their data to the reader when a reader queries. Since tag's ability to transmit is weak, forward range is wider than backward range. For example, in the RFID systems using 915 MHz [2,3], tags have the backward range within a 3-meter radius when readers have the forward range within a 100-meter radius [21]. Therefore a reader may not identify tags when some tags received queries from reader transmit their data to the reader. The communication channel between the readers and the tags is insecure since the communication between the readers and the tags uses RF signals. On the contrary, it is assumed that the communication channel between the back-end databases and the readers is secure.

2.2   The Security Requirements of the RFID System

The RFID system can bring about privacy problems as this system can identify tags without physical contact. Especially, since readers and tags communicate in insecure channel, the RFID systems must be designed to be secure against attackers that are described in these paragraphs [21].

(1) Eavesdropper

The eavesdroppers can't take part in the RFID system protocol but can eavesdrop on communication between readers and tags. By eavesdropping, the eavesdropper can take secret information and perform replay attack. So the RFID system should be designed that the eavesdroppers don't get any secret information from the eavesdropped information and it is secure against the replay attack.

(2) Active attacker

The active attackers can take part in the process of the RFID systems actively. The active attackers can't physically contact with tags. However the active attackers can query to the tags and respond to the readers. So the attackers can perform spoofing attack such that the attackers collect transmitted data from the tags by disguising as the right readers then the attackers disguise as the right tags using these data [22]. Besides, the attackers can track the location of the tags disguising as the right readers and getting responses from the tags continuously. Therefore, the RFID system should be designed that the active attackers can't disguise the right tags using the data collected from the right tags and the active attackers can't know that different responses of a tag are from the same tag.

(3) Tracker

The trackers know that when, from where and how much information is transmitted since trackers can perform traffic analysis. Then the trackers can track the location of the user. Therefore, the RFID system should be designed that the trackers can't know that different responses of a tag are from the same tag.

(4) Denier

The deniers can't take any information in the process of the RFID systems. However the deniers damage such as losing data through interrupting the transmitted information among the entities. Since the deniers don't violate user's privacy but they interrupt systems to perform, the RFID system should be designed to detect attacks such as interrupting the transmitted information.

3 Related Works

In the RFID system, the communication between readers and tags is performed at insecure channel through RF signals. So it is open to the attack mentioned in subsection 2.2. In addition, low-cost RFID system for supply chain management is difficult to adapt cryptographic approach for secure communication since the tag has a cost limit [17]. To resolve this problem, many kinds of security technologies for the RFID system are proposed. The physical technologies for security in

Table 1. Problems of the physical technologies in the RFID system

Security technologies	Problems
Kill command	It is impossible to reuse tags.
	It has difficulty to verify that 'Kill' command is performed.
Faraday cage	It has limitation of the form of 'Faraday cage'.
Active jamming	It has legal problems such as interrupting the lawful processes.
Blocker tag	It is needed additional 'Blocker tag'.

RFID system are the 'Kill command' approach [22], the 'Faraday cage' approach [13], the 'Active jamming' approach [11], and the 'Blocker tag' approach [11] and so on. However the physical technologies to protect RFID system have problems such that additional devices are needed or the form of the protection devices is limited or legal problems exist. Therefore, in the recent RFID system, the authentication technologies using cryptographic approach are proposed. Until now, the hash-lock protocol [18, 19, 21, 22], the randomized hash-lock protocol [21, 22], the external re-encryption protocol [10], the hash-chain protocol [14], and the hash-based ID variation protocol [9] are proposed. However previous protocols have many problems that protocols are vulnerable to replay and spoofing attacks or tag can be tracked. In this section, we analyze the problems of the previous RFID authentication protocols.

3.1   The Hash-Lock Protocol

The hash-lock protocol [18, 19, 21, 22] uses $metaID$ to hide tag's real ID. However $metaID$ is fixed. So attacker can track the tags and protocol is vulnerable to replay attack. In addition, protocol is vulnerable to spoofing attack when attacker disguises the right reader and receives the $metaID$ from the tag then disguises the right tag and gets the key from the right reader sending this $metaID$. Fig. 2 shows the process of the hash-lock protocol.

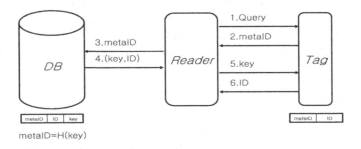

Fig. 2. The hash-lock protocol

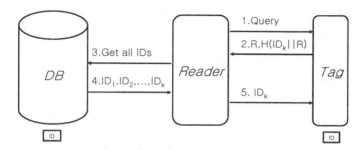

Fig. 3. The randomized hash-lock protocol

3.2   The Randomized Hash-Lock Protocol

In the randomized hash-lock protocol [21, 22], the tag makes random number then sends it to the reader as a response on every session. However ID_k is sent to the tag through the insecure channel. So the tag can be tracked. In addition, the protocol is vulnerable to replay attack since attacker can disguise the right tag when the attacker overhears the tag's response $R, H(ID_k\|R)$ then sends it to the reader. Besides the protocol is vulnerable to spoofing attack since the attacker can disguise the tag. For example, the attacker disguises the right reader and receives the response $R, H(ID_k\|R)$. Then the attacker sends $R, H(ID_k\|R)$ to the right reader as a response when the right reader queries. Fig. 3 shows the process of the randomized hash-lock protocol.

3.3   The External Re-encryption Protocol

The external re-encryption protocol [10] is theoretically more secure than previous protocols because of using a public key cryptography technique to protect the tag's ID. However the external devices such as a reader to perform encryption and decryption instead of the tags since the public key cryptography needs much computation and the tags can't compute the public key encryption and decryption. In this protocol, the encrypted tag's ID is fixed. So it has a problem that the tag's data is often rewrites to protect the secret information. Besides the protocol isn't suitable for ubiquitous environment as the protocol needs the external devices and the user's action for re-encryption.

3.4   The Hash-Chain Protocol

In the hash-chain protocol [14], the tag always sends different responses when the reader queries using two different hash function. So the attackers don't know what tag responds although the attackers know the tag's response $a_{t,i}$. The attacker can't know that different responses of a tag are from the same tag. However the attackers can disguise the right tag when the attackers resend $a_{t,i}$ to the reader. Therefore, the protocol is vulnerable to replay and spoofing attacks. In addition, the hash-chain protocol has a heavy burden on back-end database to authenticate tags since the protocol computes hash function i times on every

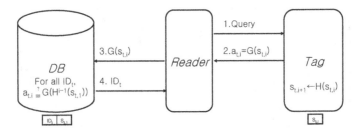

Fig. 4. The hash-chain protocol

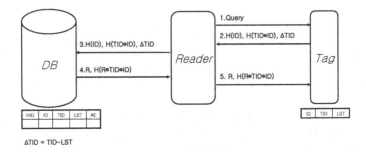

Fig. 5. The hash-based ID variation protocol

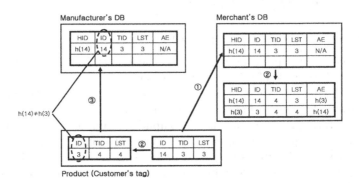

Product (Customer's tag)

Fig. 6. The unsuitability of the hash-based ID variation protocol for the distributed database environment. ① When a customer contacts the merchant for warranty service, the merchant can examine the genuineness of the product(the customer's tag). ② Then the data of the product and merchant's database are updated. ③ When the merchant sends the product to the manufacturer for the warranty service, the manufacturer can't examine the genuineness of the product since the ID of the product is different from the ID in the manufacture's database.($h(14) \neq h(3)$)

tag. Besides, the cost of the tag increases as the tag should include two different hash functions. Fig. 4 shows the process of the hash-chain protocol.

3.5   The Hash-Based ID Variation Protocol

The hash-based ID variation protocol [9] exchanges ID as a tag's identification information on every session like the hash-chain protocol. This protocol is secure against replay attacker since the tag's ID is renewed by random number R and TID and LST are updated. TID means that the last transaction number and LST means that the last successful transaction number. However the attackers can be authenticated when the attackers disguise the right reader and receives $H(ID), H(TID \oplus ID), \triangle TID$ from the tag then sends them to the reader as a response before the tag performs the next authentication session. In this time, if the attackers don't transmit the information described at step 5 in Fig. 5, the tag regards that the information is lost then the tag don't update its ID. So the attackers can track the location of the tag since $H(ID)$ is fixed before the tag performs the next authentication session and updates its $H(ID)$. Besides IDs of the the back-end database and tag are updated on every session. So this protocol isn't suitable for ubiquitous computing environment that the distributed databases exist. Fig. 5 shows the process of the hash-based ID variation protocol and Fig. 6 shows that this protocol is not suitable for ubiquitous computing environment using distributed databases. In Fig. 6, the data of the product and the two databases are taken from [9].

4   The Proposed Protocol

The proposed protocol uses the challenge-response method [12]. First, the reader queries to the tag with a random number. Then the tag responds using this random number and random number generated by itself. So the protocol is secure against the replay and spoofing attacks which are pointed at previous protocols. In addition the protocol has a merit that it can be applied to a ubiquitous environment that databases are distributed. This is different from the Hash-based ID Variation protocol since the proposed protocol doesn't update ID of the tag.

4.1   Structure

In the proposed protocol, the back-end database stores ID and the other information of the tags and authenticates tag using only hash function computation. The reader generates only one random number and requires only temporary memory to store data that is transmitted between tags and back-end database. The parameters used in the proposed protocol are showed in the next. And Fig. 7 shows the process of the proposed protocol.

[Parameters]

- $Query$: Requesting the responses of the tags.
- ID: The secret authentication information of the tags such as EPC[6, 16]. L bits.

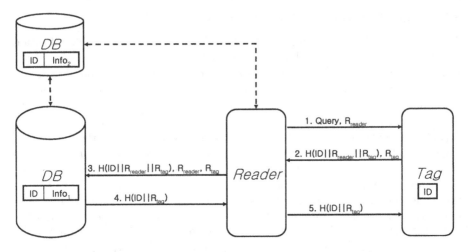

Fig. 7. The proposed protocol

- $H()$: The one-way hash function. $H : \{0,1\}^* \longrightarrow \{0,1\}^L$.
- R_{reader}: The random number that is generated by the reader and is transmitted to the tags on every session. M bits.
- R_{tag}: The random number generated by the tags. N bits.
- $\|$: Concatenate function.
- $\longrightarrow$: Transmitting.
- $\stackrel{?}{=}$: Comparison.

4.2   Authentication Phase

(Step 1: the reader) The reader broadcasts to the tags with a *Query* and a random number R_{reader}.

$$\text{reader} \longrightarrow \text{tags: } Query, R_{reader}$$

(Step 2: the tag) The tag concatenates a random number R_{tag} generated by itself, a challenge R_{reader}, and ID then hashes them. Then the tag transmits $H(ID\|R_{reader}\|R_{tag})$ to the reader as a response to *Query* with R_{tag}.

$$\text{tag} \longrightarrow \text{reader: } H(ID\|R_{reader}\|R_{tag}), R_{tag}{}^1$$

---

[1] However, the number of gates to compose low-cost tag is 7.5-15Kgates. In these gates, the number of gates that can be used to implement cryptographic technology is 2.5-5Kgates [20]. So the number is not enough to generate a random number R_{tag} using random number generator. Therefore, to improve the efficiency of the proposed protocol, the tag may concatenate *key* that is embedded in the tag when the tag is produced, a random number R_{tag}^{i-1} generated in the former session and R_{reader} received from reader then hashes them to generate a new random number R_{tag}^i for the current session. When the tags produce R_{tag}^i, R_{tag}^0 is $H(key)$, where *key* is a secret information.

(Step 3 : the reader) The reader transmits R_{reader} to the back-end database with $H(ID\|R_{reader}\|R_{tag})$ and R_{tag} received from the tag.

$$\text{reader} \longrightarrow \text{back-end database: } H(ID\|R_{reader}\|R_{tag}), R_{reader}, R_{tag}$$

(Step 4 : back-end database) For all IDs stored in the back-end database, the back-end database concatenates ID, R_{reader} and R_{tag} then hashes them. Then the back-end database compares it with $H(ID\|R_{reader}\|R_{tag})$ received from the reader to authenticate the tag.

back-end database:

$$\text{computed } H(ID\|R_{reader}\|R_{tag}) \overset{?}{=} \text{received } H(ID\|R_{reader}\|R_{tag})$$

If the authentication is successful, the back-end database sends $H(ID\|R_{tag})$ to the reader.

$$\text{back-end database} \longrightarrow \text{reader: } H(ID\|R_{tag})$$

(Step 5 : reader, tag) The reader transmits $H(ID\|R_{tag})$ received from back-end database to the tag.

$$\text{reader} \longrightarrow \text{tag: } H(ID\|R_{tag})$$

The tag concatenates its ID and R_{tag} generated in step 2 then hashes them. Then the tag compares it with $H(ID\|R_{tag})$ received from the reader to authenticate back-end database. If the authentication is successful, the tag authenticates back-end database and the authentication session is successfully finished.

$$\text{tag: computed } H(ID\|R_{tag}) \overset{?}{=} \text{received } H(ID\|R_{tag})$$

4.3   Security Analysis

The previous protocols are vulnerable to the replay attack, spoofing attack and can be tracked by an attacker. In the proposed protocol, the tag transmits different response on every session using a random number received from the reader. So the proposed protocol is secure against replay attack and spoofing attack. In addition, the proposed protocol protects tracking by the attackers.

In this section, we analyze how the proposed protocol is secure against the attacks described in 2.2.

(1) Security against the spoofing attack

The attacker performs the following attack.

① The attacker disguises as a right reader then sends Query and R_{reader} to the tag.

② The attacker gets $H(ID\|R_{reader}\|R_{tag}), R_{tag}$ from the tag as a response.

③ In the next session, when the right reader transmits $Query, R'_{reader}$, the attacker responds with $H(ID\|R_{reader}\|R_{tag}), R_{tag}$ in order to disguise as a right tag.

If R_{reader} is different from $R'_{reader}(R_{reader} \neq R'_{reader})$, the probability that attacker disguises as a right tag is negligible because of the collision-resistance property of hash function. So the proposed protocol is secure against spoofing attack.

(2) Security against the replay attack

The attacker performs the following attack.

① After the reader transmits $Query, R_{reader}$ to the tag, the attacker eavesdrops $H(ID\|R_{reader}\|R_{tag}), R_{tag}$ that is the response of the tag.
② In the next authentication session, when the reader transmits $Query, R'_{reader}$, the attacker responds with $H(ID\|R_{reader}\|R_{tag}), R_{tag}$ in order to disguise as a right tag.

If R_{reader} is different from $R'_{reader}(R_{reader} \neq R'_{reader})$, the probability that attacker disguises as a right tag is negligible. So the proposed protocol is secure against replay attack. Besides if the one-way hash function such as MD5 [15], SHA-1 [7] is secure, the attacker doesn't know ID of the tag because of the one-wayness property of hash function. So it is impossible to produce a right response $H(ID\|R'_{reader}\|R_{tag})$.

(3) Security against the traffic analysis and tracking

The attacker performs the following attack.

① To receive responses, the attacker disguises the reader then transmits fixed $Query$ and R_{reader} to the tag or overhears the information between the reader and the tag.
② The attacker analyzes the response of the tag, $H(ID\|R_{reader}\|R_{tag}), R_{tag}$ to know which tag sends it.

Since $H(ID\|R_{reader}\|R_{tag})$ is produced using a random number R_{tag} and ID that the attacker doesn't know, $H(ID\|R_{reader}\|R_{tag})$ becomes different on every session. Therefore if the one-way hash function is secure, the attacker doesn't know which tag responses with $H(ID\|R_{reader}\|R_{tag})$.Therefore the attacker is impossible to analyze the traffic and to track the location of the tag.

(4) Security against the interruption of transmitted information

The proposed protocol provides a mutual authentication between the reader and the tag. If the message loss occurs, the reader or the tag can detect it. Besides the ID of the tag is fixed so that the loss of the information in the back-end database doesn't occur. However in the Hash-based ID Variation protocol, the loss of the information in the back-end database may occur.

Table 2. Comparison of the security ($\bigcirc$: *secure*, $\times$: *not secure*)

Attacks	Hash-lock	Randomized hash-lock	Hash-chain	Hash-based ID variation	Proposed protocol
Spoofing	$\times$	$\times$	$\times$	$\times$	$\bigcirc$
Replay	$\times$	$\times$	$\times$	$\bigcirc$	$\bigcirc$
Traffic analysis	$\times$	$\times$	$\bigcirc$	$\bigcirc$	$\bigcirc$
Weak anonymity	$\times$	$\times$	$\bigcirc$	$\bigcirc$	$\bigcirc$
Strong anonymity	$\times$	$\times$	$\bigcirc$	$\times$	$\bigcirc$
DB sync	Not need	Not need	Not need	Need	Not need

Table 2 shows the security of the proposed protocol comparing with the previous RFID authentication protocols. In Table 2, 'Weak anonymity' means that the recipient of response generated by the tag can verify that it is a valid response of the query, but cannot discover which tag made it. And 'Strong anonymity' means that the recipient of a response generated by the tag can verify that it is a valid response of the query, but cannot decide whether two responses have been generated by the same tag. In addition, 'DB sync' means that the necessity of sync between the back-end database and the tags in order to protect the loss of information. Only in the hash-based ID variation protocol, the loss of information in the back-end database is considered since the authentication information of the tag becomes different on every session. Otherwise, the authentication information of the tag is fixed. So the loss of information in the back-end database does not matter.

4.4   Efficiency of the Proposed Protocol

In the proposed protocol, the tag needs a random number generator. But if we use $R_{tag}^0 = H(key)$, $R_{tag}^i = H(key \| R_{tag}^{i-1} \| R_{reader})$ as R_{tag} to improve the efficiency of the proposed protocol, the tag needs to embed only one hash function. So, it is suitable for low-cost tag. In the proposed protocol, the tag performs 2 hash operations and generates a random number using a random number generator.(In the improved version, the tag performs 3 hash operations but no random number generator is needed.) The reader generates a random number only one time. And the back-end database averagely performs $\frac{\text{the number of IDs}}{2}$ hash operations in order to authenticate tag. In addition, the additional one hash operation is needed to generate the authentication information of the back-end database.

If the size of ID, key, R_{reader} and R_{tag} is equal to L bits, the tag needs $2L$ bits memory to store ID, R_{tag}(In the improved version, additional L bits memory to store key is needed) And the back-end database needs L bits memory per one tag to store ID of each tag.

Table 3 shows the efficiency of the proposed protocol comparing with the previous RFID authentication protocols. In Table 3, It is assumed that the size of the secret information $ID, S_{t,i}$ and the one-way hash function is equal to $H : \{0,1\}^* \longrightarrow \{0,1\}^L$. In addition, it is assumed that TID and LST in Hash-based ID Variation are L bits.

Table 3. Comparison of the efficiency

	Memory(bits)		Computation(times)			Suitability to distributed database environment
	Tag	Back-end database	Tag	Reader	Back-end database	
Hash-lock	2L	4L	H : 1	-	-	○
Randomized hash-lock	1L	1L	R : 1, H : 1	H : $\frac{\text{The number of IDs}}{2}$	-	○
Hash-chain	1L	2L	H : 2		-	H : $\frac{\text{The number of IDs}}{2} \times i$ ○
Hash-based ID variation	3L	8L	H : 3	-	R : 1, H : 3	×
Proposed protocol	1L (3L)*	1L	R : 1, H : 2 (H : 3)*	R : 1	H : $\frac{\text{The number of IDs}}{2} + 1$	○

H : the hash function operation, R : generating a random number
* in the improved version.

In this paper, it is not considered the memory of the tag's information since the tags' information such as producer, production date, price in the back-end database are variable each back-end database.

In the hash-based ID variation protocol, the back-end database needs two records per tag to prevent message loss. However the back-end database needs only one record per tag in the proposed protocol since the ID of the tag is fixed. Therefore the quantity of total information in back-end database is smaller than that of the Hash-based ID Variation protocol. Besides, the proposed protocol is suitable for ubiquitous computing environment that the distributed databases exist. On the contrary, the Hash-based ID Variation protocol that the ID of the tag becomes different on every session is not suitable for ubiquitous computing environment.

5   Conclusion

Many people have been researching the RFID system as a technology to realize ubiquitous computing environment. However the automatic identification of the RFID system brings on not only convenience of the life but also various privacy problems. So in order to resolve these problems, many technologies have been proposed. But the previous security technologies still have security problems and are not suitable for ubiquitous computing environment.

In our proposed protocol, the tag responds using two random numbers received from the reader and generated by the tag on every session. So the tag can differently responds on every session and the protocol is secure against replay attack, spoofing attack and tracking.

Since the proposed protocol is secure and efficient and it considers distributed database environment, it is expected that the proposed protocol is variously utilized to realize ubiquitous computing environment.

References

1. Associated Press, "Benetton undecided on use of 'smart tags' ", 8 April 2003.
2. Auto-ID Center, "860MHz-960MHz Class I Radio Frequency Identification Tag Radio Frequency and Logical Communication Interface Specification Recommended Standard, Version 1.0.0", Technical Report MIT-AUTOID-TR007, 2002.
3. Auto-ID Center, "860MHz-930MHz Class 0 Radio Frequency Identification Tag Protocol Specification Candidate Recommendation, Version 1.0.0", Technical Report MIT-AUTOID-TR016, 2003.
4. CNET, "Wal-Mart cancels 'smart shelf' trial", http://www.cnet.com, Jul. 2003.
5. EAN International and the Uniform Code Council. http://www.ean-int.org.
6. EPCglobal, "EPC Tag Data Standards Version 1.1 Rev.1.24", http://www.epcglobalinc.org.
7. Federal Information Processing Standards (FIPS), Secure Hash Standard (SHA-1), Technical Report 180-1, National Institute of Standards and Technology(NIST), April 1995, supersedes FIPS PUB 180, 1993.
8. K. Finkenzeller, RFID Handbook, John Wiley and Sons, 2003.
9. D. Henrici, P. Müller, "Hash-based Enhancement of Location Privacy for Radio-Frequency Identification Devices using Varying Identifiers", Proceedings of the Second IEEE Annual Conference on Pervasive Computing and Communications Workshops (PERCOMW'04), pp.149-153, IEEE, 2004.
10. A. Juels, R. Pappu, "Squealing Euros: Privacy protection in RFID-enabled banknotes", Financial Cryptography'03, LNCS 2742, pp.103-121, Springer-Verlag, 2003.
11. A. Juels, R. L. Rivest, and M Szydlo, "The Blocker Tag : Selective Blocking of RFID Tags for consumer Privacy", In Proceedings of 10th ACM Conference on Computer and Communications Security, CCS 2003, pp.103-111, 2003.
12. W. Mao, Modern Cryptography Theory and Practice, Prentice Hall PTR, 2004.
13. mCloak: Personal/corporate management of wireless devices and technology, 2003. http://www.mobilecloak.com.
14. M. Ohkubo, K. Suzuki, and S. Kinoshita, "Hash-Chain Based Forward-Secure Privacy Protection Scheme for Low-Cost RFID", Proceedings of the SCIS 2004, pp.719-724, 2004.
15. R. L. Rivest, "The MD5 Message Digest Algorithm". Technical Report RFC 1321, MIT Lab for Computer Science and RSA Laboratories, April 1992.
16. S. Sarma, D. L. Brock, and K. Ashton, "The Networked Physical World Proposals for Engineering the Next Generation of Computing, Commerce and Automatic-Identification", Technical Report MIT-AUTOID-WH-001, 2001.
17. S. Sarma, "Towards the 5 cent Tag", Technical Report MIT-AUTOID-WH-006, 2001.
18. S. E. Sarma, S. A. Weis, and D. W. Engels. "RFID systems, Security and Privacy Implications", White Paper MIT-AUTOID-WH-014, MIT AUTO-ID CENTER, 2002.
19. S. E. Sarma, S. A. Weis, and D. W. Engels, "RFID Systems and Security and Privacy Implications", CHES 2002, LNCS 2523, pp.454-469, Springer-Verlag, 2003.

20. S. E. Sarma, S. A. Weis, and D. W. Engels, "Radio-Frequency Identification : Secure Risks and Challenges", RSA Laboratories Cryptobytes, vol. 6, no. 1, pp2-9, Spring 2003.
21. S. A. Weis, "Security and Privacy in Radio-Frequency Identification Devices" MS Thesis, MIT, May 2003.
22. S. A. Weis, S. E. Sarma, R. L. Rivest, and D. W. Engels, "Security and Privacy Aspects of Low-Cost Radio Frequency Identification Systems", Security in Pervasive Computing 2003, LNCS 2802, pp.201-212, Springer-Verlag, 2004.

Security Concept of the EU-Passport

Dennis Kügler

Federal Office for Information Security (BSI),
Godesberger Allee 185-189,
53175 Bonn, Germany
dennis.kuegler@bsi.bund.de

With the introduction of biometrics into passports, the next generation of passport books will become pervasive computing devices. In more detail passports will be equipped with contactless RF-chips not only storing digitized biometrics of the holder but also providing fundamental security mechanisms to protect the authenticity, originality, and confidentiality of the data stored on the chip.

To allow global interoperable border crossing the International Civil Aviation Organization (ICAO) has developed a specification for the security features that must be supported by both the RF-chips and the corresponding readers. In a nutshell, the ICAO specification determines the facial image as mandatory biometric, and a digital signature (Passive Authentication) must be used to protect the authenticity and integrity of all data stored on the RF-chip. To support verification of those signatures a global Public Key Infrastructure is also set up.

Besides those mandatory features two optional security mechanisms are also specified that may be supported by an RF-chip: Active Authentication may be implemented to allow readers to check that the chip is genuine and Basic Access Control may be implemented to protect against skimming and eavesdropping on the air interface.

This talk presents the available security mechanisms in detail and discusses their effectiveness against potential threats. The main focus is however on the security concept of the EU-passport, which does not only incorporate fingerprints as mandatory secondary biometric but also provides even more advanced security mechanisms.

D. Hutter and M. Ullmann (Eds.): SPC 2005, LNCS 3450, p. 85, 2005.
© Springer-Verlag Berlin Heidelberg 2005

Efficient Cooperative Signatures: A Novel Authentication Scheme for Sensor Networks[*]

Stefaan Seys[**] and Bart Preneel

K.U.Leuven, Department Electrical Engineering-ESAT, SCD/COSIC,
Kasteelpark Arenberg 10, B-3001 Leuven, Belgium
{stefaan.seys,bart.preneel}@esat.kuleuven.ac.be

Abstract. This paper describes an efficient and strong authentication mechanism for ad hoc sensor networks. Our protocol focuses on providing strong authentication and privacy for requests from query nodes to the network and for the corresponding responses. Our scheme uses the asymmetrical energy consumption of the well known public key cryptosystems RSA and Rabin. As the sensor nodes are assumed to be power-restrained, we only employ efficient public key operations at their side of the protocol, this leaves us only with the public operations encryption and signature verification. We have extended this set with a novel building block that allows nodes to sign messages cooperatively. We show that our protocol is robust against attacks from both outsiders and insiders.

1 Introduction

As technology advances and integration of low-power radio, computing and sensor technology becomes reality, the road is paved for distributed sensor networks (DSNs). These networks will typically consist of 1000's of ultra-low power nodes, with limited communication means and CPU power [1, 5, 12, 10, 14].

Distributed sensor networks can be used in a wide range of applications, including military sensing, environment monitoring, collecting vital signs of patients, smart houses, etc. As sensor networks will be deployed and possibly left unattended in hostile environments, security is very important.

In this paper we focus on the key operation of a sensor network: pulling data from it. We propose a novel scheme that allows low-power devices to cooperatively send an authenticated answer to the requests from query nodes.

1.1 Network Operation

Our security architecture is designed with the following network infrastructure in mind. The majority of the nodes in the sensor network, *sensor nodes*, mea-

---

[*] This work was supported by the Concerted Research Action (GOA) Mefisto-2000/06 of the Flemish Government.
[**] Research financed by a Ph.D. grant of the the Institute for the Promotion of Innovation through Science and Technology in Flanders (IWT-Vlaanderen).

D. Hutter and M. Ullmann (Eds.): SPC 2005, LNCS 3450, pp. 86–100, 2005.

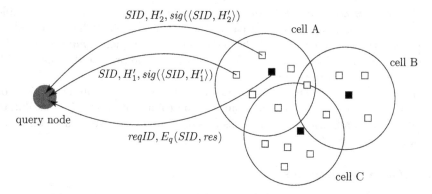

Fig. 1. Example network with three cells. Every cell has one manager node (black square)

sure whatever property they are designed to measure, for example, temperature, pressure, light intensity, etc. These sensor nodes are organized in *cells* (sometimes referred to as clusters). One node in each cell will act as a *cell manager*. The cell manager is responsible for collecting information from the sensor nodes in its cell and forwarding it to a *query node* or *sink node*. A query node requests (pulls) a specific cell manager for an update, while a sink node is used when an event is triggered by a sensor node and the update information is pushed to the sink node. Obviously a single node can act as both a query and a sink node. Figure 1 shows an example network topology with three cells. When a query node sends a request to the cell manager to pull data from the sensors, the cell manager broadcasts the request to the rest of its cell. Next to requests from query nodes, an update can be triggered by any sensor and will be forwarded to the cell manager. Sensors within a cell collect data, and locally process it resulting in a single response or update that is transmitted to a query or sink node respectively. The response/update is transmitted to the query/sink node by the cell manager. The cell manager also ensures that every node in its cell gets a copy of the final result, as this is required for our authentication scheme.

We propose an energy-efficient security architecture for sensor networks that provides the following security properties:

1. Query nodes can authenticate their requests.
2. The confidentiality of the response/update data can be guaranteed (only the query/sink node can read it).
3. Sensors in a cell *have* to cooperate in order to authenticate the response/update. This prevents that a single malicious node in the network can provide the query or sink nodes with incorrect information.

1.2   Assumptions

This paper is focused on providing strong authentication for the messages transmitted between a cell and a query or sink node. A number of additional measures needs to be taken to make the complete network operation secure.

- *Secure intra-cell communications.* Our scheme depends on nodes to be able to securely communicate with each other within a cell. It has little use to protect the confidentiality of the response to some query *only* between the cell manager and the query node – it also has to be protected while the cell is negotiating on the response.
- *Robust routing scheme.* Query nodes need to be able to contact the sensor nodes and vice versa. To make our scheme robust, it should be possible to adapt the configuration of the cells as sensor nodes can stop functioning or become corrupted.

1.3   Our Contributions

We present an authentication protocol that forces multiple nodes to cooperate in order to be able to authenticate a message. This prevents a single compromised or malicious node (or even a small subset of nodes) from sending authenticated messages. Moreover, our scheme is designed to work in the setting of power-constrained devices such as sensor nodes: the low-power devices only use the efficient *public* operations of RSA or of the Rabin public key cryptosystem, or symmetric building blocks. To the best of our knowledge no design has been proposed in the literature that can offer similar properties.

1.4   Notation

We will use the following notations:

- N_x: nonce generated by X,
- $Sig_x(m)$: signature on message m using X's private key,
- $E_x(m)$: public key encryption of m using X's public key,
- $E_K[m]$: symmetric encryption of m using symmetric key K,
- $\text{MAC}_K[m]$: Message Authentication Code of m using symmetric key K,
- $\langle a, b \rangle$: concatenation of a and b.

2   Efficient Encryption and Signature Verification

We use the asymmetric computational cost of the RSA and Rabin public key cryptosystems [7]. The textbook version of the RSA public key encryption scheme works as follows:

- Each user generates two large primes p and q.[1]
- Each user picks a public exponent e and computes the inverse $d = e^{-1}$ mod $\phi(pq)$, with $\phi()$ indicating the Euler function.
- The public key for a user is the pair $(n = pq, e)$; the private key consists of the prime factors p and q, or the pair (n, d).
- The encryption c of a message m is equal to $c = m^e \bmod n$.
- The decryption m of a ciphertext c is equal to $m = c^d \bmod n$.

---

[1] *"large"* in this context means 512 or more bits.

In order to make RSA more efficient, popular choices for the RSA public exponent e are either 3 (not recommended) or 65535 ($= 2^{16} - 1$), while the value d has about the same bit length as the modulus n. This means that the computational effort of encrypting (public operation) is much less than decrypting (private operation).

The textbook version of the Rabin public key encryption scheme is very similar to RSA, but it uses the even public exponent $e = 2$.[2] This is not a special case of RSA as this function is not 1-to-1: every ciphertext $c = m^2 \bmod n$ results in four possible plaintexts. Redundancy in the plaintext is required to ensure that only one square root is a legitimate message. Rabin encryption (public operation) is extremely efficient as it only involves a single modular squaring. By comparison, RSA with $e = 3$ requires an additional modular multiplication. Rabin decryption (private operation) is comparable in efficiency to RSA decryption.

The same efficiency difference holds for the RSA and Rabin signature schemes, where signing is equivalent to "decrypting" (private operation) and verifying is equivalent to "encrypting" (public operation). In all cases the public operation is very efficient, while the private operation is rather inefficient and requires a large computational effort [16]. While public key operations are sometimes considered too expensive for ultra low-power devices such as sensor nodes, we argue that RSA with a small public exponent or the Rabin public key cryptosystem allow the use of the *public* operations in these power-restrained devices.

3   Lamport One-Time Digital Signatures

Lamport proposed a so-called one-time signature scheme based on a general one-way function (OWF) F [6]. Lamport's scheme can be used to sign a single bit in the following way: the secret key consists of two random values x_0 and x_1, while the public key is the pair $\{F(x_0), F(x_1)\}$. The signature for bit b is x_b. For signing longer messages, several instances of this scheme are used. Lamport's scheme was further generalized in [2, 3, 8, 15]. There are other approaches like [9, 11] but these are not suitable for our purposes.

3.1   Lamport Scheme Using the Winternitz Improvement

One generalization of the Lamport scheme attributed by Merkle to Winternitz [8] is to apply the OWF F to the secret key iteratively a fixed number of times, resulting in the public key. Briefly the scheme works as follows. Suppose we wish to sign a m-bit message M. First the message M is split in m/t blocks of size t bits. Let these parts be $M_1, \ldots, M_{m/t}$. The secret key is $sk = \{x_0, \ldots, x_{m/t}\}$ where x_i is a l-bit value . The public key is $pk = \{F^{(2^t-1)m/t}(x_0), F^{2^t-1}(x_1), \ldots F^{2^t-1}(x_{m/t})\}$[3]. The signature of a message M

---

[2] Note that all possible RSA public exponents e are odd.
[3] Note that $F^2() = F(F())$ is applying the OWF F twice iteratively.

is computed by considering the integer value of the blocks $\text{Int}(M_i) = I_i$. The signature $Sig(M)$ is composed of $m/t + 1$ values $\{s_0, \ldots, s_{m/t}\}$ where, for $i \geq 1$, $s_i = F^{2^t - 1 - I_i}(x_i) = F^{-I_i}(y_i)$, while $s_0 = F^{\sum_i I_i}(x_0)$ for $1 \leq i \leq m/t$. The signature length is $l(m/t + 1)$. On average, computing a signature requires $2\frac{2^t m}{t}$ evaluations of F. To verify a signature, one splits the message M in m/t blocks of size t bits. Let these parts be $M_1, \ldots, M_{m/t}$. One then verifies that pk equals $\{F^{2^t - 1 - \sum_i I_i}(s_0), F^{I_1}(s_1), \ldots, F^{I_{m/t}}(s_{m/t})\}$ for $1 \leq i \leq m/t$. It is possible to prove that forging a signature of a message M' given a message M, a valid signature $Sig(M)$ and the public key requires inversion of the function F.

In practice we assume that F maps 64 bits to 64 bits. Since collision resistance is not required from F we believe that this parameter is sufficient. In order to prevent attackers from building a large table of evaluations of F, F can be made different for each signature by defining $F(x)$ to be $G(\text{Salt}||x)$, where G is a one-way 128 bits to 64 bits function and Salt is generated at random by the signer and transmitted to the verifier. Suitable F's can be constructed from efficient block ciphers such as AES or from fast hash functions such as SHA-1.

Further we assume that the message M that needs to be signed is hashed with a cryptographic hash function such as SHA-1 before it is fed to the signing algorithm. If the length of the message is smaller than the output of the hash function, then the hash function is not applied. This ensures that the input length of the signing algorithm is at most the output length of the hash algorithm being used.

Note that the secret key $sk = \{x_0, \ldots, x_{m/t}\}$ can be generated with a good pseudo-random generator using a single seed x. This means that storing the secret key only requires l bits instead of $(m/t)l$ bits. Obviously this is not true for the public key.

3.2   Merkle Trees

One disadvantage of the Lamport scheme is the size of the public key. All verifiers need an authenticated copy of this public key in order to verify the validity of a signature. Merkle proposed the use of binary trees to authenticate a large number of public keys with a single value, i.e., the root of the tree [8]. A Merkle tree is a complete binary tree with a n-bit value associated to each node such that each interior node value is a OWF of the node values of its children (Fig. 2):

$$P[i,j] = F\big(\langle P[i,(i+j-1)/2], P[(i+j+1)/2,j]\rangle\big).$$

The N values that need to be authenticated are placed at the N leaves of the tree. Although the leaf value may be chosen arbitrarily, usually it is a cryptographic hash of the values that need to be authenticated. In this case these values are called *leaf-preimages*. A leaf can be verified with respect to a publicly known root value and the *authentication path* of the leaf. We assume that the public keys of the Lamport one-time signature scheme (Sect. 3.1) are stored at the leaf-preimages of the tree (one public key per leaf-preimage).

Authentication Paths. Let sib_i be the value of the sibling of the node on height i on the path from the leaf to the root. A leaf has height 0, the OWF of two leaves has height 1, etc., and the root has height H if the tree has 2^H leaves. The authentication path is then the set $\{sib_i \mid 0 \leq i \leq H\}$. For example, the gray nodes in Fig. 2 are the authentication path for leaf y_3.

A leaf may be authenticated as follows: First apply the OWF to the leaf and its sibling sib_0, then apply the OWF to the result and sib_1, etc., all the way up to the root. If the calculated root value is equal to the published root value, then the leaf value is accepted as authentic. This operation requires $\log_2(N)$ invocations of the OWF.

Authentication Path Generation. The goal of *Merkle tree traversal* is the sequential output of the leaf values and their authentication paths. In [8], Merkle presents a straightforward technique that requires a maximum of $2\log_2(N)$ invocations of the OWF per round, and requires a maximum storage of $\log_2^2(N)/2$ outputs of the OWF. In [4], Jakobsson et al. present an algorithm which allows a time-space trade-off. When storage is minimized, the algorithm requires about $2\log_2(N)/\log_2(\log_2(N))$ invocations of the OWF, and a maximum storage of $1.5\log_2^2(N)/\log_2(\log_2(N))$ outputs of the OWF. Finally in [13], Szydlo presents an algorithm that requires $2\log_2(N)$ time and a maximum storage of $3\log_2(N)$. All three Merkle tree traversal algorithms described here start with the calculation of the tree root. During this root calculation, the initial internal state of the algorithms are also calculated and stored in memory. This initialization requires $N-1$ invocations of the OWF.[4] The initial state storage requirements are maximized as stated before.

3.3   Public Key Chaining

Another means for producing multiple one-time signatures associated to a single public key is the use of public key chaining. In this technique the public keys are still computed by applying a OWF F multiple times to the private key, but now the OWF is applied s times more than in the simple case of Sect. 3.1). This enables us to use the same private key s times. Figure 3 shows an example of this process. The columns in Fig. 3 represent OWF-chains starting from the top, going downwards. The public key of the first signature to be generated with the private key sk is depicted by the bottom row pk. Recall that $s_i = F^{-I_i}(y_i)$, this means that computing a signature is equivalent with going up the chain I_i times; this is depicted by the arrows pointing up.[5] For the next signature, the public key becomes the *previous* signature, and the signature is computed by going up the chains I_i times starting from that point, etc. The disadvantage of this technique is that the computational effort for the signatures is larger

---

[4] The cost of this initial setup is not included in the time and storage requirements stated previously.

[5] In practice the signer has to start from the private key and compute downwards since the function F is irreversible.

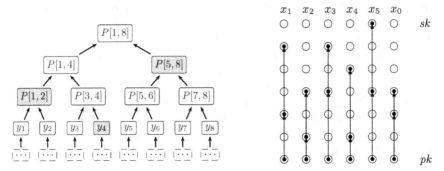

Fig. 2. Merkle tree with 8 leaves. The root $P[1,8]$ can be used to authenticate the complete tree

Fig. 3. Public key chaining: the previous signature becomes the public key for the following signature. This process continues until the secret part of one of the chains becomes to short

as the chains are longer. This technique provides a means to exchange storage requirements for computation time.

4   One-Time Cooperative Signature Scheme

4.1   High Level Overview of the Protocol

Figure 4 depicts the preparation phase of the signature scheme. First an error-correcting code is applied to strengthen the scheme. Let $H' = ECC(H)$ be the result of applying the error-correcting code ECC to the cryptographic hash H of the original message M. Now we split H' in k parts $H'_1, \ldots, H'_k$. Every node is assigned a subset of these parts to sign using the scheme explained in Sect. 3.1. Let k be the number of users in a group, and b the maximum allowed number of non-cooperative users in this group.

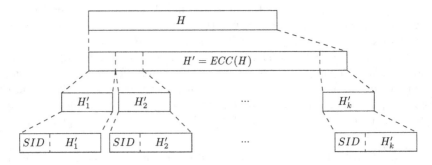

Fig. 4. Preparation phase of the signing process

4.2   Error-Correcting Codes

The use of an error-correcting code that can recover the original message from a fraction $\frac{k-b}{k}$ of the code words provides the following properties:

- *Robustness.* If at least $k - b$ parts of the signature arrive unaltered, a valid signature can be recovered from them.
- *Honest insider detection.* If no more than b out of k users misbehave (i.e., by signing a different message or by creating an invalid signature), the honest users can be identified using their valid partial signatures.

We use a concrete example to further clarify this. Suppose we have a group of $k = 15$ users and use a cryptographic hash function with a 160-bit output. Every user computes the hash value of the original message M resulting in the 160-bit message hash H. Further suppose that we want to be able to reconstruct a valid signature even if $b = 3$ out of the 15 users refuse to cooperate. One error-correcting code that can achieve this property is a (45,27) Reed-Solomon code over $GF(2^6)$ [17]. This code operates in the q-ary alphabet ($q = 2^6$) and encodes 27 information symbols into 45 code symbols, having a fractional redundancy of 40%, and guarantees a 9 symbol-error-correcting capability. As each user is supposed to sign its 3 designated code words, 3 malicious users cannot corrupt more than 9 code words and hence the signature can be recovered from the remaining 36 code words. Adapting the scheme to the group size k and threshold b is simply a matter of selecting a suitable error-correcting code.

Note that our scheme requires that more than half of the users behave correctly. If more than half of the users in a cell behave incorrectly, they can cooperate and jointly sign some altered message $\widehat{M}$, regardless of the error-correcting code that is used.

4.3   Partial Signatures

After applying the error-correcting code, user i uses the following scheme to sign its designated part H_i' of H'. First i increments the Signature Identifier (SId) and concatenates it with its identity ID_i resulting in SID_i. This SID_i together with H_i' are signed using the scheme explained in Sect. 3.1. The SId is used to link the different partial signatures with each other. Without this link an adversary could collect partial signatures on *different* messages and try to combine them to create a signature on a new message[6]. The identity ID_i is included in the signature in order to allow a user to *prove* that he created a valid partial signature on the message M. Finally the user transmits $\langle M, SID_i, H_i', Sig_i(\langle SID_i, H_i' \rangle) \rangle$ to the verifier.

Note that in many cases, depending on the k and b parameters, the length of H_i' together with SID_i is less than 160 bit. This means that the computational cost of a partial signature is less than the cost of a normal individual signature.

---

[6] Note that if a hash function is applied to the message before it is signed, the adversary will only obtain a valid signature on a message hash. She still needs to invert the hash function in order to get a signature on a message itself. This is referred to in the literature as existential forgery.

4.4   Verification

Upon receiving the message M, its multiple parts H_i' of H', and their corresponding partial signatures $Sig_i(\langle SID_i, H_i'\rangle)$ from the different cooperating signing users in a group, the verifier uses the following protocol to verify the correctness of the *complete* signature on the message M.

First the verifier checks if $Sig_i(\langle SID_i, H_i'\rangle)$ is a valid signature on $\langle SID_i, H_i'\rangle$ for all the individual partial signatures using the protocol described in Sect. 3.1. Next the verifier checks whether there are enough valid signatures, if so, the verifier recombines the different H_i' (replacing missing or invalid parts with 0's) into $\bar{H}'$. Enough here means at least $k - b$ valid parts. The verifier now decodes this $\bar{H}'$ into $\bar{H}$ using the error-correcting code. Finally the verifier checks whether $\bar{H}$ equals the cryptographic hash of the received message M. Depending on the result of this verification process, the verifier can conclude the following:

1. If there are sufficient valid partial signatures and $\bar{H}$ equals the computed H, then the combination of the different partial signatures is accepted as a valid signature on the message M, and the users that *did* generate a valid partial signature can be identified;
2. if there are sufficient valid partial signatures but $\bar{H}$ is not equal to the computed H, then the cooperating users signed different messages (indicating an attack by users inside the group), or the message was altered (indicating a Denial of Service (DoS) attack by insiders or outsiders);
3. if there are insufficient valid partial signatures, then this indicates a DoS attack by insiders or outsiders.

4.5   Informal Security Analysis

The one-time signatures on the H_i''s protect them from being altered by an adversary. This means that the verifier can be assured of the validity of the received H_i' and the identity ID_i of the user that signed it. The use of unique identifiers that link the partial signatures make it impossible to combine partial signatures on different messages in order to create a signature on some new message. These measures prevents *outsiders* from altering the signed messages or creating a valid signature on a new message.

The scheme also protects against a limited number of maliciously *collaborating insiders*. If no more than b malicious insiders do not follow the correct signing process, then they cannot prevent the rest of the users to create a valid signature. The valid partial signatures can be used to identify the honest users. If more than b malicious insiders do not follow the correct signing process, then they can prevent the others from creating a valid signature (DoS attack). If more than $k - b - 1$ malicious insiders collaborate to sign an altered message $\widehat{M}$ (while the remaining honest users faithfully sign M), then the attackers will succeed and can produce a valid signature on $\widehat{M}$. Note that in this case the verifier will incorrectly conclude that the honest users are trying to disrupt the signing process. It is easy to see that our scheme can only support thresholds b smaller than $k/2$.

5 Security Architecture

In the previous sections we have showed how we can achieve the following *efficient* public key operations: (1) encryption, (2) signature verification and (3) signature generation (cooperative or individual). In this section we propose a scheme that uses these building blocks to provide strong authentication for query-response conversations between query (sink) nodes and cells in the sensor network. Note that in our setting the low-power devices do not possess an asymmetric decryption (private) key since we assume that the decryption operation is too power consuming.

Our scheme requires the following Public Key Infrastructure (PKI) to be in place:

1. Every query and sink node has a private/public key pair for signing and another pair for encryption, both accompanied by a certificate signed by some third party.
2. Every sensor node has an authenticated copy of this third party's public key in order to be able to verify the certificates of the query or sink nodes. Note that signature verification is an efficient operation.
3. Every sensor node has a number of private/public key pairs to be used with the one-time signature scheme explained in Sect. 4. In Sect. 5.2 we show how these key pairs can be renewed.

5.1 Strong Authentication Between Query Nodes and Cells

Using the proposed building blocks, implementing the authentication scheme itself is straightforward.

Authenticated Requests. When a query node Q wishes to send an authenticated request *req* to a manager node M, it uses the following protocol:

$$Q \longrightarrow M : \quad reqID, req, Sig_q(\langle reqID, req \rangle) \ .$$

The *reqID* is incremented for every request and stored in memory by both the query node and the manager nodes. Only requests with an *reqID* larger than the one in memory are accepted. The signature in combination with the *reqID* ensure the manager node that the request is not a replay and that it originated from a valid query node. If freshness of the request must be guaranteed, then a three-message challenge/response can be used:

$$
\begin{aligned}
Q &\longrightarrow M : \quad \text{notify} &(1)\\
Q &\longleftarrow M : \quad N_m &(2)\\
Q &\longrightarrow M : \quad req, Sig_q(req, N_m) &(3)
\end{aligned}
$$

Here the first message is only necessary to notify the manager node that the query nodes wishes to send an authenticated request. In the push model towards a sink node this message is not necessary.

Authenticated Replies or Updates. For this purpose we developed the Cooperative Signature Scheme explained in Sect. 4. Obviously our scheme can be used in any low-power setting were a single device is not trusted to sign a message individually. As we explained, we assume that upon arrival of a valid request, the manager node broadcasts the request to the cell, and the cell locally computes the best result from the collective data. The manager ensure that all nodes in its cell know this final result *res*. Once the final result is established, the manager node replies to the request with the following message: $\langle reqID, E_q(\langle SID, res \rangle) \rangle$. This message contains the identity of the corresponding request and the encryption (with the query nodes public key) of the final result and the *SID* that will be used for the cooperative signatures.

All nodes in the cell employ the cooperative signature scheme in order to create the partial signatures on the final result *res*. These partial signatures $\langle H'_i, Sig_i(\langle SID, H'_i \rangle) \rangle$ are transmitted by every node in the cell to the query node (see Fig. 1). The query node collects all partial signatures and verifies the correctness of the complete signature on the result *res* it received from the manager node. Note that the result of this verification process might be used to distinguish between honest nodes and possibly uncooperative sensor nodes.

5.2   One-Time Secret Key Updates

Two important aspects in the use of one-time signature schemes is (1) generating public keys, and (2) providing the verifier with an authenticated copy of these public keys [8]. In our architecture we efficiently solve this problem by reversing it: we let the verifier (query nodes) generate the public key and transmit an authenticated and encrypted version of the corresponding private key to the signers (sensor nodes). This has multiple advantages:

1. The computational burden of generating the random private keys and computing the corresponding public keys is off-loaded from the low-power sensor nodes. When Merkle trees are used, computing the root node and the initial internal state of the tree traversal algorithm is also off-loaded from the sensor nodes.
2. The verifier automatically obtains an authenticated copy of the public key.
3. The private key *sk* can be generated from an *l*-bit seed $\underline{sk}$. This means that transmitting the private key to the signer is more efficient than transmitting the public key to the verifier. This is true particularly in this case where there is only one dedicated verifier.

The disadvantage is that the secret key is known by two parties, but in this scenario that is not an issue, as the query nodes are assumed to be trusted.

Public Key Authentication Using Public Key Chaining. The query node Q first generates n private keys sk_i from the seeds $\underline{sk}_i$ and computes the public keys pk_i. Protocol (1) shows the scheme we propose in order to install these new key pairs when authenticating public keys using public key chaining. First a symmetric session key K is established between the sensor node S and the query node Q. The signature in message (2) is required to provide the query node with prove that this session key K is really generated by sensor node S. In the last message, the query node transmits an encrypted set of new private keys, and authenticates them with a MAC. Both the encryption key and authentication key are derived from the session key K.

Note that this protocol is only efficient if multiple secret keys are transferred using the session key K since one signature is required in message (2). Even the small sensor nodes should be able to store multiple private keys simultaneously since only a single l-bit seed has to be stored per private key (the sensor nodes do not need to store or compute public keys in this case). The query node has to store the bottom rows of all n key chains, i.e., all the public keys (see Fig. 3).

Protocol (1): One-time Secret Key Update Protocol when Using Key Chaining

---

Pre-protocol setup: The query node Q prepares n fresh private/public key pairs (sk_i, pk_i) that are to be used by sensor node S. The private keys sk_i are generated by the seed values $\underline{sk}_i$.

Conventions: K_1 and K_2 are two distinct keys derived from the session key K.

Protocol messages:

$$
\begin{aligned}
Q \longrightarrow S : \quad & N_q & (1) \\
Q \longleftarrow S : \quad & N_q, N_s, E_q(K), Sig_s(N_q, N_s, K) & (2) \\
Q \longrightarrow S : \quad & E_{K_1}[\underline{sk}_1, \ldots, \underline{sk}_n], \mathrm{MAC}_{K_2}[\underline{sk}_1, \ldots, \underline{sk}_n, N_s] & (3)
\end{aligned}
$$

Result: Node S can now use the new secret keys to sign messages.

Public Key Authentication Using Merkle Trees. When using Merkle trees to authenticate the public keys, the query node Q first generates n private keys sk_i from the seeds $\underline{sk}_i$ and computes the public keys pk_i as before. The hashes of these public keys $h(pk_i)$ are then placed at the leaves of a Merkle tree. Finally the query node calculates the root of the tree and the initial internal state $Init$ of the tree traversal algorithm. The sensor node requires the following information in order to sign messages and compute authentication paths: the $\underline{sk}_i$'s, the $h(pk_i)$'s and $Init$. Note that both $\underline{sk}_i$ and $h(pk_i)$ are short bit-strings (compared to a complete public/private key) and that the size of $Init$ is maximized by $3 \log_2(n)$ l-bit values when using Szydlo's tree traversal algorithm.

The protocol messages of Protocol (1) can be reused when using Merkle trees when replacing message (3) by:

$$
Q \longrightarrow S : \quad E_{K_1}[m], \mathrm{MAC}_{K_2}[m] \text{ with } m = \langle \{\underline{sk}_i, h(pk_i)\}_{1 \leq i \leq n}, Init \rangle .
$$

After successful completion of the private key update protocol the query node only has to store the root of the Merkle tree in order to be able to verify signatures. When using Merkle trees, the sensor node has to regenerate the public key when signing a message and include it in the signature as the verifier (i.e., the query node) needs the public key to verify the validity of the signature.

Comparison. When using public key chaining, generating signatures requires multiple evaluations of the OWF F as the signer has to work his way down the chains starting from the top (Fig. 3). Next to this the verifier needs to store the current public key in memory.

The use of Merkle trees requires that the signer computes the public key and the authentication path and includes both in the signature. On the other hand, the verifier only needs to store the root of the tree. The size of message (3) of Protocol 1 when using Merkle trees will be about double the size of this message when using public key chaining.

The optimal choice depends on multiple factors such as the number of verifiers, relative cost of communications and computations, specific scenario in which the protocol is used, etc.

6   Related Work

Zhou and Haas present a distributed key management service based on threshold cryptography [18]. In particular the functionality of the Certification Authority (CA) is distributed among multiple nodes in the network (servers). A node has to collect and combine partial signatures on its certificate from a subset of these servers. Distributing the secret key of the CA prevents an attacker from compromising the whole PKI by capturing a single node. This scheme relies heavily on demanding public key operations, while our scheme only uses efficient operations. Moreover, in the scheme of Zhou and Haas, the workload for every partial signer is exactly as large as in the case when he would sign the message individually. Hence the cost of a cooperative signature is k times larger than the cost of a normal signature. In our scheme the cost of a partial signature will normally be smaller than the cost of a normal signature, so the nodes actually distribute the workload amongst each other.

7   Conclusions

In this paper we have described an efficient and strong authentication mechanism that enables query nodes and cells to securely exchange request/response conversations. As the sensor nodes are assumed to be power-restrained, we only employ efficient public key operations at their side of the protocol. We have developed and presented a new building block that allows nodes to sign messages cooperatively and have shown that our protocol is robust both against attacks from outsiders as from insiders.

References

[1] F. Bennett, D. Clarke, J. Evans, A. Hopper, A. Jones, and D. Leask, "Piconet: embedded mobile networking," *IEEE Personal Communications*, vol. 4, pp. 8–15, Oct. 1997.

[2] D. Bleichenbacher and U. Maurer, "Directed acyclic graphs, one-way functions and digital signatures," in *Advances in Cryptology – CRYPTO '94* (Y. Desmedt, ed.), vol. 839 of *Lecture Notes in Computer Science*, pp. 75–82, Springer-Verlag, 1994.

[3] S. Even, O. Goldreich, and S. Micali, "On-line/off-line digital signatures," in *Advances in Cryptology – CRYPTO '89* (G. Brassard, ed.), vol. 435 of *Lecture Notes in Computer Science*, pp. 263–275, Springer-Verlag, 1990.

[4] M. Jakobsson, T. Leighton, S. Micali, and M. Szydlo, "Fractal Merkle tree representation and traversal," in *Topics in Cryptology – RSA Conference Cryptographers' Track (RSA-CT '03)*, vol. 2612 of *Lecture Notes in Computer Science*, Springer, 2003.

[5] J. Kahn, R. Katz, and K. Pister, "Next century challenges: Mobile networking for "smart dust"," in *Proceedings of the 5th International Conference on Mobile Computing and Networking (MobiCom '99)*, pp. 483–492, ACM Press, Aug. 1999.

[6] L. Lamport, "Constructing digital signatures from a one way function," Technical Report CSL-98, SRI International, Oct. 1979.

[7] A. Menezes, P. van Oorschot, and S. Vanstone, *Handbook of Applied Cryptography*. CRC Press, 1997.

[8] R. C. Merkle, "A certified digital signature," in *Advances in Cryptology – CRYPTO '89* (G. Brassard, ed.), vol. 435 of *Lecture Notes in Computer Science*, pp. 218–238, Springer-Verlag, 1990.

[9] A. Perrig, "The BiBa one-time signature and broadcast authentication protocol," in *Proceedings of the 8th ACM Conference on Computer and Communications Security (CCS '01)*, ACM Press, New York, NY, USA, 2001.

[10] J. Rabaey, J. Ammer, J. da Silva, D. Patel, and S. Roundy, "Picoradio supports ad hoc ultra-low power wireless networking," *IEEE Computer Magazine*, July 2000.

[11] L. Reyzin and N. Reyzin, "Better than BiBa: Short one-time signatures with fast signing and verifying," in *Proceedings of the 7th Australian Conference on Information Security and Privacy* (J. Seberry, ed.), vol. 2384 of *Lecture Notes in Computer Science*, pp. 144–153, Springer-Verlag, 2002.

[12] R. Szewczyk and A. Ferencz, "Power evaluation of smartdust remote sensors," CS252 project reports (final), Berkeley Wireless Research Center, 2000.

[13] M. Szydlo, "Merkle tree traversal in log space and time," in *Advances in Cryptology – EUROCRYPT '04* (C. Cachin and J. Camenisch, eds.), vol. 3027 of *Lecture Notes in Computer Science*, pp. 541–554, Springer, May 2004.

[14] University of California, "Wireless integrated network sensors (WINS)." ⟨http://www.janet.ucla.edu/WINS/⟩.

[15] S. Vaudenay, "One-time identification with low memory," in *Proceedings of EU-ROCODE '92* (P.Camion, P.Chappin, and S.Harari, eds.), no. 339 in CISM Courses and lectures, pp. 217–228, Springer-Verlag, 1992.

[16] M. J. Wiener, "Performance comparison of public-key cryptosystems," *RSA Laboratories' CryptoBytes*, vol. 4, no. 1, pp. 1+3–5, 1998.

[17] S. G. Wilson, *Digital Modulation and Coding*. Prentice Hall, 1996.

[18] L. Zhou and Z. Haas, "Securing ad hoc networks," *IEEE Network Magazine Special Issue on Network Security*, vol. 13, no.6, 1999.

Ephemeral Pairing on Anonymous Networks[*]

Jaap-Henk Hoepman

Nijmegen Institute for Computing and Information Sciences (NIII),
Radboud University Nijmegen,
P.O. Box 9010, 6500 GL Nijmegen, the Netherlands
jhh@cs.ru.nl

Abstract. The *ephemeral pairing problem* requires two or more specific physical nodes in a wireless broadcast network, that do not yet know each other, to establish a short-term relationship between them. Such short-lived pairings occur, for example, when one pays at a check-out using a wireless wallet. This problem is equivalent to the *ephemeral key exchange* problem, where one needs to establish a high-entropy shared session key between two nodes given only a low bandwidth authentic (or private) communication channel between the pair, and a high bandwidth shared broadcast channel.

We study this problem for truly anonymous broadcast networks, discuss certain impossible scenarios and present several protocols depending on the type of communication channel between the nodes.

Keywords: Authentication, identification, pairing, key exchange, anonymous networks.

1 Introduction

The *ephemeral pairing problem* (introduced in [Hoe04]) consists of establishing a short-term relationship between two or more specific physical nodes in a wireless broadcast network that do not yet know each other. Ephemeral pairings occur, for example, when one pays at a check-out using a wireless wallet. As opposed to paying with a smart card by inserting it into a specific terminal, using a wireless connection (like Bluetooth[1] or IrDA[2]) gives no guarantee that two physical nodes that want to communicate with each other are actually talking to each other. Without any countermeasures one might end up paying for the customer at the check-out next to you.

To achieve such short-lived pairings, we do not wish to rely on any secret information shared a priori among the nodes. For the large scale systems where we expect the ephemeral pairings to play a part, such a secure initialisation might

---

[*] Id: pairing.tex,v 2.7 2005/01/18 15:25:17 jhh Exp

[1] See http://www.bluetooth.com.

[2] See http://www.irda.org.

D. Hutter and M. Ullmann (Eds.): SPC 2005, LNCS 3450, pp. 101–116, 2005.
© Springer-Verlag Berlin Heidelberg 2005

be costly and carry a huge organisational burden. Instead, we allow the nodes in the system to exchange *small* amounts of information reliably and/or privately.

Two typical application scenarios may help to understand the issues involved.

Consider for example the case where someone wishes to pay using a wireless wallet at a checkout counter of a large supermarket. There are many checkouts, and many customers paying simultaneously. To pair the wallet with the right checkout counter, the counter could generate a small random number every time a new customer arrives, and show this number on its display. Subsequently, the customer enters this number on his wallet to initiate the pairing. In this case, the customer knows the source of the random number and uses the number displayed by the counter at which it wants to pay. In other words, the random number is *authentic*. However, eavesdroppers may also be able to read the number from the display, and hence the number is not *private*. If eavesdropping is made impossible, the communication is both authentic and private.

As an example for the private case[3] consider the following. Instead of a display at each counter, the supermarket installs a single ticket dispenser ahead of all the counters (similar to systems used to assign waiting numbers to customers in e.g., a large post office). The ticket dispenser provides the customer with a ticket on which the random number is printed, together with the number of the counter to pay at. Authenticity of the information cannot be assumed, for instance because attackers may reinsert old or forged tickets in the machine. However, the information can be considered private (provided the user does not drop the ticket on the floor right after entering it on his wallet).

Because the devices are human operated, and the operators are involved in the exchange of the information, the numbers of bits that can be transferred is low (comparable to the size of typical passwords), and certainly much less than the number of bits required for strong cryptographic keys. Therefore, one cannot expect to be able to use such private or authentic communication mechanisms (called channels from now) to establish cryptographic keys directly. We do note that typically the numbers transferred over these channels are machine generated. Several realistic methods for implementing such private or authentic low bandwidth channels exist [Hoe04].

In more abstract terms then, this problem can be phrased as an *ephemeral key exchange* (denoted by φKE) problem: given a low bandwidth authentic (or private) communication channel between two nodes, and a high bandwidth broadcast channel, can we establish a high-entropy shared secret session key between the two nodes without relying on any a priori shared secret information? Here, the low bandwidth channel models the (implicit) authentication and limited information processing capabilities of the users operating the nodes.

There are numerous applications that require a solution to the ephemeral pairing problem, e.g., connecting two laptops in a business meeting, exchanging electronic business cards using PDAs, buying electronic tickets at a box office

---

[3] This example is admittedly slightly more contrived — indeed authentic communication appear to occur more naturally in real applications.

and checking them at a venue, unlocking doors using a wireless token (making sure the right door is unlocked), etc. In most of these applications, indeed by the very nature of the problem, the cooperation of the user/owner of the device is required to successfully establish a pairing. For instance, the user may be asked to select a pattern from a list that corresponds to the pattern shown on the remote device. Alternatively, the user may be asked to copy and enter a pass-code. We stress that in all these cases, the number of bits that can be handled by the user is very limited and that these bits do not have enough entropy to secure the communications directly. This is the main motivation for the model and the problem statement of establishing a high bandwidth secure communication channel between two nodes using only a low bandwidth authentic/private channel.

1.1   State of the Art

Stajano and Anderson [SA99] introduced the (long-lived) pairing problem that occurs when separate devices need to establish a long term relationship that allow one of the devices to exert control over the other (e.g., a remote control and the corresponding TV set). These pairings are supposed to exists over pro-longed periods of time, and therefore the setup of such a pairing is allowed to be quite involved.

In [Hoe04] it was shown that solutions to the ephemeral pairing problem can sometimes be based on Encrypted Key Exchange (EKE) [BM92] protocols, suggesting a relationship between these two problems. An extended discussion on this, and a review of the state of the art regarding EKE is also presented there. The solutions of [Hoe04] only apply to non-anonymous broadcast networks.

In this paper we study ephemeral pairing on anonymous broadcast networks. The difference between the anonymous and non-anonymous case is the following. In the non-anonymous case, participants only need to receive messages from a identified sender. If no such message is received, or if the adversary forged a sender identity (which is detected in subsequent stages of the protocol), the protocol simply aborts. In the anonymous case, participants may receive many messages, and it is not a priori clear which messages are intended for them. Therefore, they have to collect all messages they receive, and based on their content decide which message to accept (if any). This influences the design of the protocols. One could, in principle, use the 'secure' point-to-point channel for coordinating a session identifier directly, but in order to save this limited resource only for the purpose of key-exchange we choose not to do so. We note that the power of the adversary is the same in both models (it can arbitrarily change the source and destination in the non-anonymous model, and doesn't have to in the anonymous case).

Balfanz et al. [BSSW02] study essentially the same problem, but assume that the low-bandwidth communication channel is large enough to pre-authenticate public keys (either by sending whole keys, or hashes of these keys), that can sub-sequently be used in a standard public key authentication protocol. Gehrmann et al. [GMN04, GN04] describe the ISO/IEC standards for manual authentication of wireless devices, that allow for smaller bandwidth on the communication channel, but require the channel to be private.

A more rigorous and formal treatment of the security of EKE protocols was initiated by Lucks [Luc97], and expanded on by several authors [BMP00, BPR00, Sho99, CK01, GL03]. Due to space constraints the security proofs in this paper are informal, but will be based on Bellare *et al.* [BPR00] in the full version.

1.2   Summary of Results

In this paper we present several ephemeral key exchange protocols for completely anonymous broadcast networks, for different combinations of the point-to-point communications channels between the two nodes. These are presented in Sect. 4. Before that, we describe the model in Sect. 2, and present some impossibility results for certain types of point-to-point channels in Sect. 3. We conclude with directions for further research in Sect. 5.

2   Model and Problem Statement

Consider n physically identifiable nodes communicating over a public and insecure broadcast network, each attended by a human operator. The operators (and/or the nodes they operate) can only exchange *small* amounts of information reliably and/or in private. The ephemeral pairing problem requires two or more nodes (to be determined by their operators) to securely establish a shared secret.

As discussed in [Hoe04], this problem can be seen in more abstract terms as an ephemeral key exchange (φKE) problem. Consider Alice and Bob, connected through a high bandwidth broadcast network. In this paper, the broadcast network is completely anonymous. Alice and Bob also share a low bandwidth communication channel over which they can exchange at most η bits of information per message. This channel is either

authentic, meaning that Bob is guaranteed that a message he receives actually was sent by Alice (but this message may be eavesdropped by others), or
private, meaning that Alice is guaranteed that the message she sends is only received by Bob (but Bob does not know the message comes from Alice).

Given these connections, Alice and Bob are required to establish an authenticated and shared σ bits secret (where $\sigma \gg \eta$). They do not share any secrets a priori, and do not have any means to authenticate each other, except through the low bandwidth channel.

The adversary may eavesdrop, insert and modify packets on the broadcast network, and may eavesdrop on the authentic channel or insert and modify packets on the private channel. Note that, by assumption, the adversary cannot insert or modify packets on the authentic channel. Also, the adversary may subvert any number of nodes and collect all the secret information stored there.

Security of our protocols is defined as in the encrypted key exchange model developed by Bellare *et al.* [BPR00], where the adversary is given the task to distinguish an actual session key from an arbitrary random value for any instance of the protocol run of his choice.

In our analysis we will bound the advantage of the adversary for a particular protocol using s, t and the number of active attacks (denoted by q) performed by the adversary. Here, s and t are the security parameters of the φKE protocol. s roughly corresponds to the size of the session key to be established, and determines the advantage of a passive adversary. t roughly corresponds to the capacity of the channel between two principals, and mostly determines the advantage of an active adversary. Actually, q corresponds to the number of instances that are attacked actively by the adversary (and that involve one or more message insertions or modifications).

We work in the random oracle model, and assume hardness of the Computational Diffie Hellman problem.

We use the following notation throughout the paper. In the description of the protocols, ac is the authentic channel, pc is the private channel, and bc is the broadcast channel. Assignment is denoted by := Receiving messages from the channel or the broadcast network can be done in a blocking fashion (indicated by **receive**) or in a non-blocking fashion (indicated by **on receiving**).

In message flowcharts, $\xrightarrow{\;m\;}$ denotes sending m on the private or authentic channel, while $\xRightarrow{\;m\;}$ denotes broadcasting m on the broadcast channel. The receiving party puts the message in the indicated variable v at the arrowhead.

3   Impossibility Results

In this section we show a few straightforward impossibility results. The φKE problem[4] cannot be solved using only a single uni-directional point-to-point channel between Alice and Bob that is either authentic or private. Even an authentic channel from Alice to Bob and a private channel from Bob to Alice is not strong enough. An authentic channel from Alice to Bob and another private channel from Alice to Bob *is* strong enough however (even though there is no point-to-point channel from Bob to Alice, see Sect.4.3).

Theorem 1. *The φKE problem cannot be solved using a single private channel from Alice to Bob and a single authentic channel from Bob to Alice.*

Proof. Suppose there is a protocol solving the φKE problem using a single private channel from Alice to Bob and a single authentic channel from Bob to Alice. Now, instead of Alice, let the adversary start a session with Bob. Because Alice and Bob do not a priori share any secret information, and because the adversary can use the private channel to Bob and the authentic channel from Bob in exactly the same way as Alice does, Bob cannot distinguish the adversary from

---

[4] To be more precise, the following results only hold for the general (two-sided) version of the problem, not the one-sided version (see [Hoe04] for the difference between these two).

Alice in this session. This contradicts the requirement that at the end of the session Alice and Bob share a secret session key.

The following two facts are easy corollaries of this theorem.

Corollary 1. *The φKE problem cannot be solved using a single private channel from Alice to Bob.*

Corollary 2. *The φKE problem cannot be solved using a single authentic channel from Bob to Alice.*

4 φKE Protocols for Anonymous Networks

In this section we present three φKE protocols. In the first protocol Alice and Bob are connected by a bidirectional private channel. The second protocol covers the case where Alice and Bob are connected by a bidirectional authentic channel. In the third protocol there are two channels, one authentic and the other private, both running from Alice to Bob. All protocols assume an anonymous broadcast network.

In all protocols, Alice and Bob are required to generate a (small entropy) password to be exchanged over the low bandwidth communication channel. We stress that this password is machine generated, at random, at the start of each protocol run, and hence that these passwords can be assumed to statistically independent. It is only the transmission of these passwords over the low bandwidth channel that requires (in the application of this model in a practical setting) human intervention. It is also this same human handling of these passwords that requires them to have only a small number of bits.

The main problem handling an anonymous broadcast network is to ensure that a participant in the protocol can immediately reject messages that are obviously not intended for it. Without such precautions, even honest but ignorant nodes can easily disrupt the protocol through the messages they themselves legitimately send over the broadcast network. The protocols to be presented next try to derive a common session identifier as soon as possible, to be used as a header on messages on the broadcast channel. Note that simply transmitting such session identifiers on the point-to-point communication channel is not a good option, as it wastes bits to be used for authenticating the shared session key.

In all protocols we use the following. G is a group of order at least 2^{2s} with generator g for which the Computational Diffie Hellman (DDH) problem is hard. A possible candidate is the subgroup of order q in $\mathbb{Z}_p^*$ for p, q prime and $p = 2q+1$. Naturally, exponentiations like g^x are computed in the group G.

Passwords are selected uniformly at random from a set P, of size 2^t.

Furthermore, we use several hash functions h_i with varying domains and ranges, which are modelled as random oracles. The domain and range of hash functions h_1, h_2 is specified for each protocol separately. All protocols use hash functions $h_3, h_4, h_5 : G \mapsto \{0,1\}^\sigma$, and $h_6 : G \mapsto I$ (where I is a suitably large session identifier set). We use the following property

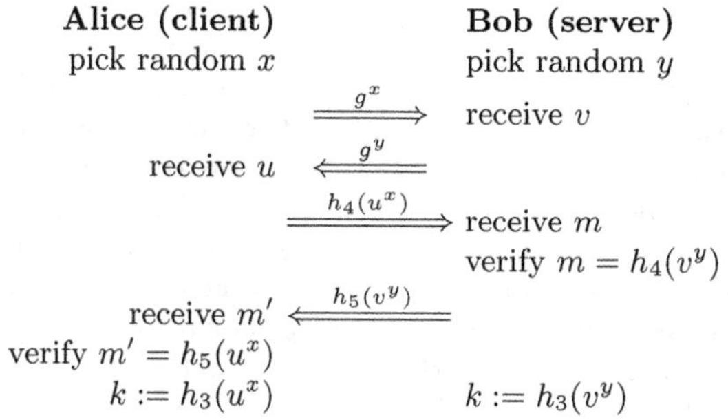

Alice (client)   **Bob (server)**
pick random x pick random y

$$\xrightarrow{\quad g^x \quad}\ \text{receive } v$$

$$\text{receive } u \xleftarrow{\quad g^y \quad}$$

$$\xrightarrow{\quad h_4(u^x) \quad}\ \text{receive } m$$
$$\text{verify } m = h_4(v^y)$$

$$\text{receive } m' \xleftarrow{\quad h_5(v^y) \quad}$$
$$\text{verify } m' = h_5(u^x)$$
$$k := h_3(u^x) \qquad\qquad\qquad k := h_3(v^y)$$

Fig. 1. Diffie-Hellman key exchange with key validation

Property 1. Let G, A and B be groups. Let X be a uniformly distributed random variable over G, let $h : G \mapsto A$ and $h' : G \mapsto B$ be random oracles and let $a \in A$ and $b \in B$ be arbitrary. Then

$$\mathbf{Pr}\left[h(X) = a\,|\,h'(X) = b\right] = \mathbf{Pr}\left[h(X) = a\right] = 2^{|A|}\ .$$

We write bc_s for the broadcast channel restricted to only carry messages with session identifier s: if a messages m is received from bc_s, it was sent with that session identifier[5].

Consider the Diffie-Hellman key exchange with validation[6] in Fig. 1, with G of order at least 2^{2s} and h_3, h_4, and h_5 as defined above. Then under the assumption that the Computational Diffie Hellman problem over G is hard we have [BPR00, Sho99]

Proposition 1. *The advantage of any adversary attacking the Diffie-Hellman key exchange with key validation in Fig. 1 — i.e., distinguishing $h_3(g^{ab})$ from a random element of $\{0,1\}^{2s}$, when given $g^a, g^b, h_4(g^{ab}), h_5(g^{ab})$ — is at most $O(2^{-s})$.*

4.1 φKE for a Bidirectional Private Channel

The φKE protocol for a bidirectional private channel (see Prot. 4.1 for the protocol and Fig. 2 for the corresponding message exchange graph) proceeds in five phases: authenticate, commit, synchronise, exchange and validate. In the exchange phase, Alice and Bob use a Diffie-Hellman type key exchange [DH76] to establish a shared session key. This key is then used to derive a session iden-

---

[5] We stress that this doer *not* guarantee that only an honest party generated this message: s is public, and hence the adversary can generate messages with that identifier as well.

[6] The validation phase only prevents a man-in-the-middle attack if somehow the shares g^x and/or g^y are authenticated. This principle is used in our protocols later on.

Authenticate
$\quad$ $H := \emptyset$
$\quad$ pick random x
$\quad$ pick random p
$\quad$ **send** p **on** pc
$\quad$ **receive** π **from** pc
Commit
$\quad$ **broadcast** $h_1(g^x, \pi)$ **on** bc
$\quad$ **for** c milliseconds **do**
$\quad\quad$ **on receiving** m **from** bc **do**
$\quad\quad\quad$ **if** $|H| < z$
$\quad\quad\quad\quad$ **then** $H := H + \{m\}$
$\quad$ **abort if** $|H| = \emptyset$
Synchronise
$\quad$ **broadcast** p **on** bc
$\quad$ **receive** q **from** bc
$\quad$ **abort if** $q \neq \pi$

Key exchange
$\quad$ $u := \perp$
$\quad$ **broadcast** g^x **on** bc
$\quad$ **for** c milliseconds **do**
$\quad\quad$ **on receiving** m **from** bc **do**
$\quad\quad\quad$ **if** $h_1(m, p) \in H$
$\quad\quad\quad\quad$ **then** $u := m$
$\quad$ **abort if** $u = \perp$
Key validation
$\quad$ $\iota := h_6(u^x)$
$\quad$ $k := \perp$
$\quad$ $j := \begin{cases} 0 & \text{if client} \\ 1 & \text{if server} \end{cases}$
$\quad$ **broadcast** $h_{4+j}(u^x)$ **on** bc_ι
$\quad$ **receive** m **from** bc_ι
$\quad$ **if** $h_{5-j}(u^x) = m$
$\quad\quad$ **then** $k = h_3(u^x)$
$\quad$ **else abort**

Protocol 4.1: φKE for bidirectional private channel

tifier ι (to distinguish relevant messages on the broadcast network)[7]. Both parties engage in a verification phase to ensure that they share the same session key [BPR00].

To identify and authenticate the share sent by the other party, Alice and Bob exchange random passwords through the bidirectional private channel in the authenticate phase. Alice hashes the password received together with her own share, and broadcasts the resulting hash on the network, to commit to the value of the share to be exchanged later on. They use the hash function $h_1 : G \times P \mapsto G$ in this phase.

The commit and exchange phase have to be separate, or else the adversary can still perform a dictionary attack to retrieve the exchanged password and substitute a suitable share of his own choice in both the commitment (that also serves to authenticate the share) and the share itself. Because Alice and Bob cannot reliably setup a session identifier at or before the exchange phase, Bob cannot distinguish Alice's commitment from other commitments broadcast on the network. Therefore, Bob accepts at most z of them.

To separate the commit and exchange phase, and to ensure that no commits will be accepted when the other party starts the key exchange phase, a separate synchronisation phase is introduced. In this phase, both parties reveal their password over the broadcast channel, and the other party only starts the exchange phase if it receives the same password as in the authentication phase. Observe

---

[7] Note that it is not possible to use $h_6(\pi)$ (with π as exchanged through the private channel) as a session identifier: this session identifier could then be used to verify all tries for the password in a dictionary attack.

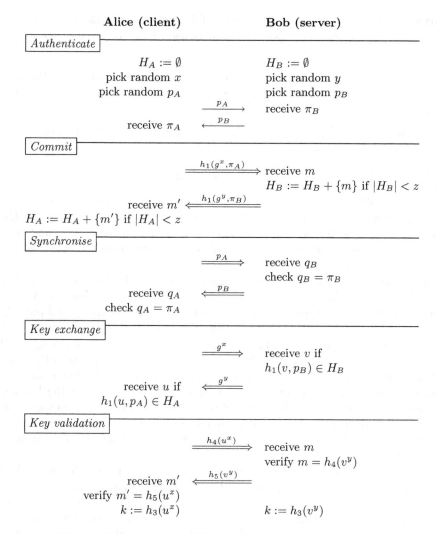

Fig. 2. Message flow of φKE for bidirectional private channel

that a password has lost all value once the commit phase for which it is used as authenticator is closed.

In the key exchange phase, Bob only accepts a share that together with Bob's own password hashes to a value in the set of commitments received previously. Because Bob only accepts z commitments, an active adversary may plant at most z commitments for its *own* share (using z different guesses for the password sent by Alice), thus limiting its chances to attack the protocol. For all our protocols a good value for z is one that allows some honest concurrent activity on the broadcast channel, while still limiting the advantage of the adversary.

Obviously, by limiting the number of commitments that Bob accepts, we allow the adversary to preempt the protocol by filling all commitment slots with garbage. This prevents Alice from successfully pairing with Bob. However, as this is but one of the many possible (and easier) denial of service attacks, we will not consider this issue further here.

Analysis. It is easily shown that using Prot. 4.1, honest Alice and Bob can exchange a shared session key. Next, we prove security of the protocol in the presence of an active and/or passive adversary.

Theorem 2. *The advantage of an adversary attacking Prot. 4.1 mounting at most q active attacks is at most*

$$O(1 - e^{-zq/2^t}) + O(2^{-s}) \ .$$

Proof. We split the proof in two cases. We first consider the case where the session key k generated by an oracle[8] is not based on a share g^a sent by the adversary, but instead derived from a value x of his own choosing, and then consider the case where the adversary manages to convince the oracle to use such a share of his own choosing.

If the session key generated by an oracle is not based on a share g^a sent by the adversary, but instead derived from a value x of his own choosing, then k depends on private random values x, y unobserved by the adversary and publicly exchanged shares g^x and g^y using a Diffie-Hellman (DH) key exchange. Any adversary attacking Prot. 4.1 can be converted to an adversary attacking a DH key exchange with validation (see Prop. 1) as follows. Given a run over the basic DH key exchange, generate random passwords p_A and p_B, and insert $h_1(g^x, p_A)$ and $h_1(g^y, p_B)$, p_A and p_B at the appropriate places in the run of the DH key exchange with validation before analysing the run. Hence the advantage of the adversary to distinguish the session key cannot be higher than its advantage in breaking the Diffie-Hellman key exchange with validation, which is at most $O(2^{-s})$ by Prop. 1.

In the other case, in order to convince an oracle of A to use the share g^a of the adversary in the second phase of the protocol, the adversary must ensure that $h_1(g^a, p_A) \in H_A$ for values H_A, p_A used in this oracle A. Note that due to the properties of the private channel, p_A is unknown to the adversary. Hence the adversary has probability $2^{-\eta}$ to guess it right and authenticate its own share g^a using $h_1(g^a, p)$ in the commit phase. As $|H_A| \leq z$, the adversary can try at most z different values for p. Hence the total probability that a share of the adversary is accepted is at most $z2^{-\eta}$.

For each active attack then the probability of success is $z2^{-\eta}$. Success with one instance is independent of success in any other instance. Hence, with q attempts, the probability of success becomes (cf. [Fel57])

$$1 - (1 - z2^{-\eta})^q \approx 1 - e^{-z2^{-\eta}q}$$

With $t = \eta$ this proves the theorem.   □

---

[8] In the Bellare *et al.* [BPR00] model, the participants in the protocol are modelled as oracles to which the adversary has access. We use the same terminology here.

Commit
  $H := \emptyset$
  pick random x
  broadcast $h_1(g^x)$ **on** bc
  for c milliseconds **do**
    on receiving m **from** bc **do**
      if $|H| < z$
        then $H := H + \{m\}$
  send close **on** ac
  receive close **from** ac
  abort if $|H| = \emptyset$
Authenticate
  send $h_2(g^x)$ **on** ac
  receive β **from** ac
  $\iota := \beta$
  $\omega := h_2(g^x)$

Key exchange
  $u := \perp$
  broadcast g^x **on** bc_ω
  receive m **from** bc_ι
  if $h_1(m) \in H$ and $h_2(m) = \beta$
  then $u := m$
  else abort
Key validation
  $k := \perp$
  $j := \begin{cases} 0 & \text{if client} \\ 1 & \text{if server} \end{cases}$
  broadcast $h_{4+j}(u^x)$ **on** bc_ω
  receive m **from** bc_ι
  if $h_{5-j}(u^x) = m$
  then $k = h_3(u^x)$
  else abort

Protocol 4.2: Anonymous φKE for bidirectional authentic channel

4.2 φKE for a Bidirectional Authentic Channel

This protocol (see Prot. 4.2 and Fig. 3) again proceeds in four phases: commit, authenticate, exchange and validate (but with the first and second phase changing order). The exchange and verification phase are essentially equal to that of the previous protocol, except that Alice and Bob use session identifiers ι and ω derived from the authentication messages exchanged earlier.

To avoid man-in-the-middle attacks, the shares used in the key exchange phase must be authenticated. However, the capacity of the authentic channel is too small to do so directly. Instead, it is used to authenticate a small hash of the share to be used later on. This is not enough to ensure security: the adversary can trivially (in an expected $2^{\eta-1}$ number of tries) find a share of his own that matches the authenticator that will be sent by Alice. Therefore, Alice and Bob must first commit to a share using a much larger hash value (against which it is infeasible to find collisions) but that has to be sent over the broadcast channel. The hash functions used for this are $h_1 : G \mapsto G$ and $h_2 : G \mapsto \{0,1\}^\eta$.

But even then a problem remains. For the adversary may try to commit to 2^η shares, corresponding to a specific authenticator value[9]. After the commit phase, when Alice reveals the authenticator a, the adversary simply reveals the share w with $h_2(w) = a$. This scenario can be prevented[10] by limiting the number of commitments accepted to a constant $z \ll 2^\eta$.

---

[9] The adversary can easily do this by spending an expected $2^{\eta-1}$ amount of work to find a candidate for each possible authenticator value, thus using a total expected $2^{2\eta-1}$ amount of work.

[10] This allows for an obvious denial-of-service attack. However, as the adversary is also capable of blocking any value sent by Alice, he already has the power to prevent Alice from connecting to Bob.

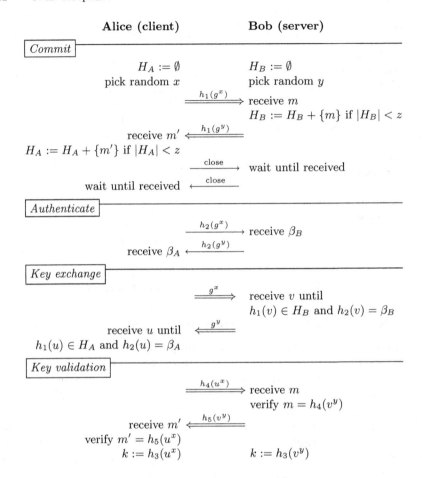

Fig. 3. Message flow of φKE for a bidirectional authentic channel

In Prot. 4.2, the security parameters are determined by the size of the session key established and the capacity of the authentic channel. We set $s = \sigma$ and $t = \eta$.

Analysis. It is straightforward to show that in an honest execution of Prot. 4.2, if Alice and Bob want to exchange a key, at the end of the protocol they do actually share the same key.

Security of Prot. 4.2 is proven as follows.

Theorem 3. *The advantage of an adversary attacking Prot. 4.2 mounting at most q active attacks is at most*

$$O(1 - e^{-zq/2^t}) + O(2^{-s}) .$$

Proof. We split the proof in two cases. We first consider the case where the session key k generated by an oracle is not based on a share g^a sent by the

Client (Alice):

Authenticate (1)
   $H_A := \emptyset$
   pick random x
   pick random p
   send p **on** pc
Commit
   broadcast $h_1(g^x)$ **on** bc
   for c milliseconds **do**
      on receiving m **from** bc **do**
        if $|H_A| < z$
          then $H_A := H_A + \{m\}$
   abort if $|H_A| = \emptyset$
Authenticate (2)
   send $h_2(g^x)$ **on** ac
Synchronise
   send close **on** ac
   receive q **from** bc
   abort if $q \neq p$
Key exchange
   $u := \perp$
   broadcast g^x **on** bc
   receive m **from** bc
   if $h_1'(m,p) \in H_A$
   then $u := m$
   else abort
Key validation
   broadcast $h_4(u^x)$ **on** bc
   receive m **from** bc
   if $h_5(u^x) = m$
      then $k = h_3(u^x)$
      else abort

Server (Bob):

Authenticate (1)
   $H_B := \emptyset$
   pick random y
   receive π_B **from** pc
Commit
   broadcast $h_1'(g^y, \pi_B)$ **on** bc
   for c milliseconds **do**
      on receiving m **from** bc **do**
        if $|H_B| < z$
          then $H_B := H_B + \{m\}$
   abort if $|H_B| = \emptyset$
Authenticate (2)
   receive β_B **from** ac
Synchronise
   receive closed **from** ac
   broadcast π_B **on** bc
Key exchange
   $v := \perp$
   broadcast g^y **on** bc
   receive m **from** bc
   if $h_1(m) \in H_B$ and $h_2(m) = \beta_B$
   then $v := m$
   else abort
Key validation
   broadcast $h_5(v^x)$ **on** bc
   receive m **from** bc
   if $h_4(v^x) = m$
      then $k = h_3(v^x)$
      else abort

Protocol 4.3: φKE for a private plus an authentic channel

adversary and derived from a value a of his own choosing, and then consider the case where the adversary manages to convince the oracle to use such a share of his own choosing.

If the session key generated by an oracle is not based on a share g^a sent by the adversary and derived from a value a of his own choosing, then the proof is almost equal to that of theorem 2.

In the other case, in order to convince an oracle of A to use the share g^a of the adversary in the third phase of the protocol, the adversary must ensure that both $h_1(g^a) \in H_A$, and $h_2(g^a) = \beta_A$ holds for values H_A, β_A used in this oracle. Note that β_A is unknown in the commit phase. Moreover, property 1 guarantees it is independent of values exchanged during the commit phase. Therefore, for each value g^a committed by the adversary in the commit phase, the probability

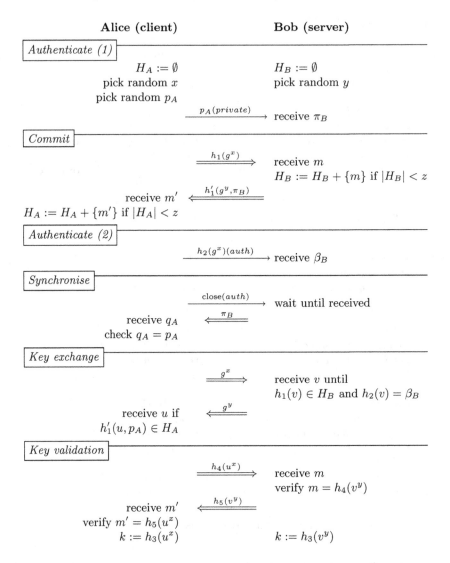

Fig. 4. Message flow of φKE for a private plus an authentic channel

that $h_2(g^a) = \beta_A$ is $2^{-\eta}$. As $|H_A| \leq z$, the adversary can commit at most z shares with different hash values for h_2. Hence the total probability that a share of the adversary is accepted is at most $z2^{-\eta}$. With the same estimate as used in the proof of Theorem 2, and with $t = \eta$, this proves the theorem. $\square$

4.3 φKE for a Private Channel Plus an Authentic Channel

In [Hoe04], it was shown that a *single* channel that is both authentic and private can be used to solve the φKE problem straightforwardly using an Encrypted

Key Exchange (EKE) protocol [BM92, KOY01, Jab96] as a building block. A combination of techniques from the previous two protocols can be used to show that with two channels both from Alice to Bob, one of which is authentic while the other is private, one can implement φKE. The complete protocol is shown in Prot. 4.3 and Fig. 4. The analysis is very similar to the previous two protocols, and is therefore omitted here.

5   Conclusions and Further Research

We have shown that the ephemeral pairing problem, and the corresponding ephemeral key exchange problem can also be solved in completely anonymous broadcast networks. Generalisations of the ephemeral pairing problem to larger groups of nodes need to be investigated, as well as the possibilities to weaken the cryptographic assumptions and to simplify the protocols.

References

[BSSW02] BALFANZ, D., SMETTERS, D. K., STEWART, P., AND WONG, H. C. Talking to strangers: Authentication in ad-hoc wireless networks. In *NDSS* (San Diego, CA, USA, 2002).

[BPR00] BELLARE, M., POINTCHEVAL, D., AND ROGAWAY, P. Authenticated key exchange secure against dictionary attacks. In *EUROCRYPT 2000* (Bruges, Belgium, 2000), B. Preneel (Ed.), LNCS 1807, Springer, pp. 139–155.

[BM92] BELLOVIN, S. M., AND MERRITT, M. Encrypted key exchange: Password-based protocols secure against dictionary attacks. In *IEEE Security & Privacy* (Oakland, CA, USA, 1992), IEEE, pp. 72–84.

[BMP00] BOYKO, V., MACKENZIE, P., AND PATEL, S. Provably secure password-authenticated key exchange using Diffie-Hellman. In *EUROCRYPT 2000* (Bruges, Belgium, 2000), B. Preneel (Ed.), LNCS 1807, Springer, pp. 156–171.

[CK01] CANETTI, R., AND KRAWCZYK, H. Analysis of key-exchange protocols and their use for building secure channels. In *EUROCRYPT 2001* (Innsbruck, Austria, 2001), B. Pfitzmann (Ed.), LNCS 2045, Springer, pp. 453–474.

[DH76] DIFFIE, W., AND HELLMAN, M. E. New directions in cryptography. *IEEE Trans. Inf. Theory* **IT-11** (1976), 644–654.

[Fel57] FELLER, W. *An Introduction to Probability Theory and Its Applications*, 2nd ed. Wiley & Sons, New York, 1957.

[GMN04] GEHRMANN, C., MITCHELL, C. J., AND NYBERG, K. Manual authentication for wireless devices. *RSA Cryptobytes* **7**, 1 (2004), 29–37.

[GN04] GEHRMANN, C., AND NYBERG, K. Security in personal area networks. In *Security for Mobility*, C. J. Mitchell (Ed.). IEEE, 2004.

[GL03] GENNARO, R., AND LINDELL, Y. A framework for password-based authenticated key exchange. Tech. rep., IBM T.J. Watson, 2003. Abstract appeared in EUROCRYPT 2003.

[Hoe04] HOEPMAN, J.-H. The ephemeral pairing problem. In *8th Int. Conf. Fin. Crypt.* (Key West, FL, USA, 2004), LNCS 3110, Springer, pp. 212–226.

[Jab96]   JABLON, D. P.   Strong password-only authenticated key exchange. *Comput. Comm. Rev.* (1996). http://www.std.com/~dpj and www.integritysciences.com.

[KOY01]   KATZ, J., OSTROVSKY, R., AND YUNG, M.   Efficient password-authenticated key exchange using human-memorable passwords. In *EUROCRYPT 2001* (Innsbruck, Austria, 2001), B. Pfitzmann (Ed.), LNCS 2045, Springer, pp. 475–494.

[Luc97]   LUCKS, S. Open key exchange: How to defeat dictionary attacks without encrypting public keys. In *The Security Protocol Workshop '97* (1997), pp. 79–90.

[Sho99]   SHOUP, V. On formal models for secure key exchange. Tech. Rep. RZ 3120 (#93166), IBM, 1999. Invited talk at ACM Computer and Communications Security conference, 1999.

[SA99]   STAJANO, F., AND ANDERSON, R. The resurrecting duckling: Security issues for ad-hoc wireless networks. In *Security Procotols, 7th Int. Workshop* (1999), B. Christianson, B. Crispo, and M. Roe (Eds.), LNCS, pp. 172–194.

EPC Technology

Christian Floerkemeier[1] and Frederic Thiesse[2]

[1] Institute for Pervasive Computing,
Department of Computer Science, ETH Zurich, Switzerland
floerkem@inf.ethz.ch
[2] Institute for Technology Management,
University of St. Gallen, Switzerland
frederic.thiesse@unisg.ch

1 Introduction

Radio Frequency Identification (RFID) technology has been widely used in applications such as car immobilizers, animal tracking and access systems since the late 90s. For the adoption of RFID in less specialized applications domains such as supply chain operations, however, there was a need for a low cost, standardized RFID technology with a read range of more than two meters. Since 1999, work at the Auto-ID Center and its successor organization EPCglobal has focused on turning this vision of low cost tags and readers into reality by developing the appropriate standards [2]. In the four years of its operation the Auto-ID Center became a collaborative effort of six universities including MIT, the University of Cambridge and the University of St. Gallen and more than 100 global companies such as Coca-Cola, Gillette, IBM, Intel, Pfizer, Procter & Gamble, UPS, and Wal-Mart. Since November 2003, EPCglobal Inc., a joint venture between EAN International and the Uniform Code Council, two of the earliest sponsors of the Auto-ID Center, has carried forth the development and commercialization of the technology, while the universities involved continue the RFID research as the Auto-ID labs.

2 EPC Network

The heart of the Auto-ID Center infrastructure, also called the EPC Network, is the Electronic Product Code (EPC). Like a European Article Number, the EPC uses a set of numbers to identify an item's manufacturer and the product category. The EPC, however, also contains a serial number that identifies individual items. The EPC is the only data stored on the microchip of the RFID tag and it serves as a pointer to additional information accessible via the web. The Auto-ID Center believed that less expensive tags could be produced by limiting memory space on the tags to this 96 Bit number [1]. In cooperation with its industry partners the Auto-ID Center developed three protocols for communication between tags and readers, both at HF and UHF frequencies. More recently, the UHF Class 1 Generation 2 protocol has been developed by EPCglobal and

D. Hutter and M. Ullmann (Eds.): SPC 2005, LNCS 3450, pp. 117–118, 2005.

its member companies that will supersede the previous UHF protocols. It specifically addresses the different radio regulations across the globe and adapts well to dense reader environments. To move and manage all the data generated by the tags and readers, the Auto-ID Center also developed a corresponding network infrastructure. It consists of a middleware component called Savant that filters the RFID data and converts them into application level events, a directory service called Object Naming Service, and a backend system called EPC Information Service to provide persistence. To standardize the mark-up of RFID data, the Auto-ID Center developed a common XML-based vocabulary called PML Core. This has recently been superseded by the Reader Protocol that additionally also provides a standardized reader interface to RFID middleware.

3   Challenges Facing the EPC Technology

One obstacle to achieve low cost tags - less than five cent - is today still a lack of volume. Volumes in the billions of RFID tags are required to make the microchip in an RFID tag cheap. The assembly of the tiny RFID microchip with the larger tag antenna remains another challenge. A state of the art RFID microchip is less than 1 mm2 in size and thus at least two orders of magnitude smaller than traditional high volume microchips such as CPUs or memory chips, which makes the assembly process non-trivial. A number of companies have invested in producing mass assembly inexpensive tags, but none of the assembly technologies are proven today given the relatively small volume of tags sold. Another obstacle obstructing the wide-spread adoption of long-range RFID operating at UHF frequencies is the problem of low read rates in challenging environmentsmeaning tags that are in the range of the reader are not successfully detected - e.g., in the vicinity of metallic objects and organic materials. At UHF frequencies organic materials absorb the power radiated by the reader, while metallic objects reflect the incident electromagnetic wave. In both cases this can lead to a failure to power a tag and thus a failed detection. The intended deployment of RFID-based tracking solutions in today's retail environments epitomizes for some the dangers of an Orwellian future: Unnoticed by consumers, embedded microchips in our clothes and groceries can unknowingly be triggered to reply with their EPC, potentially allowing for a fine-grained yet unobtrusive surveillance mechanism that would pervade large parts of our lives.

References

1. S. Sarma. Towards the five-cent tag. Technical Report MIT-AUTOID-WH-006, Auto-ID Center, 2001.
2. S. Sarma, D.L. Brock, and K. Ashton. The networked physical world. Technical Report MIT-AUTOID-WH-001, Auto-ID Center, 2000.

Exploiting Empirical Engagement in Authentication Protocol Design*

Sadie Creese[1], Michael Goldsmith[2,3], Richard Harrison[1], Bill Roscoe[2,4], Paul Whittaker[2], and Irfan Zakiuddin[1]

[1] QinetiQ, Malvern, UK
{S.Creese, R.Harrison}@eris.QinetiQ.com
I.Zakiuddin@signal.QinetiQ.com
[2] Formal Systems (Europe) Ltd
{michael, paulw}@fsel.com
http://www.fsel.com
[3] Worcester College, University of Oxford
[4] Oxford University Computing Laboratory
Bill.Roscoe@comlab.ox.ac.uk

Abstract. We develop the theme of an earlier paper [3], namely that security protocols for pervasive computing frequently need to exploit empirical channels and that the latter can be classified by variants of the Dolev-Yao attacker model. We refine this classification of channels and study three protocols in depth: two from our earlier paper and one new one.

1 Introduction

1.1 Pervasive Computing Environments and Security

The pervasive computing paradigm predicts a future in which wireless communicating and computing devices are ubiquitous throughout our environment. This will in turn facilitate the formation of dynamic networks operating independently of back-bone infrastructures, offering the capacity for short-lived relationships operating over hybrid resources and perhaps utilising local distributed processing services. It will also offer the ability to connect to infrastructures where they exist via a wide variety of means, providing major opportunities for service-based business models. The exact form of such devices will vary from the embedding of such functionality within already commonplace electronic objects, to enhancing the functionality of previously non-electronic devices, and to the creation of new bespoke devices designed to offer specific communications and computing services (perhaps on a nano scale).

---

* This research is conducted as part of the FORWARD project which is supported by the U.K. Department of Trade and Industry via the Next Wave Technologies and Markets programme: www.forward-project.org.uk.

D. Hutter and M. Ullmann (Eds.): SPC 2005, LNCS 3450, pp. 119–133, 2005.

It is clear that the pervasive computing paradigm offers huge opportunity, as evidenced by the level of international research being focused on the domain. Successful exploitation of such opportunity will require both a trust in the technologies on the part of the user community, and that the technologies are dependable and worthy of such trust. Information security is a fundamental component of dependability in pervasive computing environments.

However, it is also clear that there are significant challenges to be addressed if we are to secure information in such potentially complex computing environments. The connectivity offered and required in order to benefit from the pervasive nature of computing resources and services may also offer a malicious intruder more options for unauthorised access. Services offering bespoke functionality and information may in turn require access to increased stores of personal or organisation details, which once networked may potentially be accessible from an unknowable set of interfaces and users. Information may exist in unknown locations for indeterminate durations.

A key concept in security of any type is authentication: you must be able to decide whether a user (human or otherwise) is authorised to access a resource. Without the ability to authenticate we would be unable to implement a useful security policy[1]. It is likely that we will require mechanisms both for authenticating the identity of a device or user ("which" or "who"), and for authenticating how a device or user will behave ("what"). We are concerned here with the former, the challenge of identity authentication in pervasive computing environments and in particular where no previous knowledge of the device or user exists.

This is a particularly challenging problem as it necessitates either:

- that there exists an accessible trusted third party who can vouch for a claimed identity based upon some pre-agreed information or token (such as a public-key or a biometric),
- or that there is some mechanism for bootstrapping trust between strangers (human or devices) where there exists no trusted third party who can verify identities.

Neither of these options are entirely unproblematic. To implement a trusted third party solution one would first need to ensure that all devices can be guaranteed access when they require it. It would not be possible to construct a centralised model, where there exists one such authority, as the number of devices to be verified may be so large that it becomes impossible to guarantee bandwidth, freshness of mirror sites and even the existence of unique naming policies. If we are to implement many such identity verification authorities then we will require interoperability between authorities, and associated access. Finally, even if a device has a unique name it may not be possible for another user or device to establish what that name is, and so to refer to the device.

The FORWARD project is investigating how we might bootstrap security by utilising authentication protocol services built upon empirically verified proper-

---

[1] A security policy which simply specifies that everyone or anything has access would of course not require an authentication mechanism.

ties of our local environment. This has the benefit both of reducing overheads associated with network communications, and that users will be interacting as part of the service via their primary senses collecting empirical evidence (such as feeling, hearing, seeing)[2]. Core to our design methodology is the use of formal analysis in order to better understand protocols' behaviour and facilitate high-assurance design.

We previously presented [3] a variant hybrid threat model precisely for reasoning about and analysing such services. The threat model includes mechanisms for representing the various types of security property that we might assume of the various empirical communications. This in turn enables the formal analysis of any authentication protocols developed, and an understanding of the corresponding levels of resilience offered by such authentication methods. Whilst in [3] we presented a number of suggested protocols for example pervasive computing scenarios, we had at that time not utilised the variant threat model to formally analyse their behaviours.

In this paper we present refinements to the variant threat models, report on our analysis of two protocols specifically for authentication between two devices in a local (line-of-sight) environment, and present an overview of the methodology for formally analysing authentication protocols utilising such empirical engagements between two devices.

We begin with a discussion of formal analysis in general, and the refinements to the variant threat models. In §3 we present an overiew of variants of the two protocols designed for device authentication in local environments (presented in [3]), and discuss the potential for design modifications. In §2.1 we briefly discuss our chosen formalism for analysis – the process algebra CSP (Hoare's Communicating Sequential Processes [5, 7]), and the accompanying tool support from FDR and Casper [8] – we outline our analysis methodology, and we present the results of such analysis on these protocols. Finally, we present our conclusions and directions for further work.

2   Refinements to the Variant Threat Models

Formal analysis itself depends on a (formal) representation (*viz.* a model) of the subject that is both[3]:

- *faithful* in the sense of capturing the behaviour that needs to be analysed in a traceable way; and
- *clear* to an analyst that the model is correct and the analysis useful.

---

[2] The use of such human verifiable properties should help make the experience of using such services more intuitive and perhaps easier.

[3] Tractability of the model is an important concern as well; but tractability is closely linked to the verification technology that is used. Moreover, an unfaithful and tractable model is useless; and a faithful, tractable, but unclear model is only a little better.

If we do not achieve this then the benefits of the analysis may not be realised in the design.

Any solution that we might propose must be flexible enough to capture:

- The varying assumptions that determine how users and electronic devices may interact to ensure successful initialisation of the link.
- The range of entities that can form the participants in the protocol, and their associated behaviours.

As formal specification and analysis depend crucially on capturing these assumptions and the objectives that the protocol is trying to achieve, the first of these points is particularly important. A fundamental requirement in any formal analysis of security properties is to construct an appropriate threat model for the environment in which the system is designed to operate. The threat model encapsulates the capabilities of an attacker, and so an incorrect threat model may lead to either:

- too weak an attacker where security can be proven in the formal model, but does not hold in the actual implementation environment; or
- too strong an attacker, which can then place restrictive constraints on the design that impact resource usage and overall functionality, when that could have been avoided.

The type of security service with which we are concerned is that of authenticated cryptographic key agreement. Currently, the *de facto* standard threat model for analysing key-agreement protocols is the Dolev-Yao model [4].

The Dolev-Yao model supposes an intruder who effectively controls the communications network, and is therefore capable of

- overhearing messages between legitimate principals
- intercepting messages and preventing their delivery to their intended recipient
- synthesising – within the limitations of the cryptographic mechanisms involved – messages from data initially known to him together with fragments of any previous messages and delivering them, apparently originating either from an identity under his control, or indeed from any other principal.

In essence this is the most potent malicious attacker that a protocol can possibly need to cope with; in effect the worst-case scenario. However, designing protocols which can withstand attack of this nature is certainly erring on the safe side: a protocol which exhibits no flaws under these assumptions will *a fortiori* be secure against a less potent attacker.

Here we are concerned with the ubiquitous arena, where most communications are through the essentially broadcast medium of wireless. The attacker can interfere with communications, attempting to subvert or disrupt the protocol that the principals are using for authentication. The facilities at the attacker's disposal depend very much on the nature of the communications that he is trying to attack. When two people physically exchange PGP keys[4] (and thus use

---

[4] www.pgpi.org

empirical engagement to initialise an authenticated link), the scope for disruption of that authentication protocol is very limited. It is in effect assumed that the two participants share a "channel" that has very few vulnerabilities. If the keys were exchanged in a digital communication using clear text then the scope for disruption would be much wider. So, in this case, empirical engagement has been used as a secondary channel for bootstrapping security. We may remark that this approach is consonant with many less theoretically-inspired suggestions in the literature [9, 1, 2, 6–etc].

In [3] we observed that this type of empirical engagement may be increasingly possible for bootstrapping security in the pervasive computing environment. There we presented a series of protocols which depend upon the existence of such engagements for their correctness. The scenarios envisaged all relied on locally-verifiable empirical data, and accompanying assumptions regarding the restricted powers of the attacker.

When considering how empirical engagement might be used as part of an authentication protocol, it is clear that the vulnerabilities associated with empirical engagement are likely to be diverse and context-specific. Thus our strategy for developing clear and faithful models of empirical engagement in authentication starts by noting that such interactions can be captured as a form of communication channel with specific properties, and for security analysis the most important of these properties are the channel's vulnerabilities. From the viewpoint of formal analysis these vulnerabilities are equivalent to the attacker's capabilities.

We incorporate the vulnerabilities of a channel into a modified threat model, which restrains the capabilities of an attacker appropriately. In the pervasive computing environment we observe that there are potentially two types of communications channel:

- A high bandwidth bidirectional medium with low or unreliable security. This represents the *network* wireless communications medium, such as wireless LAN, Bluetooth, or IrDA.
- The second type represents *empirical* channels, such as reading a message on the printer display panel, physically punching in a code on the printer control panel, or checking that the flashing light is present as in the first example below.

We shall call the high-bandwidth digital communications channel N (for "network") and the "empirical" channel E. This channel can be considered more costly, as a human is necessarily "in the loop" and the channel is therefore low-bandwidth and consumes the scarce resources of intellect and attention. However, the E-channel can thus offer various forms of higher security; it may, according to the details of the scenario, operate in either or both directions.

The two (or more, if multiple empirical mechanisms are available) channels can be supposed vulnerable according to a different threat model. This flexibility can be exploited to develop cryptographic protocols which are secure where they would not be under standard Dolev-Yao assumptions.

By varying how the attacker can manipulate these two channels (the attacker's capabilities on E being the more limited), a variety of hybrid threat models can be created. In [3] we identified a number of reduced-threat variants, each specifying a restriction placed on the powers of the Dolev-Yao attacker:

- AOT_C : the attacker cannot both block and hear messages at the same time on channel C, where AOT stands for *Atomicity of Transmission*.
- NS_C : the attacker cannot spoof messages on channel C, where NS stands for *No Spoofing*.
- NOH_C : the attacker cannot overhear messages over channel C, where NOH stands for *No OverHearing*.

To this list we may add NB_C : the attacker cannot block messages on channel C, where NB stands for *No Blocking*.

These restrictions are not entirely independent of one another. Indeed, we may form a small lattice, making explicit the modality over time (or messages):

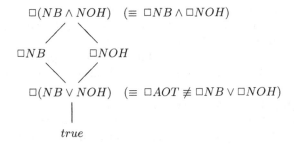

Here the top of the lattice is reliable and confidential, while the bottom allows the full Dolev-Yao powers over these aspects, with varying degrees of security in between; higher properties imply the lower. Adding NS along another dimension yields a rich variety of channel types that may be available[5]. A later paper will populate this design space with illustrative protocols.

The idea behind AOT, which is a dynamic blend of NOH and NB, is that in some circumstances it may be impractically hard for an attacker to "jam" a signal and at the same time hear the message that was being conveyed. We have received more feedback on this item than any other, mostly suggesting cunning noise-cancellation schemes which make it hard to justify the assumption that this property holds of radio traffic. We stand corrected, and seek to reduce our reliance on the notion.

2.1 Formal Analysis of Variant Threat Model Cryptographic Protocols

Our analysis is based around use of Formal Systems' refinement checker FDR, with the CSP models of the agents and the attacker typically generated by Lowe's Casper front-end tool. Space precludes a full presentation of the technology: the reader is referred to [8] for a complete exposition.

---

[5] Especially as NS is not as simple a concept as it may seem at first sight; see below.

Casper takes as input descriptions of security protocols written in a "journal" notation, together with specifications that assert the security properties claimed for the protocol. Casper compiles a given protocol description to CSP processes representing the possible behaviours of the agents when run in the presence of the Intruder – standardly a Dolev-Yao attacker. The security specifications are also compiled to CSP processes. These processes – representing the implementation and specifications of the protocol – can then be automatically compared using the CSP refinement checker FDR2.

The Casper model of the Intruder is that of the standard Dolev-Yao model, modulo perfect encryption: collision-free hash functions, strong message types, and so on. The Intruder is given complete control over the network and may *overhear*, *intercept*, *re-route*, *delay*, *reorder*, *replay*, *fake* or *obliterate* a message. Although this default model of the Intruder is sufficient for most analysis work, the tool is very flexible as regards deductions on the part of the Intruder and the user may easily extend the threat model to weaken the assumptions of perfect cryptography. However, it is harder to change the model to weaken the attacker as regards control over the network simply because the Intruder and network are one and the same entity within Casper. Lowe is working on incorporating (at least some of) the notions required here into the tool, but in the interim we have worked by modifying the resultant CSP scripts directly.

The special channel properties AOT, NS, and NOH that define the new variant threat models have been implemented approximately as recommended in [3] – we curb the powers of the Intruder by limiting its ability to *take*, *fake*, and *overhear* certain messages on the network.

The first step in implementing the special channels is to (re-)introduce, at least conceptually, a channel *comm* to represent direct, uninterrupted communication between agents. The Intruder has no control over this channel and may only overhear messages. This separates out the Intruder from the network and allows us to limit its powers by modifying the mapping of *send/receive* events for those messages sent over the special channels. To add the new channel we must first endow both agent processes and the Intruder process with the event. For agent processes, we add the channel by mapping *send/receive* events to both *send/receive* and *comm* events. For the Intruder process we do the same but for only the *hear* channel as the Intruder may only overhear the *comm* channel.

In this context it is straightforward to modify the definition of the intruder to reflect restricted powers:

- leaving the intruder's knowledge unchanged after a *take* gives the AOT semantics;
- barring communications on a subset of the message space on *fake* can model a reliable one-way NS channel;
- disconnecting both *take* and the tap on *comm* on a subset of the message space captures the confidentially of NOH transmission.

In practice for various technical reasons we in fact replace the synchronous *comm* channel with two counterparts *scomm* and *rcomm* representing the sending and receiving of a direct, uninterrupted communication. These channels have the

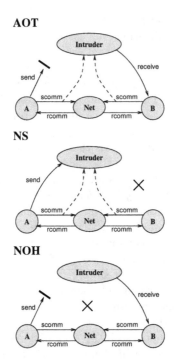

Fig. 1. Restrictions on the Intruder with a benign network process

same profiles as *send* and *receive* and are connected together with a new benign network process that adds some buffering and reordering of messages as in Figure 1. Finally, we modify the construction of the complete system process to ensure that agents and Intruder communicate over the new channels.

The next step is to define the set of network messages for each channel property *AOT*, *NS*, and *NOH*. As Casper provides names for the sets of input/output messages for each step of the protocol it is straightforward for the user to define a set-union for each property.

3   Example Protocols

In [3] we presented three protocols, addressing two different usage scenarios. Here we consider further the first of these scenarios, namely *The Wireless Printer Scenario*, the subject of the first two protocols there; and also present a variation on the first of these. This is the case of a user wishing to print a confidential document, residing on a PDA, on a public printer – imagined, for the sake of argument, to be located in an airport lounge. Communication between the printer and the user's PDA is via a wireless connection of some type (the precise communications technology is not relevant here). The user requires some assurance that the printer they are sending the document to is indeed the one they are looking at, as opposed to some other device elsewhere within communications range, and that that printer will be the only agent capable of successfully decyphering (in both the technical and colloquial senses of the word) the document.

3.1 Protocol 1.1 (NS $_E$[+AOT $_N$?])

We begin by assuming that all suitable printers are manufactured with a generic public/secret key pair. This does not offer any particular additional security in the worst case, since we assume that an intruder may have access to a suitable printer, and possibly be able to subvert it; but it clearly makes life more difficult for an attacker in practice. There is clearly plenty of scope for research into desirable degrees of assurance and the related question of the cost-benefit trade-offs for the attacker, but we do not address that issue here. Throughout we also make the assumption that the user A has a unique key certificate, $kc(A)$; and that the printer is manufactured with knowledge only of the generic key pair associated with the class of printers to which it belongs, P.

Moreover we assume that it is fitted (in a reasonably tamper-proof way) with a light which flashes while (and only while) it is printing data that it itself is communicating as part of a protocol run. This effectively gives a no-spoofing assurance that the printer expelling the paper is the one generating the contents of the paper; we discuss below, when we come to the formal analysis (§3.1), the question of the printer itself being spoofed into doing so inappropriately. An alternative mechanism might be to use the LCD panel on the printer as a reliable medium between the printer and its user. Without some such facility, it would be hard to avoid the possibility of a suborned device-in-the-middle engaging in the protocol and simply using the intended printer as a slave to reprint what the protocol requires.

A wants to check that the printer she is communicating with over the N-channel is indeed the printer B that she can see, as in Figure 2.

More specifically, the security goal is to establish a shared secret known only to the user and that specific printer (which may then be used as a symmetric-encryption key for the document, for instance).

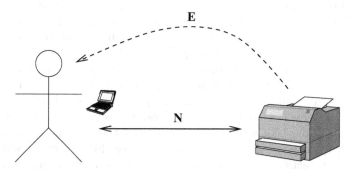

Fig. 2. A unspoofable channel E exists between the printer and the user; the network N gives a bidirectional link

Our first protocol depends on the channel E, running from the printer to the user, being impervious to spoofing, NS_E. The protocol proceeds as described below (the N or E subscript on the arrow denoting the channel over which the communication event occurs). If, however, at any stage before the protocol has completed either the user or the printer receives additional Messages 1 to 4 directed to them then the protocol will abort.

$$
\begin{aligned}
&1.\ A \rightarrow_N P(B) : \{A, kc(A), N_A\}_{pk(P)} \\
&2.\ B \rightarrow_E A \quad : \text{print } A, N_A \\
&3.\ B \rightarrow_N A \quad : \{K, N_A, N_B\}_{pk(A)} \\
&4.\ A \rightarrow_N B \quad : \{N_B, N'_A\}_K \\
&5.\ B \rightarrow_E A \quad : \text{print } N'_A
\end{aligned}
$$

Informally, the protocol proceeds as follows: In Message 1 A sends the printer her name, her key certificate and a random nonce, all encrypted with the generic printer public key. The printer then prints both A's name and the nonce, which A verifies empirically over channel E. At this stage, given that an attacker cannot spoof messages on channel E, A knows that the printer she is looking at has received Message 1 and is a printer, but she cannot exclude a corrupt printer-in-the-middle having overheard and understood Message 1. Assuming that the certificate $kc(A)$ is unforgeable, an honest B will only proceed to print a Message 2 acceptable to A if he received the intended Message 1 (from somebody).

In Message 3 the printer sends A a session key, K, the previous nonce N_A from Message 1, and a new nonce N_B, all encrypted using A's public key, extracted from the $kc(A)$ received in Message 1. A then sends a message to the printer which contains the second nonce N_B and a new nonce N'_A, encrypted using the key sent in Message 3. Since only A can have read the contents of Message 3 (it was encoded using her unique public key), it follows that only A and the device which sent Message 3 know the key K. However since an intruder knows N_A and may have blocked Message 3 from B and sent his own, A does not know that the Message 3 that she heard was actually from B.

The printer then prints the new nonce N'_A, which A verifies over channel E. Since this new nonce was sent in Message 4 and was encrypted using the key K in a message containing N_B, the printer would not print N'_A unless the Message 3 that A received really was from B. It follows that at this point A is certainly connected to B (the desired printer).

Note that the first printed output also serves to guard against spoofing on channel N, since if an attacker were to force B to abort after this point in the run, then the attacker could not get beyond this point without a further Message 2 being spotted, which A could see. This observation is somewhat application-specific, since it may not always be the case that the E-channel that B would use with an intruder would be observed by A. For this reason we additionally require that any entity in the role played by the printer here which aborts a run after Message 2 should send an E-message to A saying so.

Verification: As expected, under Dolev-Yao assumptions the protocol fails to meet any of its goals. For the basic system of one user and one printer, Casper finds an attack on secrecy in which the Intruder uses an honest printer to decode Message 1 before spoofing Messages 2 and 5 in order to get the user to accept *his* session key, K_I. Interestingly, without corrupt printers it takes a more complicated system (one in which the printer runs twice) for the Intruder to learn a real session key and for the user to claim it as secret, i.e. to think she has completed a correct protocol run.

For the authentication, Casper uses similar tricks to produce several attacks on the basic system of one user and one printer. One attack fakes Message 3 to provide the user with the Intruders own session key and nonce, then again spoofs Message 5 to convince the user that the session key originated from the intended printer.

When we consider the possibility of corrupt printers and users (by giving the Intruder appropriate secrets – namely the generic printer private key $sk(P)$), Casper finds many more attacks and clearly does not need an honest printer to learn the user's nonce N_A sent in Message 2.

Under the variant threat model with the special channel properties AOT_N and NS_E, Casper fails to find any attacks on the protocol even in the presence of corrupt users/printers, within the scope of two printers and two sequential runs.

This initial modelling (naturally) used the interpretation of the NS property as specified in [3], that is that a message received on a channel with this property must have been freshly sent by its apparent sender *to the recipient* (although it may be overheard, or indeed not received because blocked).

If, however, a weaker interpretation that omits the italicised phrase above is adopted, and so allows a message to be diverted (or in this case, the recipient to be deluded that a message physically directed to her was logically intended by the sender to be so), we may uncover the following "printer-in-the-middle" attack (assuming, perhaps unreasonably, that E-messages can also be suppressed):

$$
\begin{aligned}
&1.\ A \rightarrow_N B(P) : \{A, kc(A), N_A\}_{pk(P)}\ (\text{overheard})\\
&2.\ B \rightarrow_E A \qquad : \text{print } A, N_A\ (\text{overheard})\\
&1'.\ I \rightarrow_N B(P) : \{I, kc(I), N_A\}_{pk(P)}\ (\text{abort 1st run})\\
&X.\ B \rightarrow_E A \qquad : \text{print } A, \text{abort (suppressed)}\\
&2'.\ B \rightarrow_E I \qquad : \text{print } I, N_I\ (\text{suppressed})\\
&3'.\ B \rightarrow_N I \qquad : \{K, N_A, N_B\}_{pk(I)}\\
&3.\ I(B) \rightarrow_N A \ : \{K, N_A, N_B\}_{pk(A)}\\
&4.\ A \rightarrow_N I(B)\ : \{N_B, N'_A\}_K\\
&4'.\ I \rightarrow_N B \qquad : \{N_B, N'_A\}_K\\
&5.\ B \rightarrow_E A(I)\ : \text{print } N'_A
\end{aligned}
$$

To avoid this problem, Message 5 should (of course, by all rules-of-thumb for good protocol design) make explicit the identity A.

Within the range of instances of the scenario analysed, the property NS_E alone is sufficient to ensure the security of the protocol, and this seems likely to be the case in general; AOT_N appears superfluous. If, however, we allow the intruder to forge a key certificate for A (as would be the case if the association between identity and key is self-certified, as it is with PGP), then this exposes another printer-in-the-middle attack, which *is* ruled out by AOT_N.

$$
\begin{array}{lll}
1. & A \rightarrow_N I(P) & : \{A, kc(A), N_A\}_{pk(P)} \\
1'. & I(A) \rightarrow_N B(P) & : \{A, kc_I(A), N_A\}_{pk(P)} \\
2. & B \rightarrow_E A & : \text{print } A, N_A \\
3. & B \rightarrow_N I(A) & : \{K, N_A, N_B\}_{pk_I(A)} \\
3'. & I(B) \rightarrow_N A & : \{K, N_A, N_B\}_{pk(A)} \\
4. & A \rightarrow_N I(B) & : \{N_B, N'_A\}_K \\
4'. & I(A) \rightarrow_N B & : \{N_B, N'_A\}_K \\
5. & B \rightarrow_E A & : \text{print } N'_A
\end{array}
$$

3.2   Protocol 1.2 (NS $_E$)

The above protocol requires two communications on the empirical channel. With the same physical scenario, this can be reduced to one at the expense, potentially, of making the task of the user harder (assuming that the user has a part in the implementation of this channel, as is the case in these examples). In the example above the user has to check that various pieces of data output on the printer are correct and appear while the printer is in "security mode". The main constituents of this data are the two nonces N_A and N'_A. Conventional nonces consisting of many characters of random data are not ideal for humans to check – and they might quickly get fed up and not do it properly! However there is the opportunity to use other types of values here, perhaps pictures, words and patterns, of a type chosen to map better onto humans' capabilities.

The following protocol requires only one communication on the empirical channel, but that is a cryptographic hash value. If a human was involved in implementing the empirical channel then we would have the following choices:

- Give the user a lot of tedious checking to do.
- Use relatively small hash values that humans can check conveniently[6].
- Devise some form of hashing into user-supplied pictures, words or patterns (or combinations of these) which enables a satisfactory range of values to be discriminated between in a satisfactory manner.

Of course the practicality of doing this, and whether any consequent greater risk is acceptable, would depend on the circumstances of the particular scenario. The protocol itself is considerably simplified:

---

[6] One can argue that the presence of a human in the loop makes this less dangerous than in many circumstances, since he or she is likely to smell a rat (rather than just resetting) if presented with an incorrect value.

$$1.\ A \rightarrow_N B(P) : \{A, pkA, N_A\}_{pk(P)}$$
$$2.\ B \rightarrow_N A \quad : \{A, B, pkA, N_A, K\}_{pkA}$$
$$3.\ B \rightarrow_E A \quad : \text{print } hash(Message\ 2)$$

As in the first example, this is reliant on a no-spoofing empirical channel. In the above, N_A is a nonce, pkA is a public key chosen by A (which may or may not be the same for different sessions and other types of communication requiring public-key cryptography), and K is a session key chosen by the printer.

When A sees Message 3 (and that it agrees with the value that A has herself generated by hashing the Message 2 received), she can be sure that Message 2 really was from the printer she has the empirical channel with (namely the one she wishes to communicate with, and trusts). For the trustworthy printer B would not have sent this message (which she knows it has by non-spoofability) unless it had sent M2, which firmly ties its interest to A (as it contains A and pkA), and to this session (as it contains N_A). Furthermore A knows that B will only have sent K in Message 2, necessarily encrypted under pkA, and that therefore K is a secret shared between A and B.

Notice that if we are free to use hashing on a non-spoofable empirical channel, then we can effectively convert any full Dolev-Yao channel C in the same direction into a non-spoofable one by using the above trick. Namely each message along C is followed up by a hash of that message plus enough information to identify the recipient (if the latter is not already included). The message-then-hash order has the advantage that it bounds the time available for any intruder to look for hash collisions, unless the empirical channel is delayable. This, of course, is an advantage if the hash range (thanks to the human-factors argument above) is not as large as one would ideally like.

Here the explicitness in Message 2 is sufficient to establish the tie between A and B as being intentional, and the question of AOT_N and of the variability in the notion of NS_E does not impact the analysis.

3.3   Protocol 2 (NOH $_E$)

As a variant of this scenario, illustrated by Figure 3, we now assume that the printer has its own unique public/secret key pair, and that the E-channel communicates from the user to the printer (in the opposite direction to the first example), perhaps by discreetly pressing buttons on a front panel. If we consider a different threat model, namely that of no overhearing on channel E, we can achieve the same goal by means of a different protocol.

$$1.\ A \rightarrow_N B(P) : \{A, kc(A), N_A\}_{pk(P)}$$
$$2.\ B \rightarrow_N A \quad : \{B, kc(B), N_A\}_{pk(A)}$$
$$3.\ A \rightarrow_E B \quad : N_A'$$
$$4.\ B \rightarrow_N A \quad : hash(N_A', pk(A), kc(B), N_A)$$

In Message 1 A sends a copy of her key certificate and identity, and a nonce, encoded with the generic printer key, to the printer. The printer then replies in Message 2 with a copy of its own unique key certificate and identity, and a copy

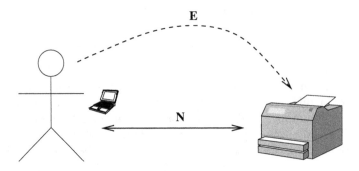

Fig. 3. Channel E now runs from user to printer, unobservable by the attacker. Channel N is bi-directional with the standard Dolev-Yao vulnerabilities

of the nonce it received from A in Message 1, all encoded with A's public key. At this stage A knows that someone has received the original message, but she cannot be sure that it is printer B.

In Message 3 A inputs a nonce N_A' into the printer directly, over the E channel. In this threat model we are assuming that this input cannot be overheard, and therefore only the printer physically interacted with can know N_A'. So in Message 4 the printer sends a hash of the nonce N_A', A's public key, the printer's key certificate sent earlier in Message 2 and the first nonce, N_A, sent by A. As a result, A knows that the printer she is communicating with over N is also the printer being communicated with on E. This message certainly originated at the physically present hardware, since only one printer can know N_A'; the inclusion of evidence of the identities of both A and B in the hash is necessary to prevent an intruder acting as a man-in-the-middle for Messages 1 and 2, and persuading each that they are engaged in the protocol with a different principal. If, for example, we were to have encrypted Message 4 under $pk(A)$, this would have opened up a man-in-the-middle attack. Of course, it is essential in this protocol that E cannot be overheard, as otherwise an imposter who had been taking part in the rest of the protocol could forge Message 4.

Since N_A' is a shared secret here, it can be used as a session key; alternatively the protocol leaves each of A and B with knowledge of each other's public keys, so they can use these.

Verification: As expected, under Dolev-Yao assumptions the protocol again fails to meet its goal. However, to find an attack Casper requires corrupt printers, i.e. Intruder knowledge of the generic printer private key $sk(P)$. This is not surprising as only Message 3 uses a special channel, and the nonce N_A that must end up in the final hash originates from the encrypted Message 1 (where it is associated with the users identity). When we do allow for corrupt printers, the Intruder overhears the nonce N_A and has only to wait for the user to send Message 3 (N_A') before faking the response in Message 4.

With the special channel property NOH_E, Casper failed to find any attacks on the protocol.

4   Conclusions and Further Work

- We have established the utility and viability of mechanical checking of protocols using empirical engagement to bootstrap authentication.
- The multi-party scenario from [3] does not fit so neatly into the Casper paradigm, and its verification will be the subject of a future report.
- Similarly, we plan a further paper on the population of the variant-threat lattice with plausible mechanisms and illustrative protocols.
- All the mechanisms considered so far use locality (and location-limited channels) to establish firm identification of parties to one another. We also intend to explore the possibility of using reduced-threat channels over a distance.

References

1. N. Asokan and Philip Ginzboorg. Key-agreement in ad-hoc networks. *Computer Communications*, 23(17):1627–1637, 2000.
2. D. Balfanz, D. Smetters, P. Stewart, and H. Wong. Talking to strangers: Authentication in ad-hoc wireless networks, Feburary 2002. In Symposium on Network and Distributed Systems Security (NDSS '02), San Diego, California.
3. S. Creese, M. H. Goldsmith, Bill Roscoe, and Irfan Zakiuddin. The attacker in ubiquitous computing environments: Formalising the threat model. In Theo Dimitrakos and Fabio Martinelli, editors, *Workshop on Formal Aspects in Security and Trust*, Pisa, Italy, September 2003. IIT-CNR Technical Report.
4. D. Dolev and A.C. Yao. On the security of public key protocols. *IEEE Transactions on Information Theory*, 29(2), 1983.
5. C.A.R. Hoare. *Communicating Sequential Processes*. Prentice Hall International, 1985.
6. Tim Kindberg and Kan Zhang. Validating and securing spontaneous associations between wireless devices. In 6th *Information Security Conference (ISC'03)*, number 2851 in LNCS. Springer-Verlag, October 2003.
7. A.W. Roscoe. *The Theory and Practice of Concurrency*. Prentice Hall, 1998. ISBN 0-13-6774409-5, pp. xv+565.
8. P.Y.A. Ryan, S.A.Schneider with M.H. Goldsmith, G. Lowe, and A.W. Roscoe. *The Modelling and Analysis of Security Protocols: the CSP Approach*. Addison-Wesley, 2001.
9. Frank Stajano and Ross Anderson. The resurrecting duckling: Security issues for ad-hoc wireless networks. In B. Christianson, B. Crispo, and M. Roe, editors, *Security Protocols, 7th International Workshop Proceedings*, pages 172–194. Springer LNCS, 1999.

Supporting Dynamically Changing Authorizations in Pervasive Communication Systems

Adam J. Lee, Jodie P. Boyer, Chris Drexelius, Prasad Naldurg,
Raquel L. Hill, and Roy H. Campbell

Department of Computer Science,
University of Illinois at Urbana-Champaign, Urbana, IL 61801
{adamlee, jpboyer, drexeliu, naldurg, rlhill, rhc}@cs.uiuc.edu

Abstract. In pervasive computing environments, changes in context may trigger changes in an individual's access permissions. We contend that existing access control frameworks do not provide the fine-grained revocation needed to enforce these changing authorizations. In this paper, we present an authorization framework, in the context of the Gaia OS for active spaces, which integrates context with authorization and provides fine-grained control over the enforcement of dynamically changing permissions using cryptographic mechanisms. Our design, implemented in middleware, addresses the limitations of traditional authorization frameworks and the specific access control needs of pervasive computing environments. As part of our proposed framework, we define cryptographic protocols that enforce access to the system's communication channels and provide secure delivery of messages. We also provide a proof of correctness of key agreement and freshness using the standard BAN deduction system.

1 Introduction

In pervasive computing environments, a change in context may affect the access permissions of users to different system resources. These context changes may occur often, and the management of access control policies for these environments is inherently more complex. The problem of enforcing access control policies for traditional information systems is well studied. We contend that existing authentication and authorization frameworks for these systems such as Kerberos [1, 2] and public-key certification hierarchies [3] are not adequate for pervasive computing scenarios. To illustrate, in Kerberos, the tickets that represent a user's right to access a service are issued with fixed expiry times, which cannot be determined in advance as a function of changing context. The problem of revocation in hierarchical PKI systems is well known [4]. While the authors in [5] explore the authentication problem for pervasive computing, our focus in this paper is on the adequate enforcement of dynamically changing authorizations, driven by changing context.

D. Hutter and M. Ullmann (Eds.): SPC 2005, LNCS 3450, pp. 134–150, 2005.

We explore these authorization issues in the context of our prototype smart room, consisting of a variety of computing and communication services that can be configured for different activities depending on the context. This infrastructure is orchestrated by Gaia OS [6], which brings the functionality of an operating system to physical spaces. In addition to common operating system functions, such as events, signals, file system, security, processes, process groups, etc., Gaia extends typical operating system concepts to include context, location awareness, mobile computing devices and actuators like doorlocks and light switches.

To illustrate the problem in this setting, consider a typical scenario where users, applications, or sensors may initiate events that trigger a change in context. For example, a smoke detector may generate an emergency alarm event triggered by an actual fire which disables electronic doorlocks and allows occupants of the environment to safely exit the building. This emergency alarm event can be implemented in Gaia as a control message to a software-controlled doorlock service, which in turn sends an unlock control message to the individual doorlocks.

Such event notification messages disseminate context information and have the potential to change the operating characteristics of their environment. Authorization to send these notifications should be tightly controlled. Without such protection, the system is vulnerable to attack. For example, an attacker can trigger an emergency alarm by forging the appropriate event, and open the doors to gain physical access to the environment. An attacker could also repeatedly send lock messages to the doorlock service to keep the doors in a locked state, thereby denying access to authorized users. These two examples illustrate how events that occur in virtual space may affect the physical security of that space.

Data exchanged between users and devices in the course of a pervasive computing scenario is also subject to dynamically changing authorizations depending on the context. Consider a collaborative meeting example where all users should be allowed to send messages using the event channel to a shared electronic bulletin board via their personal handheld devices. When the room is configured as a lecture hall, only a presenter should be authorized to send messages to this bulletin board. Therefore, a user's authorizations to the board should change in response to a change in context. Due to the asynchronous and distributed nature of event generation and notification, as well as data dissemination, this service in Gaia OS is implemented as publish-subscribe channels.

Given the setting, we contend that existing frameworks [1, 3, 7, 8, 9] do not provide the fine-grained revocation necessary to enforce changing authorizations. In this paper we present an access control architecture that integrates context with authorization and provides fine-grained control over the enforcement of dynamically changing permissions. Our proposed solution extends the functionality of the Gaia OS and is implemented using distributed objects. The components of our new framework can be replicated easily for load-balancing, are designed to keep minimal state, and work independently without coordination. We believe that this aspect of our design makes our system more efficient and resilient to denial of service (DoS) attacks.

The rest of the paper is organized as follows. Section 2 describes the threat model for attacks on the communication systems of pervasive computing environments. Section 3 presents the limitations of existing authorization frameworks and motivates the need for a new access control architecture, which we present in Section 4. In Section 5, we present the authorization protocols used in our framework. We present an evaluation of our architecture and protocols in Section 6 and conclude in Section 7.

2   Threat Model

In this section, we characterize the nature and scope of attacks that can be mounted against the message distribution system of our prototype pervasive computing environment. We assume that attackers can be either *passive* or *active*. Regardless of their physical location, passive attackers can listen to messages anywhere on the network but cannot change the contents of these messages. Active attackers can modify, reorder, replay, or inject messages into the network. Neither active nor passive attackers can perform cryptographic operations with keys that they do not possess. The remainder of this section discusses various attacks and the impact they have on the system.

Integrity Violations. It is important that an event published by a sender is the same event that arrives at the receiver. If no such guarantees can be made, an active attacker can change the content of messages while they are in transit. Consider an active attacker who changes the sign bit on messages sent out by a temperature sensor. This attack may cause the climate control equipment in the room to activate the heaters, which may adversely impact system hardware.

Confidentiality Violations. In many cases, the contents of both data and control messages may need to be confidential. Consider an electronic doorlock system that sends events to a central monitoring facility when any door is locked or unlocked. If these messages are sent unencrypted, unauthorized viewers can quickly learn what parts of the building are unlocked. This could lead to intrusions and theft.

Privacy Violations. While it is difficult to make strong guarantees about privacy such as unobservability, or unlinkability [10], it is important that a message distribution system provides for basic user privacy by preventing disclosure of sensitive personal information. Content publishers should be able to define which entities have access to generated information. For instance, if a user is wearing a location-tracking badge that periodically sends her GPS location, she may specify a list of authorized recipients of this data to preserve her location privacy.

Authenticity. Message authenticity is necessary in an event distribution system, since the configuration and security of the pervasive computing environment can change as a result of the messages sent. Without such guarantees, the system is open to attacks in which a malicious user injects spurious messages, claiming that they came from legitimate sources. One example of such an attack is when an intruder forges a message from a smoke detector that will trigger an alarm system. The alarm system may unlock the doors to the building to allow easier exit, or in this case, entrance to an unauthorized user.

Denial of Service. In addition to traditional denial of service (DoS) attacks, the context-sensitive nature of pervasive computing environments exposes these systems to additional avenues of DoS. For instance, a clever attacker might realize that access permissions in the system change with context. The attacker can repeatedly trigger context changes to force management overheads associated with permission revocation and acquisition on the system. If these overheads are too high, such an attack could impact the distribution of events.

In the rest of this paper, we describe the design and implementation of our secure event distribution system and evaluate the architecture and protocols that we present to show that our system is robust enough to resist the threats outlined in this section. In the next section, we examine the shortcomings of existing security solutions, explore the limitations that they impose when deployed in pervasive computing environments, and motivate the need for our new authorization framework.

3   Related Work

In this section, we present the limitations of existing authorization and authentication frameworks with respect to enforcing dynamically changing permissions in pervasive environments. These frameworks include Kerberos [1, 2], SESAME [7], hierarchical PKI [3], SDSI/SPKI [9], and KeyNote [8]. We also distinguish how this work differs from other efforts to incorporate contextual changes into access control frameworks for pervasive environments.

Kerberos and SESAME. Kerberos is a distributed authentication and authorization framework that enforces access control through the use of time-limited tickets. SESAME provides functionality beyond the scope of Kerberos such as scalability when multiple networks are connected. However, the basic SESAME Security Architecture is essentially an extension of Kerberos. Kerberos service tickets and SESAME certificates are valid for a fixed time interval starting at a predetermined time. Explicit revocation before ticket expiration is not possible. To combat this problem, Kerberos and SESAME administrators may decrease the time interval between ticket activation and expiration. This strategy now acts as revocation mechanism for all tickets, regardless of whether or not permissions have actually changed. This negatively impacts the usefulness of tickets and increases the burden on clients wishing to access resources in both Kerberos and SESAME. This derived revocation mechanism does not solve the revocation problem since there is still no direct link between ticket expiration and context-driven permission changes. Role-based extensions to Kerberos and SESAME including [11] still suffer from the same fundamental revocation limitation as the basic Kerberos and SESAME architectures.

Hiearachical PKI. Unlike Kerberos and SESAME, hiearachical PKI systems do have the ability to revoke access rights. However, critical analysis in [4] suggests that distribution of key revocation information may be prohibitively expensive on a large scale. Each time permissions change, a message reflecting the new permission state must be distributed to each host in the system. The dynamic nature of pervasive environments makes this framework insufficient for the revocation needs of these environments.

SDSI/SPKI. SDSI/SPKI suffers from the same revocation issues outlined above for hierarchical PKI. Though SDSI/SPKI does not support certificate revocation lists (CRLs), a service may exist that provides a list of principals whose keys have been revoked. To maintain system-wide consistency, service providers must continually poll the list of revoked certificates. SDSI/SPKI is not appropriate for ubiquitous environments since certificates may be revoked often.

KeyNote. Similar to the limitations of the other authorization and authentication frameworks addressed above, KeyNote does not provide sufficient credential revocation mechanisms to handle changing context information. Like Kerberos and SESAME, KeyNote allows credentials to exist for a limited window of time, but explicit revocation is not possible. The KeyNote interpreter, a component used to verify credentials, may be informed of authorization revocation. Similar to SDSI/SPKI above, this places the burden on clients to perform certificate verification. Since we wish to eliminate this client-side burden, the KeyNote framework is insufficient for our needs.

In [12] the authors propose a security middleware for Gaia, that consists of a network of Middleboxes, reconfigurable computing and communications nodes that act as proxies or access points for critical services and mediate access to services by authenticating requesters and negotiating security requirements. Our system implements the generic proxy behavior of Middleboxes and mediates communication between publishers and subscribers by brokering information published by publishers to authorized, registered subscribers. In [13] the authors argue that traditional authentication frameworks that attempt to prove the validity of a claimed identity are not sufficient for pervasive environments, and that contextual attributes like location and manufacturer's certificates should be authenticated to establish higher levels of assurance. This work focuses on establishing trust as opposed to handling dynamically changing permissions. In

[14], the authors propose extensions to RBAC that facilitate context-aware access control policies. In their system, users can assume multiple roles, and changes in user permissions are communicated to applications for which the associated roles are active. The authors do not provide a mechanism by which applications can enforce dynamically changing permissions.

In the next section, we introduce our authorization architecture, which is designed to overcome the revocation granularity limitations of existing authorization and authentication frameworks. We also provide implementation and analysis details to validate our proposed concepts.

4   Architecture

Gaia OS [6] is a middleware meta-operating system that exposes APIs which allow users to locate and interact with applications, manage the context of the system, create and utilize communication channels, and otherwise interface with the pervasive computing environment in a meaningful way. Gaia OS utilizes publish-subscribe "event channels" to control the system and disseminate information to interested parties. The specific solution that we present is designed to secure these channels.

4.1   System Architecture

We rely on cryptographic mechanims to enforce dynamic authorizations. If an individual has sufficient rights to an information resource, the system can encrypt the information and provide the user with a secret decryption key. This ensures that only authorized individuals have direct access to sensitive data, and anyone snooping on the communication channels is denied access. Dynamic au-

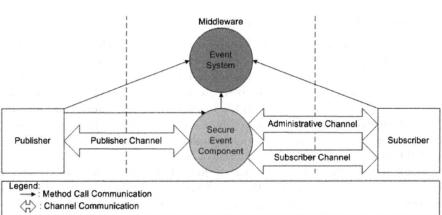

Supporting Dynamically Changing Authorizations

Fig. 1. System Architecture

thorization is achieved by controlling the distribution of keys, and key freshness and agreement are essential for proper enforcement of access control policies. Key revocation, an integral part of key management, is used in our framework to deny access when permissions change.

We present a key distribution and management protocol to achieve dynamic authorization in pervasive computing environments. Our proposed solution accounts for denial of service, failures of commodity hardware and the dynamic nature of pervasive systems. Our framework is distributed and provides multiple key management entities. Each management entity maintains minimal state to facilitate bootstrapping, data migration and replication as well as allows the system to handle attacks on individual components. Figure 1 presents the architecture of the secure publish-subscribe system that we have developed for Gaia OS. We now describe the components of this system.

Publisher. Publishers are the information providers in our system. They create channels, determine the access control polices for these channels, and publish data. Example publishers include sensors, messaging clients, and other system components.

Subscriber. Subscribers are the event consumers in our system. Any subscriber can register to consume events that they are authorized to view.

Event System. The Event System is the underlying messaging system provided by Gaia. This component provides functionality for creating, destroying, and managing event channels.

Secure Event Component (SEC). In our system, there are one or more SECs. These components act as distributed reference monitors for the event channels in the system. Each SEC manages access control for one or more event channels. When a channel is created, its creator pushes access control lists (ACLs) controlling read and write access to the new channel. The SEC is responsible for enforcing these ACLs. We describe the SEC in further detail next.

4.2   Secure Event Component

The Secure Event Component (SEC) stores encryption keys, checks access rights, and brokers messages securely from publishers to authorized subscribers. A particular configuration of an active space may have multiple SECs that generate and manage symmetric keys used to secure specific event channels. The symmetric keys are stored in a hash table to allow efficient storage and lookup. These symmetric keys must be stored in a secure manner, e.g., using tamper-resistant hardware. Details of the cryptographic protocols between the SEC and the publishers and subscribers are presented in Section 5.

Users in our system can authenticate and obtain their credentials using a public/private key pair issued by the Gaia Certificate Authority. Once the user's identity is established, an attribute certifier, which is not discussed in detail in this paper, can issue them credentials bound to the current context by a counter which attest to various attributes, including their roles in the system. Each device or service maintains an access list, which associates a set of permissions with each role.

When the context of the space changes, the underlying Gaia access control architecture [15] changes the user-role assignment of affected users, according to a meta policy specified by the administrator of the space. The privileges assigned to roles in a space are relatively static, but principals can move in and out of roles in a dynamic fashion, triggered by changes to the current configuration of the space. A Gaia administrator is responsible for setting up these policies. In [15] we show how our access control framework, based on RBAC, can be used to specify such context-sensitive policies correctly. In this paper, we present a set of mechanisms to guarantee that the permissions that are being enforced are current.

To create a secure event channel, user Alice authenticates with the SEC and receives a symmetric key that she can use to publish to the SEC over a newly created channel. When Bob wants to subscribe to the events published by Alice, the SEC checks Bob's current role permissions to verify whether he possesses the necessary permissions. If authorized, the SEC creates a new channel, negotiates a symmetric key with Bob (one per channel), decrypts the message it receives from Alice and re-encrypts it with Bob's key, and sends it on the appropriate channel.

The binding between a user and their current role can change at any time due to a change in context. The SEC is notified by Gaia's access control service when existing user-to-role mappings are altered by a role change in the system. If any user-role assignments are changed for a particular subscriber channel, the SEC revokes the symmetric key and denies unauthorized access to this information. It is important to note that publishers are unaffected by this change, as the Secure Event Component decouples the publish and subscribe operations by using different keys to communicate with publishers than with subscribers.

In the next section, we present the details of our cryptographic protocols, highlighting their key acquisition and revocation features.

5   Protocol Details

In this section, we explain the details of the cryptographic protocols used in our system. These protocols are used to negotiate and transfer keys from the SEC to the publishers and subscribers. We also describe protocols for sending messages and requesting new keys. Finally, we discuss how key revocation works in our system.

It should be noted that throughout this section, we assume that the publisher creates the channels in the system and provides an ACL used to restrict the set of potential subscribers. A straightforward extension of these protocols would allow a third party to create a channel and provide ACLs for both publisher and subscriber groups. Due to space limitations, however, this extended set of protocols is not discussed.

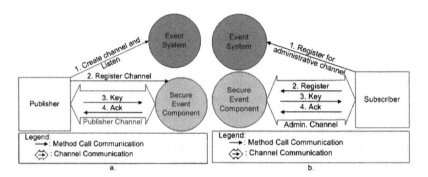

Fig. 2. a. The messages required to create a channel. b. The messages required to register as a subscriber for a channel

5.1   Notation

The following notation is used throughout the remainder of this document:

- P is a publisher, S is a subscriber and M is the SEC.
- $ID(B)$ refers to user B's identity certificate, which is publicly available from a trusted Certificate Authority (CA) in the system.
- $Attr(B)$ refers to object B's attribute certificate (e.g., its system role binding).
- PK_B refers to B's public key and PK_B^{-1} refers to B's private key.
- K_{PM} is a symmetric key shared between the publisher P and the SEC M.
- $K_{SM}(P)$ refers to a symmetric key that is shared between the SEC and the subset of authorized subscribers. Note that $K_{SM}(P) \neq K_{PM}$.
- N_B is a nonce generated by user B.
- $\{C\}_K$ refers to the message C encrypted with key K, whereas $\langle C \rangle_{K'}$ refers to the message C signed by key K'.
- H refers to a cryptographic hash function, used to create a MAC.

5.2   Authorized Channel Creation

When a publisher, P, wishes to publish on a secure channel, he must first create an insecure channel. This is done with the aid of the Event System. This channel, known as the publisher channel, is used by P and the SEC to exchange messages. These messages are shown in Figure 2a. Once the publisher channel is created P and the SEC exchange a key. Key exchange begins when P sends a *secure channel* message to the SEC. This message contains the name of the SEC, a nonce, generated by P, an ID certificate for P and a hash of the message signed with P's private key. The entire message is encrypted with the SEC's public key. The SEC responds to P with a message that contains P's name, P's nonce, a new nonce generated by the SEC, a new symmetric key and a hash of the message signed with the SEC's private key. This entire message is then encrypted with P's public key. P acknowledges the receipt of the key by sending a message that contains the SEC's nonce. This message also contains a signed hash and is encrypted with the SEC's public key.

Formally:

$$P \rightarrow M : \{D = (\text{SECURECHANNEL}, \text{M}, N_P, ID(P), \langle H(D) \rangle_{PK_P^{-1}}\}_{PK_M}$$

$$M \rightarrow P : \{D = (\text{OK}, \text{P}, N_P, N_M, K_{PM}), \langle H(D) \rangle_{PK_M^{-1}}\}_{PK_P}$$

$$P \rightarrow M : \{D = (\text{ACK}, \text{M}, N_M), \langle H(D) \rangle_{PK_P^{-1}}\}_{PK_M}$$

This protocol allows for the mutual authentication of the SEC and P, along with secure key exchange. It also assures P that the SEC is an authorized system component and binds the actions of P to his identity which ensures nonrepudiation.

We model the protocols using a belief logic. The rules of the Burrows-Abadi-Needham (BAN) formal deduction system [16] are used to draw some conclusions about what guarantees these protocols provide. While the BAN system does not have an independent semantics, it is sufficient here to prove mechanically, given that the assumptions are correct, that key agreement and freshness can be achieved with our protocols. Using only the rules of inference outlined in [16], we prove that after a run of our protocol, a trusted publisher (or subscriber) in our system believes that the SEC believes that he or she shares a symmetric key with the SEC, and that this key is fresh. Likewise, we prove that a trusted SEC believes that P believes that it shares a fresh key with the publisher (or subscriber). We present details of our proof in Appendix A. Note that we cannot prove these results if either the SEC or the publishers and subscribers are malicious and lie about their beliefs.

To prove that we achieve our goals, we assume that all parties communicating can generate fresh nonces. Since each party in the system uses a cryptographic pseudo-random number generator, we feel that this is a valid assumption. Additionally, we assume that all parties can obtain the public-key certificates of the other parties through the Gaia certificate authority. Lastly, we assume that publishers and subscribers trust the SEC to generate appropriate session keys.

Validating that the key agreement and freshness properties can be achieved by our protocols provides us the assurance that our cryptographic mechanisms are being used correctly. It is important to note that these mechanisms only enforce the underlying dynamic policy changes. It is equally important to analyze whether the underlying RBAC framework itself generates the appropriate user-role assignments, consistent with the requirements and goals of our pervasive computing scenarios. We present a proof of this safety property in [15].

5.3   Authorized Client Subscription

When a subscriber, S, subscribes to a secure channel, she must first acquire an attribute certificate that serves as an attestation of her current system role. The following message exchange is similar to that in Section 5.2:

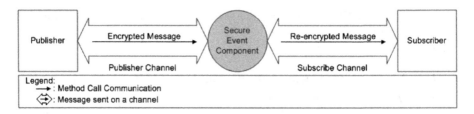

Fig. 3. The message publication sequence

$$S \to M : \{D = (\texttt{JOIN}, \ \texttt{M}, \ N_S, \ Attr(S), \ ID(S)), \ \langle H(D) \rangle_{PK_S^{-1}} \}_{PK_M}$$

$$M \to S : \{D = (\texttt{OK}, \ \texttt{S}, \ N_S, \ N_M, \ K_{SM}(P)), \ \langle H(D) \rangle_{PK_M^{-1}} \}_{PK_S}$$

$$S \to M : \{D = (\texttt{ACK}, \ \texttt{M}, \ N_M), \ \langle H(D) \rangle_{PK_S^{-1}} \}_{PK_M}$$

This exchange provides the same guarantees as those discussed for channel creation. S's attribute certificate is passed to the SEC in the first message. This allows the SEC to mediate access to the channel based on S's system role.

The client registers as a listener on the administrative channel. All three messages described above are exchanged on the administrative channel. The client does not register for the subscriber channel until the final acknowledgment is sent. Figure 2b. illustrates this process.

5.4   Publishing a Message

P publishes messages to the SEC encrypted with their shared key. The SEC subsequently decrypts these messages and re-encrypts them with the subscriber key and sends them to the subscribers.

Formally:

$$P \to M : \{\texttt{MESSAGE}\}_{K_{PM}}$$

$$M \to S : \{\texttt{MESSAGE}\}_{K_{SM}(P)}$$

This is shown in Figure 3. It is important to note that there may be many subscribers listening to the same channel.

5.5   Changing a Publisher Key

P uses a symmetric key to encrypt its messages. Keys that are used for a long period of time are susceptible it is to cryptanalysis, therefore P periodically requests a new symmetric key from the SEC. P requests a key by sending a message that contains a nonce and is encrypted using the key shared between P and the SEC. The SEC subsequently sends a new key to P. This message is encrypted with the old key and contains P's nonce and a new nonce generated by the SEC. P acknowledges the receipt of the key by sending the SEC's nonce back, encrypted with the new key.

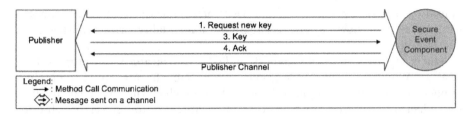

Fig. 4. The messages exchanged to get a new key

This exchange is shown as follows:

$$P \rightarrow M : \{\texttt{CHANGE},\ N_P\}_{K_{PM}}$$
$$M \rightarrow P : \{\texttt{KEY},\ N_P,\ N_M,\ K'_{PM}\}_{K_{PM}}$$
$$P \rightarrow M : \{\texttt{KEYACK},\ N_M\}_{K'_{PM}}$$

All of these messages are sent between SEC and P using the publish channel as shown in Figure 4.

5.6   Handling a Role Change

In a pervasive computing environment, an individual may have several roles and her active role binding may change for a variety of reasons. The same user may have the role of a lecturer in a smart classroom, and the role of a researcher when a meeting is scheduled in the same room.

Role changes in this system are handled by a unilateral revocation of the keys on the channels affected by the role change. For example, only lecturers may have access to the overhead projectors, so if a lecturer's role changes to a researcher, the projector's publisher key is revoked. In order to accomplish this, the SEC receives a message from a trusted authority, namely the Gaia context system, informing it of the role change. Students subscribed to the projectors display channel need not change their roles or keys.

Unilateral key revocation allows the overhead of revocation to be distributed among the affected entities. These entities are required to reacquire the attributes necessary to continue to use the event channel. This means that the SEC does not need to track the roles and permissions of users subscribed to the channel and also allows key revocation to be fast and efficient.

In the next section, we will evaluate our solution and protocols and show how it meets the needs of pervasive computing environments.

6   Evaluation

In this section, we revisit our threat model and argue informally about how our authorization framework addresses our original goals and overcomes the limitations of existing solutions. We revisit each of our threats from Section 2 in turn and examine how we address integrity, confidentiality, privacy, authenticity, and DoS concerns.

Our framework relies on standard public-key certificates for identity authentication. When a new user, Alice, joins our system, she is required to obtain a public-key certificate from our (offline) CA and include this in her communication when she first attempts to contact any server, tries to publish, or subscribe to the event channels. We propose that the user's identity is verified out-of-band before the certificate issued. All trusted entities in the system, including the SEC and the event managers also publish their public keys so that anyone wishing to communicate with them can use their public key to send them encrypted messages. However, relying on public-key encryption for all confidentiality requirements can be expensive. Therefore the public-key encrypted channels are only used to exchange symmetric keys securely as outlined in our protocols previously.

With the public-key infrastructure, we can also provide integrity protection, non-repudiation, and mutual authentication. For integrity, Alice can create a MAC using a cryptographic hash function and sign this MAC with her private key used for digital signatures. A verifier on the other end can validate the integrity by recomputing the MAC and checking it with the decrypted value embedded in the message. This mechanism can also be used to provide non repudiation of origin. Mutual authentication can be accomplished by a standard challenge-response protocol used in this fashion. Our protocols are optimal in the number of rounds required for mutual authentication.

While our use of the PKI is fairly standard during protocol initiation, all subsequent messages between two mutually authenticated parties are protected by encryption using symmetric session keys for performance reasons. The novelty in our framework is in the use of these keys to enforce authorizations. For example, whenever subscriber authorizations change due to changes in system context, the publishers in our protocol are unaffected. The mediators or the SECs simply change the encryption keys on the channel they share with the subscribers, enforcing this policy change without sacrificing security guarantees. In this case, the subscribers are burdened with the responsibility of obtaining new keys by re-authenticating with the attribute certifiers according to their new roles. This unilateral revocation of keys may inconvenience affected subscribers, requiring them to buffer some event messages from the SECs and delay their processing. On the other hand, when a publisher's authorizations change, subscribers are unaffected. We picked this trade-off deliberately to cause the least amount of impact on the rest of the system, and maximize the precision of enforcement of dynamic access control policies.

Our use of group keys, i.e., one key per role, simplifies key distribution and management. In our initial prototype, we do not optimize group key revocation and sharing. In the future, we plan to explore different hierarchical key distribution frameworks, especially multicast and group-key management [17, 18, 19, 20] to optimize this aspect of our protocols.

With respect to the DoS problem, we believe that our distributed mediators (the SECs) make it difficult for an attacker to mount DoS attacks against our infrastructure. In particular, an attacker would need to expend a large amount of resources to target all the different components to cause service outages. Since our protocols themselves are soft-state and our entities can bootstrap easily without needing to coordinate with each other or worry about consistency issues, we claim our solution is resilient to DoS attacks.

However, we realize that a dedicated insider can repeatedly change the context to trigger key revocation and deny service to legitimate users. While our system provides non-repudiation at session start-up, such an attacker can hide behind the group or role set that he or she belongs to due to our use of symmetric keys at this point. At this point, we may need to look at publish behavior of individual users by analyzing audit logs to catch the culprit. Maintaining these logs becomes more crucial in this context. While our use of symmetric keys at this point makes it harder to catch an attacker quickly in this scenario, we still have accountability at a per-user level.

In the next section, we summarize our work and present our conclusions.

7 Conclusion

In this paper we present an access control architecture that integrates context with authorization and provides fine-grained control over the enforcement of dynamically changing permissions. The foundation of this access control architecture is our secure message distribution system which consists of protocols for gaining authorized access to communications channels and securely transmitting messages throughout the system. Our secure message distribution system addresses the threats to the underlying communication system of pervasive computing environments, as well as the limitations of existing access control frameworks.

We have implemented our access control architecture in the Gaia meta-operating system as distributed objects. Our access control and messaging protocols secure Gaia's publish/subscribe communication system. We also present a proof of correctness of our cryptographic protocols using BAN logic.

Our design includes distributed reference monitors, authorization servers, and key managers, which afford maximum flexibility to handle dynamically changing permissions securely. Our SECs maintain ACLs and are directly responsible for enforcing access policy. This design choice enables distributed enforcement of policies without sacrificing consistency. The components of our architecture can be replicated easily for load balancing, are designed to be soft-state, and work independently without coordination. We believe that this aspect of our design makes our system more efficient and resilient to denial of service (DoS) attacks.

References

1. Kohl, J., Neuman, B.C.: The Kerberos Network Authentication Service (Version 5). Internet Request for Comments RFC-1510 (1993)
2. Neuman, B.C., Ts'o, T.: Kerberos: An Authentication Service for Computer Networks. In: IEEE Communications. Volume 32. (1994) 33–38
3. Housely, R., Ford, W., Polk, W., Solo, D.: Internet X.509 Public Key Infrastructure Certificate and CRL Profile. Internet Request for Comments RFC-2459 (1999)
4. : Public key infrastructure study. National Institute of Standards and Technology (1994)
5. Creese, S., Goldsmith, M., Rosco, B., Zakiuddin, I.: Authentication for pervasive computing. In: Proceedings of the First International Conference on Security in Pervasive Computing, Boppard, Germany, March 12-14th, LNCS, Springer. (2003)
6. Roman, M., Hess, C.K., Cerqueira, R., Ranganathan, A., Campbell, R.H., Nahrstedt, K.: Gaia: A middleware infrastructure to enable active spaces. IEEE Pervasive Computing (2002) 74–83
7. Ashley, P., Vandenwauver, M.: Practical Intranet Security: Overview of the State of the Art and Available Technologies. Kluwer Academic Publishers (1999)
8. Blaze, M., Feigenbaum, J., Keromytis, A.D.: KeyNote: Trust management for public-key infrastructures (position paper). Lecture Notes in Computer Science **1550** (1999) 59–63
9. Rivest, R.L., Lampson, B.: SDSI – A simple distributed security infrastructure. Presented at CRYPTO'96 Rumpsession (1996)
10. Pfitzmann, A., Köhntopp, M.: Anonymity, unobservability, and pseudonymity: A proposal for terminology (2000)
11. Vandenwauver, M., Govaerts, R., Vandewalle, J.: How role based access control is implemented in sesame. In: WETICE. (1997) 293–298
12. Hill, R., Al-Muhtadi, J., Campbell, R., Kapadia, A., Naldurg, P., Ranganathan, A.: A middleware architecture for securing ubiquitous computing cyber infrastructures. In: 5th ACM/IFIP/USENIX International Middleware Conference. (2004)
13. Creese, S., Goldsmith, M., Roscoe, B., Zakiuddin, I.: Authentication for pervasive computing. In: Security in Pervasive Computing. (2003)
14. Wullems, C., Looi, M., Clark, A.: Towards context- aware security: An authorization architecture for intranet environments. In: in the proceedings of the Second IEEE Conference on Pervasive Computing and Communciations Worshops. (2004)
15. Sampemane, G., Naldurg, P., Campbell, R.H.: Access control for active spaces. In: Annual Computer Security Applications Conference. (2002)
16. Burrows, M., Abadi, M., Needham, R.: A logic of authentication. In: Proceedings of the twelfth ACM symposium on Operating systems principles, ACM Press (1989) 1–13
17. McGrew, D.A., Sherman, A.T.: Key establishment in large dynamic groups using one-way function trees. IEEE Transactions on Software Engineering **29** (2003) 444–458
18. Mittra, S.: Iolus: A framework for scalable secure multicasting. In: ACM SIGCOMM '97. (1997)
19. Perrig, A.: Efficient collaborative key management protocols for secure autonomous group communication. In: International Workshop on Cryptographic Techniques and E-Commerce CrypTEC '99. (1999)
20. Steiner, M., Tsudik, G., Waidner, M.: Cliques: A new approach to group key agreement. In: 18th International Conference on Distributed Computing Systems (ICDCS '98). (1998) 380–387

A   BAN Analysis

Assumptions	Goals	Idealized Protocol
$P \models \#(N_1)$	$P \models M \models P \xleftrightarrow{K_{PM}} M$	$P \to M : \left\{ N_1, \{N_1\}_{K_P^{-1}} \right\}_{K_M}$
$M \models \#(N_2)$	$M \models P \models P \xleftrightarrow{K_{PM}} M$	$M \to P : \left\{ N_1, N_2, P \xleftrightarrow{K_{PM}} M, \left\{ N_1, N_2, P \xleftrightarrow{K_{PM}} M \right\}_{K_M^{-1}} \right\}_{K_P}$
$P \models \xmapsto{K_M} M$		$P \to M : \left\{ N_2, P \xleftrightarrow{K_{PM}} M \left\{ N_2, P \xleftrightarrow{K_{PM}} M \right\}_{K_P^{-1}} \right\}_{K_M}$
$P \models \xmapsto{K_P} P$		
$M \models \xmapsto{K_P} P$		

A.1   Analysis

After step 1 we know: $M \lhd \left\{ N_1, \{N_1\}_{K_P^{-1}} \right\}_{K_M}$

$$\frac{\overline{M \lhd \left\{ N_1, \{N_1\}_{K_P^{-1}} \right\}_{K_M}} \quad \overline{[M \models \xmapsto{K_M} M]}^{\, asmp}}{M \lhd N_1, \{N_1\}_{K_P^{-1}}}^{sees5}$$

$$\frac{\dfrac{\overline{M \lhd N_1, \{N_1\}_{K_P^{-1}}}}{M \lhd \{N_1\}_{K_P^{-1}}}^{sees1} \quad \overline{[M \models \xmapsto{K_P} P]}^{\, asmp}}{M \models P \hspace{-0.3em}\sim\hspace{-0.3em} N}^{pubkey}$$

After step 2 we know: $P \lhd \left\{ N_1, N_2, P \xleftrightarrow{K_{PM}} M, \left\{ N_1, N_2, P \xleftrightarrow{K_{PM}} M \right\}_{K_M^{-1}} \right\}_{K_P}$

$$\frac{\overline{P \lhd \left\{ N_1, N_2, P \xleftrightarrow{K_{PM}} M, \left\{ N_1, N_2, P \xleftrightarrow{K_{PM}} M \right\}_{K_M^{-1}} \right\}_{K_P}} \quad \overline{[P \models \xmapsto{P} K_P]}^{\, asmp}}{P \lhd N_1, N_2, P \xleftrightarrow{K_{PM}} M, \left\{ N_1, N_2, P \xleftrightarrow{K_{PM}} M \right\}_{K_M^{-1}}}^{sees5}$$

$$\frac{\dfrac{\overline{P \lhd N_1, N_2, P \xleftrightarrow{K_{PM}} M, \left\{ N_1, N_2, P \xleftrightarrow{K_{PM}} M \right\}_{K_M^{-1}}}}{P \lhd \left\{ N_1, N_2, P \xleftrightarrow{K_{PM}} M \right\}_{K_M^{-1}}}^{sees1} \quad \overline{[P \models \xmapsto{K_M} M]}^{\, asmp}}{\dfrac{P \models M \hspace{-0.3em}\sim\hspace{-0.3em} N_1, N_2, P \xleftrightarrow{K_{PM}} M}{P \models M \hspace{-0.3em}\sim\hspace{-0.3em} N_1, P \xleftrightarrow{K_{PM}} M}^{said}}^{sees5}$$

$$\frac{\dfrac{\overline{[P \models \#(N_1)]}^{\, asmp}}{P \models \#(N_1, P \xleftrightarrow{K_{PM}} M)}^{fresh} \quad \overline{P \models M \hspace{-0.3em}\sim\hspace{-0.3em} N_1, P \xleftrightarrow{K_{PM}} M}}{\dfrac{P \models M \models N_1, P \xleftrightarrow{K_{PM}} M}{P \models M \models P \xleftrightarrow{K_{PM}} M}^{bb}}^{nv}$$

After step 3 we know: $M \lhd \{\{N_2, P \xleftrightarrow{K_{PM}} M, P, M\}_{K_P^{-1}}\}_{K_M}$

$$\frac{\dfrac{\bullet}{M \lhd \{\{N_2, P \xleftarrow{K_{PM}} M, P, M\}_{K_P^{-1}}\}_{K_M}} \quad \dfrac{\bullet}{[M \equiv \overset{K_M}{\mapsto} M]} \; asmp}{M \lhd \{N_2, P \xleftarrow{K_{PM}} M, P, M\}_{K_P^{-1}}} \; sees5 \quad \dfrac{\bullet}{[M \equiv \overset{K_P}{\mapsto} P]} \; asmp$$

$$\frac{M \lhd \{N_2, P \xleftarrow{K_{PM}} M, P, M\}_{K_P^{-1}} \qquad [M \equiv \overset{K_P}{\mapsto} P]}{M \equiv P \mid\!\sim N_2, P \xleftarrow{K_{PM}} M, P, M} \; pubkey$$

$$\frac{M \equiv P \mid\!\sim N_2, P \xleftarrow{K_{PM}} M, P, M}{M \equiv P \mid\!\sim N_2, P \xleftarrow{K_{PM}} M, P} \; said$$

$$\frac{M \equiv P \mid\!\sim N_2, P \xleftarrow{K_{PM}} M, P}{M \equiv P \mid\!\sim N_2, P \xleftarrow{K_{PM}} M} \; said$$

$$\frac{\dfrac{\bullet}{[M \equiv \sharp(N_2)]} \; asmp}{M \equiv \sharp(N_2, P \xleftarrow{K_{PM}} M)} \; fresh$$

$$\frac{\dfrac{\bullet}{M \equiv \sharp(N_2, P \xleftarrow{K_{PM}} M)} \quad \dfrac{\bullet}{M \equiv P \mid\!\sim N_2, P \xleftarrow{K_{PM}} M}}{M \equiv P \equiv N_2, P \xleftarrow{K_{PM}} M} \; nv$$

$$\frac{M \equiv P \equiv N_2, P \xleftarrow{K_{PM}} M}{M \equiv P \equiv P \xleftarrow{K_{PM}} M} \; bb$$

Look Who's Talking - Authenticating Service Access Points

Adolf Hohl[1], Lutz Lowis[1], and Alf Zugenmaier[2]

[1] Institute of Computer Science and Social Studies,
University of Freiburg, 79098 Freiburg, Germany
{hohl, lowis}@iig.uni-freiburg.de
[2] Microsoft Research Cambridge
alfz@microsoft.com

Abstract. Pervasive computing can be divided into computing on personal wearable devices and computing in a smart infrastructure. When a wearable device communicates personal data for further processing to the infrastructure, privacy concerns arise. These concerns would be unnecessary if the behavior of services in the smart environment could be authenticated and known to be compliant to given policies. Based upon the Trusted Computing idea, we present a solution to the specific problem of service access point authentication. In contrast to previous approaches, this operating system centric approach does not only handle trusted computing enhanced applications but also deals with legacy applications providing services.

1 Introduction

The paradigm of ubiquitous and pervasive computing [1] is leading to a much greater intrusion of information and communication technology into the personal life of everyone than what we experience today. Users in a pervasive computing environment will use smart personal objects interacting with services provided by other smart devices. This can lead to a huge amount of communication between personal user devices and devices of the smart environment and thus result in accidental release of sensitive information such as personal data. While people using services in the Internet are becoming more aware of the situation and at least try to use only trustworthy services and not release sensitive information to everybody, the same problem in pervasive computing seems to be harder and even more complicated. One reason for this is the number of service-providing devices in a smart environment. For somebody using these devices it is hard to figure out who is their owner and maintainer. He may assume that devices in a smart environment located inside a building of an organization are maintained by this organization, but he cannot be sure about that. In a public space, the user can only guess who might be maintaining a certain device. It can also not be assumed that the same device in a smart environment at the time t and a later time $t + \Delta t$. Particularly an attacker with the aim of collecting information

D. Hutter and M. Ullmann (Eds.): SPC 2005, LNCS 3450, pp. 151–162, 2005.

via providing a service in a smart environment will keep his device running only as long as necessary to collect enough information and then disappear. Thus, not even the argument of security through physical proximity works [2]. Therefore, we propose the authentication of the behavior similar to that proposed by Creese [3] by providing the user with the ability to verify a service-providing device before the intended service is going to be used. This verification consists of a first step in which a challenged system provides evidence about its state and a second step in which the attestation data is interpreted. Trusted computing platforms, as they are specified by the Trusted Computing Group [4], provide a solution to attest the software components running on a system. With knowledge about the behavior of the specific software and hardware components one can decide if they are in compliance with a given policy and thereby trustworthy. Trusted Computing Group compliant hardware is available in PCs and in reference implementations of a PDA [5] and embedded devices [6]. In a prototype implementation, the authors developed a service using a personal device to access a service at a terminal [7]. In this scenario, the personal device of a service user requests a hash value of the service-providing system and proceeds only if it can identify the service as one of which the behavior is known. We continue that approach in this paper and solve the attestation problem by mapping the result of a machine attestation to the access point of a service. This approach allows reuse of legacy applications that are not aware of the attestation mechanism. Our mechanism focusses especially on avoiding man-in-the-middle attacks and prevents a user from inadvertently communicating with a service started at a later time than the time attestation took place.

The following section of the paper describes the attacker model. An overview of how Trusted Computing is used to authenticate the behavior of a service application is given in section 3. We describe security requirements which are necessary to avoid ambiguities of service access points. Section 4 describes the proposed approach and some extensions to the operating system to defeat the described attacks. A discussion in section 5, an overview of related work and an outlook conclude the paper.

2   Attacker Model

The aim of an attacker is to gain access to personal or sensitive information which is communcated by a user to a service. The position of the attacker can be between the service-providing device and the user. There he may read datagrams of the communication and insert his own datagrams or try to take over the communication with a man-in-the-middle attack. An attacker can also be located inside the service device if he gains access to it. There he can start his own services and try to get them registered with well-known service access points. He may also use denial of service of reduction of quality of service attacks on the service the user wants to talk to. We further assume that the operating system running on the service-providing device provides strong separation and isolation of processes and an attacker with access to the device itself cannot access resources of an application already running and providing a service.

We do not consider visual attacks on the user input or output, e.g. by pointing a camera on the screen.

3   Authentication of Behavior via Attestation and Interpretation

Mapping or describing the behavior of software on a computer to a policy is a complicated task. It becomes especially difficult to verify the compliance of the system's behavior with a stated policy when a system becomes more complex. From a privacy point of view, such a policy could be, for example, that a pervasive computing device does not leak its users personal data. One way to approach this problem of unknown services is to let a potential user know exactly which applications are executed on a service-providing system. With the knowledge about the behavior of the service application and the execution environment, a service user can decide to use this application or service if it complies with his personal policy. As it is unlikely that all of this information is available at the user's devices or that a user has the ability to perform this evaluation, we introduced a trusted third party which provides a mapping between rated applications and their expected behavior stated in a policy.

In the proof of concept demonstrator mentioned above we used software-based verification of a single hash value for a packed set of applications and libraries to give a challenger the ability to identify pieces of software before they are executed on the service-providing device. A user of this terminal proceeded only if the hash value was one of a terminal which complied to a certain policy.

The Trusted Computing Group specifies a mechanism in the form of a separate tamper-resistant hardware extension with a set of special purpose registers and functions. This security chip is used for measurement and as a reporting entity and it measures every piece of software or configuration which is going to be executed. These results are reported to the platform configuration registers (PCR) located on the security chip. It is then possible to decide later whether the system is in a known and trustworthy state after loading all these measured software components. The measurement starts with the core root of trust of measurement (CRTM) that checks the firmware, then the bootloader, the OS and the applications. During the boot process, every component is responsible for checking the next one loaded. Once the OS is up and running it becomes the OS's responsibility to make sure that every application is measured, i.e., its hash reported to a PCR in the security module for later evaluation. The transitive trust during boot is applied to extend the trusted domain and is illustrated in figure 1.

Due to the fact that the PCRs are hardware registers and the memory size of the TPM hardware module is limited, the TPM provides a mechanism to virtualize this limited set of registers by adding a hash value to a platform configuration register which already keeps a hash value. This mechanism is called

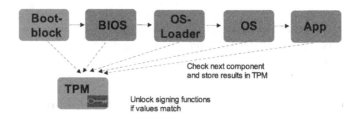

Fig. 1. *Transitive trust during system and application startup.* During boot, before the respective next component can be loaded it has to be reported to the trusted platform module (TPM) which calculates the corresponding hash and adds it to the platform configuration registers (PCR) and list of loaded components

Append to the list		Extend the PCR(reg) with TPM_Extend
$hash(executable_n)$	$executable_n$	$PCR_n(reg)=hash(PCR_{n-1}(reg) \mid hash(executable_n))$
...	...	...
$hash(executable_3)$	$executable_3$	$PCR_3(reg)=hash(PCR_2(reg) \mid hash(executable_3))$
$hash(executable_2)$	$executable_2$	$PCR_2(reg)=hash(PCR_1(reg) \mid hash(executable_2))$
$hash(executable_1)$	$executable_1$	$PCR_1(reg)=hash(PCR_0(reg) \mid hash(executable_1))$
$hash(executable_0)$	$executable_0$	$PCR_0(reg)=hash(PCR_{nil}(reg) \mid hash(executable_0))$

Fig. 2. *Extension of a PC-Register on the TPM and maintaining a hash chain.* On the left, the list of hashes is displayed, containing the hashes of the loaded executables from the first (index zero) to the last one (index n). On the right, the corresponding platform configuration register (PCR) extensions are shown, illustrating how the PCR value is updated by calculating a hash over the old value concatenated with the new value. The register number *reg* stays the same during the process, as in our case only one of the at least sixteen available PC registers is used to attest the validity of the hash chain

extension and can be used with the command *TPM_Extend*. This command concatenates an existing value in a selected PC-Register with the hash value of an application or library to load, hashes this value again and stores it in the same PCR. By keeping a list of all single hash values which were extended to a selected PCR it is possible for a challenger to verify the chain of hashes step by step and identify all executables or library parts of the system [8]. The following figure 2 illustrates this:

To decide if the platform which should process sensitive personal data behaves as it claims to, one has to know about the behavior of the software and the platform. Trusted Computing mechanisms can guarantee a proper measurement of software, but, as mentioned above, a trusted third party has to provide information on the classification of software and hardware components as conformant to a given policy or level of trustworthiness. This can be seen as a technical replacement for a trust or privacy certificate presented when a web-based service is used in the Internet. Contrary to what certificates usually are used for, here

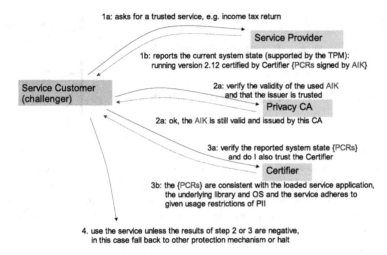

Fig. 3. *Attestation and mapping of a service-providing machine.* The customer only uses the service if the service provider is trusted, provides a valid system attestation and the service complies with the desired policies

the certificates are not interpreted as proof of identity of a device or a system but as proof of the behavior thereof.

A service user, who is interested as to whether a presented service on a machine is in conformance to his personal policy, performs the following steps.

1. He first requests the state of the machine which claims to offer the service. As a result, he gets a set of PCRs signed with an Attestation Identity Key (AIK).
2. Then the service user verifies the authenticity of the TPM to decide if the reported PCR hash values can be treated as authentic values. Obviously, the issuer of the AIK which was used to sign the PCRs in the previous step has to be issued by a trust authority, which is trusted by the challenging service user.
3. The service user then interprets the attested hash values and the hash chain. He uses local knowledge from a previous transaction or queries a third party to find out a mapping of a running service on the service-providing machine to a policy which is conformant to his personal one. The complexity of this mapping increases with the number of different software versions and patches. Research on how to simplify this is done by Haldar et al [9] and is beyond the scope in this paper.

This procedure is visualized in figure 3.

This provides a challenger with a view to the attested system at the time the PC-registers are signed. Since the attestation step has to be carried out before a service is used, there is a time window in which the system can change its configuration. For example, it is possible that a service with a known hash value

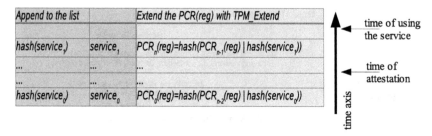

Fig. 4. *Using a different service despite of a valid machine attestation.* After attestation at time t, a second service (index 9) is started. If service 5 was stopped between t and $t + \Delta t$ and service 9 is now running on the access point the user expects service 5 to be at, the user will not be communicating with the desired service. No matter whether service 9 is a malicious service or a trusted service, this problem has to be addressed as we want the user to get the exact service he chose

was in the list of attested applications but in the meantime this service was stopped and an untrustworthy service has registered at the same service access point.

We can also consider the case where a device runs two service applications on a service-providing device, each of them being conformant to a different policy or level of trustworthiness. For a challenger and user of this service it is therefore essential to continue the usage of the service with a selected policy only. This requires a link between the attested system state and the service (and service access point) which can be validated when the service is used. This security weakness caused by the time delay is showed in figure 4.

The second reason why a link between the system state attestation and a service is necessary is to avoid a man-in-the-middle attack which could take place after a challenger has successfully attested a system and proceeds to use a service on this system. If there were no link between these two tasks, it would be possible for an attacker to take over the communication at this point.

4   Our Approach

Our approach to solve the problems mentioned in the previous section is to introduce service-dependent associations between the attestation results and individual services. This enables a challenger to detect whether he is communicating with a service application he does not expect to communicate with. It also prevents a user accidentally selecting an application or service that could not be verified as trusted which could easily happen on a system offering several services but not all of them being trusted. On the other hand, this prevents a man-in-the-middle attack where a malicious system takes over the communication after the attestation of a system but before using the application. It is not enough for the attested system to announce the location where the service can be accessed in an authentic way, because, after the attestation, the user would

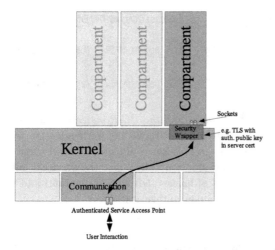

Fig. 5. *OS provided wrapper for authenticated service access points on socket request.* TLS is used to protect the communication channel between the service-providing system and the user's system. The service's public key is used as TLS server certificate so that only the intended service can decrypt incoming data correctly - without using the public key another service could be eavesdropping

have no assurance that when using the service the same service is still running at that location - a malicious service could have taken over in-between.

The solution we propose to remedy this security weakness was designed with respect to simplicity and transparency. Simplicity is achieved by using built-in mechanisms of the TPM. Transparency is achieved by exposing the usual socket interface to the application, therefore avoiding adaptations of the applications.

In order to assure that the challenger will always be communicating with the desired, specifically chosen service on a certain service access point only, we introduce a link between the attestation and the corresponding service by using cryptographic keys in the communication process (as opposed to using cryptography for authentication only). When a service is started and requests a socket from the operating system, the OS generates a private/public key pair and assigns it to the specific service running on the requested socket. The purpose is to exactly re-identify this service by using this key when it comes to the service usage. It is important to annotate that we treat the public part of this key pair as an executable file. This means that its hash value is added to the hash chain of loaded applications and the corresponding PCR is extended accordingly. This workaround is necessary because the Attestation Identity Keys which are used to attest a machine can only sign the content of a PC-register. When a machine is attested, the hash of this public key is announced and signed and a service user can check a presented key pair of a selected service by the verification of its hash value. This wrapping is illustrated in figure 5. During the authentication process, the challenger's OS receives the public key and then has to encrypt all further data sent to the service. The receiving OS, keeping a list of all service-

Append to the list		Extend the PCR(reg) with TPM_Extend
$hash(public\ key_{service\ N})$	$public\ key_{service\ N}$	$PCR_{new}(reg)=hash(PCR_{previous}(reg)\ \|\ hash(public\ key_{service\ N}))$
...	...	...
$hash(service_N)$	$service_N$	$PCR_{new}(reg)=hash(PCR_{previous}(reg)\ \|\ hash(service_N))$

Fig. 6. *Extending the hash chain and the PC-Register with a service authentication key.* Sending the service's public key without any authentication would not lead to a secure service access point as an attacker could simply insert other keys that allowed malicious services to steal information. Therefore, the service's public key is hashed and its hash added to the list of hashes (left side of diagram) and to the PCR (right side of diagram) so that it becomes authenticated

socket combinations, decrypts the data before passing it on to the service so that the service does not have to take care of decryption. While on this level only the user has to encrypt the data sent to the service and the service itself does not encrypt, on a lower level TLS [10] or alternatively some other socket layer cryptographic protocol will be used to protect the exchanged messages. The service's key pair and especially its hash serve the purpose of creating an attestation for the user that he will only be talking to the service that he verified on a certain service access point.

Since the OS provides a unique key pair for each service-socket combination, there is no way a malicious service registering to the service access point or listening to the channel could get any information other than the encrypted data as long as the OS provides strong process isolation.

The public key necessary for communication with a service is transmitted as follows: after generating the key pair, the OS adds the public key's hash to the list of hashes that is used for attestation. As writing directly into a PCR is not possible, the OS has to put the public key in a file on the harddisk first and then pretend to be loading the file as an application. This fake application is then hashed by the TPM and a PCR is extended with the hash value which is also appended to the list of hashes as is done with every application, so now the public key's hash value has been added to the list of hashes (as shown in figure 6). Together with the hash value the name of the corresponding service and its hash value are added so that the challenger knows exactly which key to use to talk to a specific, attested service. Also, the entry shows that it is a service's public key's hash and so the challenger does not have to ask the TTP about it[1].

What if an attacker manages to tamper with the list of hashes before it reaches the challenger? Changing the hash values would lead to the attestation hash becoming invalid so the challenger would not continue the communication. However, an attacker might be able to change the names of the applications on the list. In this very unlikely event, the worst that could happen would be the

---

[1] the hash would be unknown to the TTP anyway.

service not being able to decrypt the incoming data: if the challenger did not check the content of the list of hashes with the TTP, the attestation hash would verify successfully but then the challenger would use the wrong public key to encrypt the data that is about to be send to the service. If the challenger checked with the TTP, he could tell from the TTP's information on the applications' hash that the list had been tampered with.

5   Discussion

Allowing a service to execute other applications after attestation puts at risk the quality of the attestation. Imagine a service that has been loaded, successfully attested and started. Then, before or maybe even after service and user start exchanging data, the service loads a malicious application as a plugin. Although with the malicious application loaded the system's attestation would fail the next time it was checked, for now the user still thinks he is talking to an attested service running on an attested system. However, the malicious plugin could easily steal all information the service provides it with. Therefore, services loading unknown applications would either have to be banned (a rather theoretical possibility) or marked as dangerous. an alternative would be sandboxing.

The processing power needed to calculate the hashes and perform encryption should not pose a problem. Today's mobile devices might not be able to handle several encrypted connections at the same time. Because of low bandwidth, display limitations and the rather poor distribution of publicly available services so far this is not a serious issue. By the time the other problems have been solved the processing power will be more than sufficient.

From a usability point of view, our approach does not impose any burden on the user. All the necessary keys can be computed automatically without the user even noticing that they are computed, let alone the user having to click through some complicated, "cryptic" form. Furthermore, none of the keys have to be stored on a device the user would have to provide (e.g., a hard disk or smartcard), in fact, except for the TPM's keys which are stored inside the TPM itself, no keys at all need to be kept longer than the service is being used. Also, as the OS will take care of the complete attestation process, the services will not have to be changed or re-implemented.

6   Related Work

There is some work that is related to the idea of qualifying or authenticating the behavior of a device (or a service running on it) in a pervasive computing environment. This was discussed by Creese et al in [3]. The authors consider self-certifying software and hardware sending its configuration to get a clue on the behavior. However, they did not present an architecture.

Haldar et al discussed the mapping of the behavior of an application in [9]. They use a virtual machine on top of a trusted computing-capable operating system to describe and monitor the information flow inside it. They mention the need of a shared secret to prevent hijacking of a session between a challenger and the attested system.

Campadello et al [11] emphasize the need of trustworthy services with secure access points in order for customers to trust and thus use pervasive computing services.

Lie et al [12] have discussed a hardware-based approach and trust model where applications are running in an isolated and encrypted compartment and can attest themselves. This approach requires more and deeper changes to the hardware than the sole introduction of a TP module; also, it aims more at copy protection than service authentication.

An integrity measurement architecture based on the Trusted Computing Group specification and an implementation on a Linux operating system were described by Sailer et al [8]. This approach allows a system to attest its state just like it is needed for secure service access points but does not address the problem of malicious services being started *after* attestation.

7   Conclusions and Future Work

Using the proposed approach, users could be sure of talking to the exact service they had chosen to talk to while excluding men-in-the-middle attacks and malicious services[2]. Thus, users should be more willing to participate in wireless communications as many will find it easier to trust in a small piece of rather tamper-proof hardware than purely depending on their service provider's goodwill – keeping in mind that, as mentioned above, the user will often not easily be able to tell to which service provider he is about to connect to.

Protecting the services while requiring changes in the OS only, the approach would not affect the large group of application developers or hinder the development of new services. Existing legacy applications can also be used without the need of any modifications.

As there will be a huge number of smart devices offering services, it might prove useful to not solely depend on a trusted third party for information on those services' expected behavior but also use techniques like proof-carrying codes [13] or semantic type-checking languages [14] where applicable and available.

With increasingly more people using smart devices and more services being offered that companies earn money with, over time we expect users to be exposed to an increasing number of fraudulent services. Secure service access points can help avoid fraud and reduce misuse of (personal) data.

---

[2] unless the user deliberately chooses to use a service whose behavior is unknown or bad according to the TTP's evaluation.

Furthermore, we will be looking into implementing a prototype demonstrating the concept based on an operating system which supports trusted computing hardware, such as Linux [15], Perseus [16], or NetBSD [17].

Acknowledgment

Part of this work was funded by the DFG/Gottlieb Daimler and Karl Benz Foundation.

References

1. Weiser, M.: The Computer of the 21st Century (1991) Scientific American, vo.265. no.3, Sept.1991, pp 66-75.
2. Langheinrich, M.: Privacy by Design – Principles of Privacy-Aware Ubiquitous Systems. In Abowd, G., Brumitt, B., Shafer, S., eds.: Ubicomp 2001 Proceedings. Volume 2201 of Lecture Notes in Computer Science., Springer (2001) 273–291
3. Creese, S., Goldsmith, M., Roscoe, B., Zakiuddin, I.: Authentication for Pervasive Computing. In: Proceedings of the first International Conference on Security in Pervasive Computing, Boppard, LNCS 2802, Springer (2003)
4. Trusted Computing Group: TCG Backgrounder (2003) https://www.trustedcomputinggroup.org/downloads/TCG_Backgrounder.pdf.
5. IBM Corporation: Developer's view of IBM PowerPC Reference Platform (2003) http://www-306.ibm.com/chips/products/powerpc/newsletter/mar2003/ ppc_process_at_work.html.
6. Kinney, S.: Embedded Security Seminar: The Trusted Platform Module Specification and Integrating the Trusted Platform Module into Embedded Systems (2004) http://www.cmpevents.com/ESCe04/a.asp?option=G&V=3&id=271270.
7. Hohl, A., Zugenmaier, A.: Safeguarding Personal Data with DRM in Pervasive Computing. In: Proceedings of the Security and Privacy Workshop of the Pervasive 2004 Conference, Vienna. (2004)
8. Sailer, R., Zhang, X., Jaeger, T., van Doorn, L.: Design and Implementation of a TCG-based Integrity Measurement Architecture. In: 13th Usenix Security Symposium, San Diego, 2004. (2004)
9. Haldar, V., Chandra, D., Franz, M.: Semantic Remote Attestation - A Virtual Machine Directed Approach to Trusted Computing. In USENIX, ed.: Proceedings 3rd Virtual Machine Research and Technology Symposium VM'04, San Jose, Berkeley, CA, USA, USENIX (2004) 29–41
10. Dierks, T., Allen, C.: RFC 2246: The TLS Protocol Version 1.0 (1999) http://www.ietf.org/rfc/rfc2246.txt.
11. Stefano Campadello, Ronan MacLaverty, T.S.: Security and Reliability Challenges in Component-Based Software for Consumer Devices. In: The IASTED International Conference on Software Engineering, 2004 Innsbruck, Austria. (2004) http://www.nokia.com/library/files/docs/CamMacSar.pdf.
12. Lie, D., Thekkath, C.A., Horowitz, M.: Implementing an Untrusted Operating System on Trusted Hardware. In: In Proceedings of the 19th ACM Symposium on Operating Systems Principles (SOSP). (2003) http://www.eecg.toronto.edu/ lie/papers/lie-sosp2003.pdf.

13. Necula, G.C., Lee, P.: Safe Kernel Extensions Without Run-Time Checking. In USENIX, ed.: 2nd Symposium on Operating Systems Design and Implementation (OSDI '96), October 28–31, 1996. Seattle, WA, Berkeley, CA, USA, USENIX (1996) 229–243

14. Myers, A.C., Liskov, B.: Protecting Privacy using the Decentralized Label Model. ACM Transactions on Software Engineering and Methodology **9** (2000) 410–442

15. IBM Corporation: Global Security Analysis Lab: TCPA Resources (2003) http://www.research.ibm.com/gsal/tcpa/.

16. Pfitzmann, B., Riordan, J., Stueble, C., Waidner, M., Weber, A.: Die PERSEUS Systemarchitektur (2001)
http://www-krypt.cs.uni-sb.de/download/papers/PfRSWW2001a.pdf.

17. Wash, R.: TCPA support on NetBSD (2004)
http://www.citi.umich.edu/u/rwash/projects/trusted/netbsd.html.

Security Issues of Mobile Devices

Claudia Eckert

Technische Universität Darmstadt,
Fachbereich 20, FG Sicherheit in der Informationstechnik,
64289 Darmstadt, Germany
Fraunhofer Institut für Sichere Informationstechnologie (SIT),
64295 Darmstadt, Germany

The growing use of the Internet combined with new prospects provided by mobile technologies (e.g. mobile devices, mobile and wireless communication) are leading to major changes in our working and private life. People will be able to communicate anytime, anywhere and with anyone. Technological advances as well as the increased number of mobile applications drive a change in mobile end-user equipment. Smart mobile devices will be equipped with various communication technologies like GSM/GPRS, 802.11-WLAN, Bluetooth, NFC and RFID chips as well as GPS for location awareness. Mobile devices already offer a broad spectrum of functionalities including a web browser to access information resources anywhere, a JavaVM to download and execute mobile applications and an e-mail client to exchange digital content with anyone.

On the downside, once people are always on - at home, in the office, on the move - they will also face new security risks. Though most of the security issues with mobile devices are not necessarily new the specific characteristics of mobile devices (e.g. portability) require new solutions. Security issues arise in three main areas: (1) secure management of assets stored in the mobile device, (2) secure communication within trusted and non-trusted environments (including privacy issues) and (3) secure interaction with critical IT infrastructures.

Due to the characteristics of mobile devices well-known best practice security measures are insufficient (if present at all). Increasing loss statistics tell about millions of lost or stolen mobile devices which store lots of sensitive data. Strong user (not only device) authentication is required to protect the user against identity theft. Stored data (e.g. RAS passwords) must be strongly protected (e.g. file encryption) against unauthorized access. As the first PDA viruses (e.g. Brador) have been observed in the wild, mobile devices must be protected from malicious software as well. Current attacks against Bluetooth and well-known WLAN and GPRS vulnerabilities reveal the high risk that mobile devices will be taken over by attackers. We need a paradigm shift from perimeter security using central firewalls and virus checks towards decentralised controls integrated into devices. In addition, new concepts like staged controls are required to assert a required level of security. A manual patch management is no longer feasible due to the large amount of mobile devices. New approaches towards self-protecting, self-healing systems are required.

D. Hutter and M. Ullmann (Eds.): SPC 2005, LNCS 3450, p. 163, 2005.
© Springer-Verlag Berlin Heidelberg 2005

Privacy for Profitable Location Based Services[*]

Tobias Kölsch[1], Lothar Fritsch[2], Markulf Kohlweiss[2], and Dogan Kesdogan[1]

[1] RWTH Aachen University, Ahornstrasse 55, 52074 Aachen, Germany
{koelsch, kesdogan}@i4.informatik.rwth-aachen.de
[2] Johann Wolfgang Goethe University Frankfurt am Main, Gräfstrasse 78,
60054 Frankfurt am Main, Germany
{fritsch, kohlweiss}@whatismobile.de

Abstract. Location based services (LBS) are distributed multi-party infrastructures with the opportunity to generate profitable m-business applications. Also, LBS pose a great risk for their users' privacy, as they have access to private information about a person's whereabouts in a particular context. As location data is the essential input for LBS, protection of privacy in LBS is not a problem of providing anonymity by supressing data release, but a problem of identity management and control over information handling. In this paper we show a solution that ensures a LBS user's control over location information with managed identities. At the same time, our solution enables profitable business models, e.g. for mobile telephony operators. Additionally, we provide fine-grained consent management for the LBS user.

1 Introduction

Location based services (LBS) can pose a privacy risk to their users if they collect and use data against a user's intention. Most of the LBS are provided by mobile communications providers that can measure a user's whereabouts by localizing his mobile device while it uses the network infrastucture. Can LBS be delpoyed in a privacy-respecting way, and still be profitable applications on the commercial market of online-services? How does a privacy-respecting architecture look like? In this paper, we will answer the question by fulfilment of these requirements:

- Enable established business models on a secure, privacy-friendly architecture
- Ensure efficiency & economy of the solution
- No localization violates a user's consent
- Enable users to manage policies & their 'online' identities for each service provider and for each usage cycle
- Hide service usage patterns from observers & infrastructure providers
- Confidentiality of communication content against observers & infrastructure

---

[*] This work was supported by the IST PRIME project; however, it represents the view of the authors only.

D. Hutter and M. Ullmann (Eds.): SPC 2005, LNCS 3450, pp. 164–178, 2005.
© Springer-Verlag Berlin Heidelberg 2005

We use a health-related LBS as an example scenario. An *allergy warning LBS* tracks Mr. John Primeur with his mobile phone. When joining the service, John first registers a profile of his allergies. Then, at the service, data about allergenes is correlated with weather conditions in John's environment. John's position is regularly checked by localizing his mobile phone. When the weather and allergene status indicate an allergy risk for John, he receives a warning on his mobile phone. On the other hand, John dislikes the idea that his identity combined with his allergy profile could become known to the LBS, his mobile network operator, or a health insurance company.

Our paper is organized as follows. First, we give an overview over related work in the fields of LBS business models, privacy relevant research, and technological developments that are important for our design. Then, we describe and analyze our privacy-friendly approach, in particular the security protocols that ensure privacy and establish user control. Finally, we summarize our achievements.

2   Related Work

For privacy-respecting LBS architectures, this section presents relevant work and requirements in LBS business models, privacy relevant research, and technological developments of LBS infrastructures.

2.1   Related Work on Business Models

Mobile Commerce applications differ from e-commerce applications in four properties [1]. *Ubiquity / Reachability* enable applications to be used from anywhere, any time. *Context Sensitivity* supports applications provided for a particular context. *Identification / Personalization* takes advantage of mobile networks providing identity management technologies that enable personalized, authenticated, and paid-for personal applications. Finally, *Telemetry / 'Remote Control'* functions enable users to remotely control applications or processes.

Camponovo [2] describes a generic m-commerce business model as a mesh of parties of infrastructure, service, technology, user, communication and regulation domains. As LBS are a special form of m-commerce, Camponovo's model also applies to them.

Business Model Overview. Location data for LBS is either provided by the communication network or by specialized hardware at the user device. The location of a person is highly sensitive data. Thus regulation authorities have an interest in controlling its usage.

The actual LBS are offered by application providers. Due to their infrastructure, mobile operators may act as localization providers, as portal operators or even as application providers themselves.

Basic LBS Business Scenarios. LBS business models can be divided into the scenarios shown in figure 1.

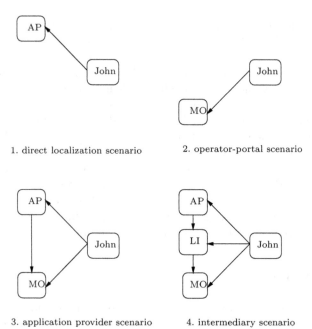

Fig. 1. Four different scenarios of LBS business models. AP: application provider, John: User, MO: Mobile Operator, LI: Location Intermediary

1. The mobile device and the application provider take care of localization and application processing. The mobile network is used as a data channel. This is the *direct localization scenario*.
2. The mobile operator does the localization and provides the application as a part of the operator's portal. This is the *operator-portal scenario*.
3. The mobile operator delivers communication and localization, but the LBS is provided by independent application providers. This is the *application provider scenario*.
4. An intermediary collects localization information from various sources (operators, GPS, WLAN), aggregates it and serves as an location broker for application providers. This is the *intermediary scenario*.

For further reading, the PRIME framework [3] provides an overview of different LBS together with their privacy and identity management requirements.

The intermediary scenario is the most interesting business model for our LBS privacy solution. The reasons are:

Interoperability: An intermediary provides an interface for LBS providers, allowing them to access location data in a unified way. *Multi-channel strategy:* An intermediary can collect location data from various sources. *Synergetic location aggregation:* An intermediary can aggregate multi-channel location information for the benefit of higher quality (see [4] for an algorithm). *Simplification:* An intermediary simplifies process handling for LBS providers by removing the need to negotiate contracts with various location sources. *Cross-Operator application:* Without an intermediary, the creation of user-to-user LBS with customers using mobile services at distinct mobile operators is much harder. *Pricing advantages:* Intermediaries provide many economic benefits in information markets. Intermediary location data can be cheaper to acquire from an intermediary than from a locaton provider for LBS that consume small amounts of location data. Other benefits of information intermediaries can be found in [5]. The allergy warning service in our example uses a location intermediary to gather location data. This service includes both the more privacy-threatening scenario of permanent tracking (Barkhuus results imply tracking as being perceived as intrusive in [6]), as well as the economically more interesting intermediary model sketched above.

2.2   LBS and Privacy

User Expectations. Research in sociology and psychology produced results about users' attitudes, assumptions and requirements. Relevant facts have been found by Kim Sheehan in [7], where four groups of consumers are found to exist: unconcerned Internet users, circumspect Internet users, wary Internet users, and alarmed Internet users. In [8], survey research found that besides the FTC's fair information practices for e-commerce [9], consumers worry about three more issues: consumer control over information-collection, information exchange between companies, and relationship towards the collector of personal information. Concerning the information to be protected, Gary Marx proposes in [10] seven distinct dimensions of personal identity. Little work has been done to assess LBS specific privacy concerns. Barkhuus and Dey found out in [6] that tracking services are perceived far more intrusive by users than other position-aware services.

Technology. Privacy enhancing technologies (PET) provide pseudonymity, anonymity and identity management in LBS. Federath et al [11] proposed the use of a trusted fixed station and Mixes [12] for hiding the linkage of real world identities to location data in todays mobile telephone networks. The idemix identity management system [13] implements cryptographic credentials for privacy protection. Researchers started to develop LBS specific PETs called mix-zones (see [14] and [15]). This allows for switching location pseudonyms in a unobservable way. Anonymity and pseudonymity are only two aspects of privacy. Additionally control over the flow of information, policies and user consent have to be considered. Policy management can be modeled with EPAL [16] or P3P [17]. Work has been done concerning requirements for LBS privacy policies. Myles et al. investigated the use of a middleware server for evaluating policy rules and Snekkenes [18] identifies concepts for formulating such policies. Usually consent is expressed by accepting the privacy policy of a service. This process may be automated by comparing the privacy policy of the service with the privacy preferences of their users. Explicit user consent is a hard requirement in many legal systems, particularly within the European Union.

Economic Aspects of Privacy. It is often stated that privacy won't sell, and that people will sell their privacy for little but 'immediate gratification'. Nevertheless privacy is a concern of many individuals and privacy legislations exist that manifest these concerns on a national and international level. In [19] Jaisingh et al. examine the effects of different privacy regimes and find evidence that a higher privacy regime increases the efficiency of the exchange of personal identifiable information. In [20] Acquisti distinguishes between on-line identities (pseudonyms) and off-line identities (real world identities). He describes the advantages of using pseudonyms and advocates a more cautious use of real world identities. Many people tend to act myoptic not heeding the long-term consequences, e.g. the build-up of information asymmetries or threats related to identity theft or credit fraud. Thus, in the on-line market merchants decide against offering privacy enhancing technologies and privacy concerned customers reduce their on-line activities.

2.3   Standards and Architectures for LBS and Privacy

Location Interoperability Forum Privacy Guidelines. The former Location Interoperability Forum (LIF), now within Open Mobile Alliance (OMA), drafted a set of privacy guidelines for location-based services in [21]. The document also contains a collection of use cases and data flow examples respecting the LIF privacy guidelines. The main privacy guidelines are: *Collection limitation:* Location data shall only be collected when the location of the target is required to provide a certain service. *Consent:* Before any location data collection can occur, the informed consent of the controller has to be obtained. Consent may be restricted in several ways, to a single transaction, certain service providers etc. The controller must be able to access and change his or her preferences. It must be possible at all times to withdraw all consents previously given, to opt-out with simple means, free of additional charges and independent of the technology used. *Usage and disclosure:* The processing and disclosure of location data shall be limited to what consent is given for. Pseudonymity shall be used when the service in question does not need to know the identity being served. *Security safeguards:* Location data shall be erased when the requested service has been delivered or made (under given consent) aggregate. Release of location information is regulated by a set of rules that govern the release of information. Users should be in control of the rules. The basic principle of LIF's concept is that location data is disclosed to an application by a *location service*. A location service consists of a *location data entity*, which already has the location data or uses a positioning method for location determination, a *location access control function* and *access control rules database*. Users have to trust the *location service*, which is placed at the network operators.

IETF Geopriv Standardization. The Internet Engineering Task Force (IETF) has initiated the Geopriv working group with the goal to generate a framework for privacy handling in LBS, resulting in RFC standards and draft papers. A good overview of Geopriv can be found in [22], where the drafts and RFCs

(IETF RFC 3693, 3694) are summarized and explained. Of particular interest are the Geopriv policy draft, the Geopriv requirements document and the Geopriv threads analysis. Geopriv processes location data by putting it into a *Location Object*. The object can carry other information like policies or intended use. The Geopriv architecture distinguishes between *Location Generator* (generates the location data), *Location Recipient* (the entity receiving the location object for LBS execution) and the *Location Server*, which is the entity deciding about releasing a *Location Object* considering the rules. Users have to trust in the policy-conformant behaviour of the *Location Server*, which is specified as an indendent entity.

GSM Association. The GSM association proposes an operator-centric architecture in [23]. Here, a *Target* is being localized upon a *Requestor*'s need. A *Clearing House* takes care of billing issues when LBS involve several operators, e.g. upon roaming with a GSM phone into a foreign network. Decisions about location release are made at the *Gateway Mobile Location Centre*, a service operated by a GSM network operator. The document mentions LBS operated by the mobile network operators as well as LBS provided by *Service Providers*, which have to cooperate with the network operators. Users have to trust the *Gateway Mobile Location Centre*, which is placed at the network operators.

OpenGIS. Within the OpenGIS standard, a location server platform called "'OpenGIS Location Services (OpenLS)"' has been specified in [24]. Here, the *GeoMobility Server* hosts a geographical information system with maps, navigaton algorithms and other geography-related services. It interfaces with a *service platform*, where the LBS is provided to the user. Location is acquired from an external source. All privacy related functionality is explicitly delegated away from OpenGIS to the operator of the service portal, where the LBS is hosted. Thus, there is no privacy architecture in OpenGIS.

Other Architectures. The academic community develops LBS platforms for various purposes, e.g. in [25], where privacy issues are deviced at the entity where the location data is available for distribution. Huber et al. describe the location trader platform as a powerful intermediary for LBS in [26], but do not specify privacy mechanisms beyond the claim that no user-specific data is stored on the platform.

3   A Privacy-Enabling LBS Architecture

3.1   Architecture Overview

This section explains our approach for a privacy-friendly LBS architecture. First, we sketch the architecture and roles, then we provide a protocol for IDM and consent managment for it. An architecture for providing LBS consists of a location source, in our case the mobile operator (MO), that is queried for our

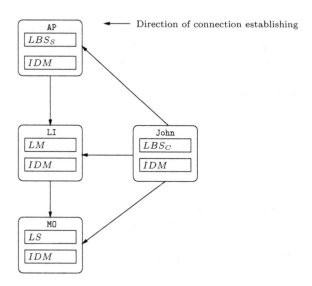

Fig. 2. The new components IDM and LM applied to the intermediary scenario

user John's location, a server operated by the application provider (AP) that provides the LBS application. We extended the basic intermediary scenario of allergy warnings with two new components. The first one is an identity management component (IDM) providing users with unlinkable pseudonyms for different business parties. The second component is the location matcher (LM). Its purpose is the secure implementation of push services. IDM and LM are used by the location intermediary (LI) to mediate between the AP's localization requests and the MO. The user is known under distinct pseudonyms to the MO and the AP. Both providers do not communicate directly with each other but use the LI. He knows the matching between the pseudonyms.

Consent Management. To subscribe to a new LBS, John creates an authorization token for the MO. The token is bound to a service specific privacy policy at the MO. This policy constrains under which conditions John may be localized, as detailed in [18]. By providing the authorization token to the AP, the user gives his consent for being localized by the AP. The consent is enforced by the MO by requiring the authorization token for location disclosure.

Location Management. If the MO has proof of John's consent, location data is released to the LI. The LI's location matcher stores user-specific areas of interest entered by the AP. The LI then queries the MO for John's location, and uses his location matcher to evaluate a push condition - e.g. John being within an area with allergenes. When John enters one of these areas, the AP is notified by the LI about John's location. A tracking AP doesn't know anything about the user's location until the user enters an area of interest. This prevents the AP from profiling John until he is in a place the service is required in.

Identity Management. In identity management systems (see [27], [28]), pseudonyms are the core mechanism of privacy aware identity management. Each pseudonym and the data linked to it comprises an on-line identity, or partial identity, of the user. The unlinkability of these partial identities is an important privacy protecting feature of our architecture. John creates a pseudonym for interaction with the MO and a different pseudonym for interaction with the AP. This is done for every new LBS John signs up to. The LI knows both pseudonyms, John's location and his areas of interest, but little more. This approach prevents the MO to learn about John's LBS usage.

3.2   A Protocol for Privacy Friendly Push Services

In this section a protocol for privacy-friendly LBS using a location intermediary LI is presented. This is done in form of a walk-through

Protocol Description. Every party involved in the protocol has an asymmetric key-pair enabling it to sign and to receive encrypted messages. Clearly this key is only used when the identity of the signer does not need to be protected, as the uniqueness of the key would lead to re-identification. This means that John can sign data sent to the MO, while he must not sign data sent to the AP.

The protocol is initiated by John, connecting to his mobile operator asking him to create a connector C_1 for a logical channel. The name of the connector must be unique, as it will be used as a pseudonym for John. Then John commits the public part of an asymmetric key-pair (E_{C_1}, D_{C_1}) and a privacy policy for the MO. E_{C_1} is used later on for authorizing access to the connector. The policy specifies the conditions for location data sent over the channel. After creating the channel connector, the MO binds John's policy and E_{C_1} to C_1 and sends a signed confirmation of the setup to John. This step is shown in Fig. 3(a).

John connects to the location intermediary and tells him to create a logical channel connector with a unique name C_2. John submits a public part of an asymmetric key pair (E_{C_2}, D_{C_2}) that will be used for authorizing access to the connector. He also submits an encrypted package that contains the name of the channel C_1, the corresponding decryption key D_{C_1}, and an authorization token A created by John stating that the MO is entitled to disclose his position. The token A must contain the name of the LI and may specify a validity period. These three items are encrypted using a symmetric cipher. The according key D is not sent to the LI. He will get access to the data only later, when the service has been initiated. Fig. 3(b) shows the described process. These two setup steps can be performed at arbitrary times before service initiation.

For service initialization John anonymously connects to the application provider and sends his allergy profile, that consists e.g. of a birch pollen allergy. John sends the name of the connector C_2 that was opened by the LI with the private key D_{C_2}, and the symmetric key D. This is depicted in Fig. 4. The AP uses John's allergy profile to find the birch pollen regions from his database and connects to the channel connector C_2. Mutual authentication between the application provider and the location intermediary is performed using some zero

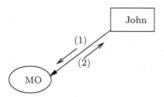

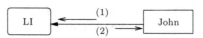

(a)   (1) John sends request to create connector, with public key to and privacy policy; (2) MO replies with confirmation of establishment of channel connector.

(b) (1) John sends request to create channel connector with public key and an encrypted data package containing information on how to connect to the channel from MO; (2) LI confirms channel connector creation.

Fig. 3. Setup of channel connectors for MO and LI

knowledge proof demonstrating that each party is in possession of its respective key. Then the areas of interest together with the location polling interval needed for the service are transmited to the LI's location matcher. Finally the AP transmits the decryption key D for decrypting the data package provided to the LI earlier to connect to the mobile operator.

The LI attaches this information together with the areas of interest to the channel C_2 and connects to the MO's channel connector C_1. He authenticates using the same method as the AP, and sends the authorization token A.

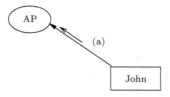

Fig. 4. Service initiation with AP: (a) John sends his allergy profile, the name of the communication channel from LI, the private key for authentication to that channel, and the decryption key for the data that is stored at LI

The LI requests John's position in the frequency specified by the application provider. The position is returned by the MO according to John's policies. If the LI finds a match of John's position and an area of interest, he notifies the AP. Now the AP sends an allergy warning to John. The warning is sent through the communication channel that has been opened by John. This anonymous channel needs to be kept open until the service is turned off.

To give John a monitor about the AP's actions, he can also connect to the channel C_2 (as he knows the keypair of the channel, authentication can also be performed), and request three types of informations: the regions of interest, the amount of map changes and the amount of events that have been sent to the AP so far.

John terminates the service by notifying the MO, who notifies the LI and closes C_1. Then the MO sends a signed confirmation to John. When the LI receives the notice of the shutdown, he closes the channel to the AP after notifying him of the impending closure. Then the LI deletes all data related to the session. Finally the AP closes the connection to John after notifying him of the closing.

All communication in the protocol is encrypted, authenticated and integrity protected. This is possible, as there is at least one asymmetric key-pair for each connection, that is used to set up secure channels. When John sets his policies with the MO, both parties have to authenticate mutually. Also note that the communication between John and the AP must be anonymized to enable to hide John's LBS usage patterns from the MO.

3.3   Security Evaluation

We evaluate the security the protocol provides against different attackers. First the strength of the approach against a global observer is inspected. Then we look at the risks arising from a single corrupt party, and finally the impact of cooperating corrupt providers will be analyzed.

Global Observer. A global observer is able to eavesdrop all communication passively. As all traffic is encrypted, the global observer does not gain information about the content of the messages. After protocol initiation he is aware of the connection between John and the mobile operator, and between John and the location intermediary. The connection between John and the application provider is not revealed to him, as communication is anonymized. Upon service shutdown there is a chain of communications: $John \rightarrow MO \rightarrow LI \rightarrow AP \rightarrow John$. This chain of events could be linked by a global observer. However this can be prevented if each party waits for random amount of time before promoting service shutdown to the next in line, thus effectively hiding one users actions in those of others.

Single Corrupt Service Provider. A single corrupt provider can be a service provider wanting to find out information about his users. It can also be an external attacker, that gained control over a providers infrstructure. A corrupt provider can change installed software and manipulate the protocol flow in order to gain further knowledge about the communication partners. We look at the different service providers in turn to find out what consequences their misbehavior could have on the users privacy.

Mobile operator: The most invading aggregation of personal information is in the hand of the MO. He usually knows John's name, address, etc and his current location. However, the information about which LBS is used by John is effectively hidden, as communication between John and the application provider is anonymized and as the LI does not reveal identifying information about the AP. The aggregation of information at the MO can be reduced if communication and location providing (together with the call routing) are done by distinct parties, e.g. by a trusted fixed station (see [11]) or by using temporal "pseudo mobile subscriber identities" instead of the usual "international mobile subscriber identities", as proposed in [29].

Location intermediary: The LI knows the areas of interest and the position of John, but he does not know who John is. If the spatial resolution is too high, deanonymization of John can be performed by physically checking who is at the specific position, or by analyzing the positions of general whereabouts and correlating them with residences in a map. These risks can be tackled by reducing the resolutions and changing the pseudonyms in unregular intervals. The policies that are connected to the communication channel C_1 control the admissible resolution. Pseudonym changes are not actively supported by the protocol. However, the pseudonym is changed each time the service is restarted or a new service is used, such that this is critical only for location based services that are used over a long period of time.

The LI knows the MO and the AP. Especially the knowledge of the AP can lead to a significant increase of available information for him as together with the areas of interest it gives a strong hint on the type of service used.

Application provider: The AP has John's allergy profile. Usually non trivial, multi dimensional sets of personal attributes permit for re-identification of an individual within large populations using pattern recognition approaches (see [30]). Another threat comes from the AP's capability to narrow down John's position by constructing the areas of interest in such a way that n overlapping areas of interest permit a subdivision of the entire area into 2^n distinguishable regions. The accuracy of the localization can be increased further by observing a succession of matching events. This can not be prevented directly by the user. But as he can check the regions of interest, the amount of map changes and the amount of events sent to the AP, he can detect anomalies and react to them by closing the communication channel.

Cooperation Between Corrupt Service Providers. Cooperating service providers can merge their data sources. They may also succeed to run cooperative attacks on the remaining communication partners in order to gain additional information. When the attacker controls the MO and the LI, John's name can be linked to all information on John, that can be deduced from the knowledge of the AP name and from the areas of interest.

If the LI and the AP cooperate, they can link his profile to his position and they can link John's mobile operator's name to the profile. When the service is used over a longer period, they can attack his anonymity directly, as discussed earlier for single cooperative corrupt providers, by finding out his name from his usual whereabouts.

If the MO and the AP want to break the anonymity gained through the protocol, they have to link the two partial identities of John. (John's name, address, etc on the one hand and his allergy profile on the other hand.) If the AP wants to know the name of John, he could send a specific area of interests to the LI and notify the MO about this choice. The MO could then, in successive time intervals, send a position within this region for every user that actually uses this LI. Then, if the LI sends a notification about a match to the AP, the deanonymization is successful. However, this attack constitutes a significant effort on the side of the MO. Another way to link both partial identities is based on timing attacks. E.g. the AP notifies the MO when the user of interest stopped the service usage. The MO then knows that John is one of the users who closed the connection to the specific LI shortly before he is notifies. This attack can be circumvented if the LI waits some random time before closing the connection to the AP, after the connection to the MO has been closed. The danger of linkability is similar to that found in MIX networks.

In the case that all three service providers cooperate, the deanonymization of John is trivial from the moment the AP has sent the decryption key D to the LI.

Anonymous Inter-provider Communication. Cooperation between the involved parties is relatively easy in the presented protocol, as the communication partners can identify each other using their connection information (on layer three of ISO/OSI network model). The cooperative attacks can be complicated by anonymizing the communication between John and the LI, and by using anonymous rendezvous-points (e.g. those presented in [31]) for the inter-provider communication. The only difference to the original protocol is that the service providers set up anonymous rendezvous-points instead of the logical channels. Now the two communication partners are effectively hindered from identifying each other using their network addresses.

Another advantage of this approach is that the LI can not use the knowledge of which AP contacted him to improve the quality of his assumptions on the kind of service that is used, and on John's profile.

The disadvantage of this approach is the increased resource consumption. This results from the computational overhead of anonymization, and the higher latencies in anonymization systems.

4   Conclusion

In this paper, we presented a new approach for implementing LBS. Our approach supports many LBS business models, as it considers infrastructure operated by mobile operators. A location intermediary mediates between operator and application providers. Thus, business scenarios can be implemented efficiently. We have designed an architecture and a protocol that help to protect user privacy. The protocol uses an intermediary that does the matching of areas of interest from the LBS provider with the user position provided by the mobile operator. The protocol divides the available identity information into multiple partial identities that can not easily be linked. A major feature of the protocol is its feasibility for contemporary mobile communication infrastructures, while it is on the other hand able to significantly reduce the information each involved party has about the user.

As a result it becomes possible to implement more efficient but still privacy friendly push services for real-world, multi-tier business models.

Cryptographic mechanisms are used not only for securing the confidentiality of communication content but for implementing identity management with pseudonyms and consent management by introducing the authorization token and anonymous channels. Our design manages the user's consent on a per service and per pseudonym basis both at MO and AP.

Future Work. Generally, in such a situation trusted hardware component at the MO or AP could be useful. Now the LM component needed for supporting push services could be running both at the MO or the AP on a trusted platform, while still assuring the partitioning of the user's data into multiple unlinkable partial identities. As of today such a trusted module for managing location information does not exist.

Our model provides little transparency for the user about which information is passed between LI and AP. We imagine using audit trails on both parties' systems to solve this problem.

In the future the protocol might also be extended to support scenarios where the position of multiple users need to be matched. Ways to provide the matching that use multi-party-protocols might be worthwhile to explore.

References

1. Turowski, K., Pousttchi, K.: Mobile Commerce: Grundlagen und Techniken. Springer, Berlin [u.a.] (2004)
2. Camponovo, G., Pigneur, Y.: Business model analysis applied to mobile business. In: ICEIS 2003. (2003)
3. PRIME WP 14.0: PRIME Public Deliverable D14.0a Framework V0. Technical report (2004) http://www.prime-project.eu.int.
4. Myllymaki, J., Edlund, S.: Location Aggregation from Multiple Sources. In Society, I.C., ed.: Proceedings of the Third International Conference on Mobile Data Management (MDM 2002), Singapore (2002)
5. Rose, F.: The economics, concept and design of information intermediaries - A theoretic approach. Information Age Economy. Physica-Verlag, Heidelberg (1999)
6. Barkhuus, L., Dey, A.: Location Based Services for Mobile Telephony: a study of users' privacy concerns. (2003)
7. Sheehan, K.: Toward a Typology of Internet Users and Online Privacy Concerns. The Information Society **18** (2002) 21–32
8. Sheehan, K.B., Grubbs Hoy, M.: Dimensions of Privacy Concern among Online Consumers. Journal of Public Policy and Marketing **19** (2000) 62–73

9. Federal Trade Commission: Privacy Online: Fair Information Practices in the Electronic Marketplace. Technical report (2000)
10. Marx, G.: What's in a name? - Some reflections on the Sociology of Anonymity. The Information Society **15** (1999)
11. Federrath, H., Jerichow, A., Kesdogan, D., Pfitzmann, A.: Security in Public Mobile Communication Networks. In: IFIP TC 6 International Workshop on Personal Wireless Communications, Aachen, Verlag der Augustinus Buchhandlung (1995) 105–116
12. Chaum, D.: Untraceable electronic mail, return addresses, and digital pseudonyms. Communications of the ACM 4(2) (1981)
13. Camenish, J., van Herreweghen, E.: Design and Implementation of the Idemix Anonymous Credential System - Research Report RZ 3419 . Technical report, Zürich (2002)
14. Beresford, A.R., Stajano, F.: Location Privacy in Pervasive Computing. IEEE Pervasive Computing **2** (2003) 46–55
15. Gruteser, M., Grunwald, D.: Anonymous usage of location-based services through spatial and temporal cloaking. In: Proceedings of First International Conference on Mobile Systems, Applications, and Services (MobiSys'03). (2003) 31–42
16. Ashley, P., Hada, S., Günter, K., Powers, C., Schunter, M.: Enterprise Privacy Authorization Language (EPAL 1.1) - IBM Research Report. Technical report (2003) `http://www.zurich.ibm.com/security/enterprise-privacy/epal/Specificatio\%n/index.html`.
17. Cranor, L., Langheinrich, M., Marchiori, M., Presler-Marshall, M., Reagle, J.: The Platform for Privacy Preferences 1.0 (P3P1.0) Specification - W3C Recommendation. Technical report (2002)
18. Snekkenes, E.: Concepts for personal location privacy policies. In: Proceedings of the 3rd ACM conference on Electronic Commerce, Tampa, Florida, USA (2001) 48–57
19. Jaisingh, J., Metha, S., Chaturvedi, A.: Privacy and Information Markets: An experimental study. In: PACIS. Volume Proceedings of the PACIS 2004., Shanghai (2004)
20. Acquisti, A.: Privacy and Security of Personal Information - Economic Incentives and Technological Solutions. In Camp, J.L., Lewis, S., eds.: Economics of Information Security. Kleuwer (2004)
21. Oinonen, K.: TR101 - LIF Privacy Guidelines. (2002)
22. Müller, M.: Standards for Geographic Location and Privacy: IETF's Geopriv. Datenschutz und Datensicherheit (DuD) **28** (2004) 297–303
23. GSM Association: Location Based Services - Permanent Reference Document SE.23. Technical report (2003)
24. Marbrouk, M., et. al.: OpenGIS Location Services (OpenLS): Core Services. (2004)
25. Synnes, K., Nord, J., Parnes, P.: Location Privacy in the Alipes Platform. Technical report, Lulea, Sweden (2002)
26. Huber, M., Dietl, T., Kammerl, J., Dornbusch, P.: Collecting and providing location information: The location trader. In: MoMuc, München, TU München (2003)
27. Clauß, S., Köhntopp, M.: Identity management and its support of multilateral security. Computer Networks (2001) 205–219 `http://drim.inf.tu-dresden.de/`.
28. Jendricke, U., tom Markotten, D.G.: Usability meets security - the identity-manager as your personal security assistant for the internet. In: Proceedings of 16th Annual Computer Security Applications Conference, New Orleans, USA (2000)

29. Kesdogan, D., Reichl, P., Junghärtchen, K.: Distributed Temporary Pseudonyms: A New Approach for Protecting Location Information in Mobile Communication Networks. Volume 1485 of LNCS., Springer-Verlag (1998)
30. Winkler, W.E.: Re-identification methods for masked microdata. Volume 3050 of LNCS., Berlin Heidelberg, Springer-Verlag (2004) 216–230
31. Dingledine, R., Mathewson, N., Syverson, P.: Tor: The second-generation onion router. In: Proceedings of the 13th USENIX Security Symposium. (2004)

On the Anonymity of Periodic Location Samples

Marco Gruteser and Baik Hoh

Winlab / Electrical and Computer Engineering Department Rutgers,
The State University of New Jersey,
94 Brett Rd, Piscataway, NJ 08854
{gruteser, baikhoh}@winlab.rutgers.edu

Abstract. As Global Positioning System (GPS) receivers become a common feature in cell phones, personal digital assistants, and automobiles, there is a growing interest in tracking larger user populations, rather than individual users. Unfortunately, anonymous location samples do not fully solve the privacy problem. An adversary could link multiple samples (i.e., follow the footsteps) to accumulate path information and eventually identify a user.

This paper reports on our ongoing work to analyze privacy risks in such applications. We observe that linking anonymous location samples is related to the data association problem in tracking systems. We then propose to use such tracking algorithms to characterize the level of privacy and to derive disclosure control algorithms.

1 Introduction

The continuous improvements in accuracy and cost of Global Positioning System (GPS) receivers are driving new location tracking applications with a massive user base. For example, in the United States, cell phone providers can determine the positions of emergency callers through Assisted GPS, and the German federal government is funding the development of a GPS-based highway toll collection system for trucks. These systems are capable of sampling location information from a large numbers of users.

We anticipate great demand for this data, going far beyond the original applications of emergency positioning or toll collection. Aside from hotly debated uses such as in law enforcement and targeted marketing, there are also clearly benevolent uses. For example, vehicles could report the location of abrupt braking activity to improve road safety, navigation systems that optimize traffic flows could alleviate congestion and pollution, or movement models collected from cell phones may help predicting the spread of infectious diseases.

Sharing location information, however, raises privacy concerns [1, 2]. For example, frequent visits to clinics signal medical problems, attending meetings may reveal political preferences, and meetings of influential business managers could indicate pending business deals. As such, the problem of sharing location information is analogous to hospitals publishing medical records to epidemiologists and other medical researchers—it can be beneficial to society but invades on privacy.

Anonymizing data provides a solution that enables data access while maintaining privacy. Sweeney [3, 4] pointed out, however, that naive anonymization strategies, such as

D. Hutter and M. Ullmann (Eds.): SPC 2005, LNCS 3450, pp. 179–192, 2005.

omitting names and street addresses, can in many cases be circumvented by a determined adversary. The combination of several factors (e.g., age, gender, zip code, race) may be sufficiently distinctive to correlate the data with other databases to reidentify individuals.

Similarly, Beresford and Stajano have reported in their pioneering work on the anonymity of location *traces* [5] how such traces can be identified. They then proposed the mix zone concept as an approach to split paths into unlinkable segments to increase privacy. In our earlier work [6], we have concentrated on the anonymity of *point* information, as used by many location-based queries. We developed mechanisms to dynamically adjust the accuracy of position information in location-based queries to maintain a predefined level of anonymity. These mechanisms were based on the assumption that queries are very sporadic and therefore can be adjusted independently. If sample points are revealed more frequently, the trajectory of a user may be used to link multiple samples and independence is not guaranteed. In this sense, time-series information like location differs significantly from medical records.

The class of applications considered here lies in between these concepts. Users report their location more frequently, so that the data cannot be anonymized as individual points, but they do not reveal a pseudonym that would link the points into location traces.

As such, this ongoing work can be viewed as bridging the gap between point anonymity and trace anonymity. We study how an adversary can exploit trajectory information to link anonymous location samples to location traces and identify multi-target tracking algorithms as a key threat. Based on these results we discuss the effect of sample rate on privacy and how formulations in multiple hypothesis tracking are helpful for deriving privacy mechanisms.

The remainder of this paper is structured as follows. Section 2 defines the class of applications and the privacy problem that this paper addresses. We introduce multi-target tracking algorithms in Sec. 3. Section 4 describes our experiments with such an algorithm on location samples collected through GPS and Sec. 4.2 discusses the results. Section 5 reviews related work before we conclude with Sec. 6.

2   Threat Assessment

We motivate the class of applications considered in this paper with an example from the automotive industry. There is interest in inferring traffic conditions from data collected in vehicles [7]. Selected vehicles could periodically send their location, speed, road temperature, windshield wiper status, and other information to a traffic monitoring facility. This data reveals the length of traffic jams (through speed and position), weather conditions such as rain (through windshield wiper activity), and slick road conditions (through frequent anti-lock braking). Using vehicles as mobile sensing platforms promises dramatic cost reductions over deploying specialized roadside sensors.

Generally, we will consider a class of remote data collection applications. This class of applications requires a large number of users to concurrently reveal anonymous location information to an external untrusted service provider. The data are collected with a well-known sample frequency f. We can characterize the data that an external service provider receives as follows. The data comprises a series of tuples containing sensor data, latitude, longitude, and time. The sensor data could be any sensor reading associated with this location such as road temperature or anti-lock braking activity. We assume, however, that the sensor readings themselves do not contain any information distinctive enough to enable tracking of individual users. Latitude and longitude can be initially determined locally on a user's device (e.g., in a car), through external infrastructure (e.g., a cell phone provider's network), or hybrid approaches. We assume, however, that the user can trust the device or infrastructure that initially senses position.

We also assume the existence of a trusted proxy that anonymizes location updates before they are passed on to the external service provider. In a cell phone based system, for example, the proxy could arguably be operated by the cell-phone provider, who operates the location tracking infrastructure and sends data to third-party application providers. Anonymizing location updates means removing identifier like user ids or network addresses, but also mixing of messages to counter timing attacks. Furthermore, this means that we will only consider applications that do not depend on user identity information.

2.1   Inference Attacks

In this paper, we will concentrate on inference attacks based on the data that the external service provider received. We will not consider attacks against the infrastructure that determines, transmits, or processes a user's location—we assume it has been appropriately secured. The inference attacks may be carried out by the service provider, malicious employees of this provider, or by anybody else who has legitimately or illegitimately gained access to this information. We are most concerned, however, with attacks that can be easily automated to monitor larger groups of individuals. We will not consider how this data could be used in targeted investigations against a specific individual.

This class of applications at first does not appear to bear any privacy risks, because each tuple is revealed anonymously. On second thought, however, it becomes clear that an adversary could link independent updates to the same user if the sample frequency f is sufficiently high compared to the user density in an area. This leads to an accumulation of path information about individual users that will likely lead to identification. For example, Beresford and Stajano [5] report that the location traces collected in an office environment through the Active Bat system could be correctly reidentified by knowing the desk positions of all workers and correlating them with the traces.

Informally, the privacy property that this research aims for is unlinkability of location samples. An adversary could employ at least three approaches to link location samples. First, trajectory-based linking assumes that a user is more likely to continue traveling on the same trajectory, rather than changing direction. The adversary could build a basic movement model that includes probabilities for altering a course from a sample user population. Second, map-based linking correlates location samples with likely routes on a road or building map. The routes can then be used to predict users' position and to link future samples. Third, empirical linking connects samples based on prior movements that have been observed at a given location.

We believe that trajectory-based linking requires the least effort for large-scale outdoor positioning systems. The adversary does not have to gather map information or collect empirical information for every intersection. Therefore, we will restrict our analysis on this approach.

3   Multi Target Tracking

The tracking systems community knows the problem of linking location samples to probable users as the data association problem in multi-target tracking systems. Radar provides one typical application: the system must assign anonymous radar echos to a set of tracked targets. The key idea of such algorithms is to compare the positions of new location samples with the predicted positions of all known targets and choose an assignment that minimizes the error.

We chose Reid's multiple hypothesis tracking algorithm [8], which is based on Kalman filtering. This algorithm is one of the basic works in the field [9–p. 325]. Although, we do not currently use its capability to maintain multiple hypotheses, we have chosen it because we plan to experiment with this feature in future work.

Here, we will summarize our implementation of the algorithm. We refer the reader to the original work [8] for a more in depth discussion and the derivation of the equations. Additional information, also on the Kalman filter, can be found in [9]. The algorithm operates in three steps: First it predicts a new system state, then generates hypotheses for the assignment of new samples to targets and selects the most likely hypotheses, and finally it adjusts the system state with information from the new samples.

We simplified Reid's algorithm in a number of points. First, we do not consider random track initiation. Second, we assume all samples are taken at a fixed sample rate. Finally, as already mentioned, after every step only one hypothesis survives, which means that at each step likelihood is calculated under the assumption that the previous assignments were correct.

3.1   State Prediction

The filter predicts state according to a process model that is described by

$$x_k = F x_{k-1} + w,$$

where x_k is the state vector of the process at step k, matrix F describes a linear prediction of the next state given the previous state, and w represents the process noise vector. A new observation vector z_k relates to the actual state through

$$z_k = H x_k + v,$$

where matrix H converts a state vector into the measurement domain and v represents the measurement noise vector. The filter assumes that the process noise and the measurement noise are independent of each other and normally distributed with covariance matrices Q and R, respectively.

When tracking only one target, the Kalman filter defines the conditional probability density function of the state vector at time instant k as a multivariate normal distribution with mean $\bar{x}$ and covariance $\bar{P}$. At each time step, the filter predicts the new target position as

$$\bar{x}^{k+1} = F\hat{x}^k \qquad \text{and} \qquad \bar{P}^{k+1} = F\hat{P}^k F^T + Q^T, \tag{1}$$

where $\hat{x}$ and $\hat{P}$ are the estimates after the last sample was received.

For two-dimensional tracking applications with only slight changes in trajectory we can model the system as

$$F = \begin{bmatrix} 1 & 0 & 1 & 0 \\ 0 & 1 & 0 & 1 \\ 0 & 0 & 1 & 0 \\ 0 & 0 & 0 & 1 \end{bmatrix} \qquad x = \begin{bmatrix} p_x \\ p_y \\ v_x \\ v_y \end{bmatrix},$$

where (p_x, p_y) represent a position and (v_x, v_y) a velocity vector. A larger process noise component captures the probability of changing directions or velocity.

3.2   Hypotheses Generation and Selection

The algorithm generates a set of hypotheses when new samples are received—one for each permutation of the sample set. A hypothesis represents a possible assignment of new samples to targets. It then calculates the likelihood for each hypothesis and selects the one with maximum likelihood.

The probability of hypothesis Ω_i at time k, given the set of measurements Z^k with cardinality M, is described by

$$P_i^k \equiv P(\Omega_i^k \mid Z^k) \approx \prod_{m=1}^{M} f(z_m) \qquad (2)$$

where f is defined by the following equation (3). Based on the observation equation in the Kalman filter, the conditional probability density function of the observation vector z_k obeys a multivariate normal distribution

$$f(z^k \mid \bar{x}^k) = N(z^k - H\bar{x}^k, B), \qquad (3)$$

where $B = H\bar{P}^k H^T + R$ and $N(x, P)$ denotes the normal distribution

$$N(x, P) = e^{-\frac{1}{2}x^T P^{-1} x} / \sqrt{(2\pi)^n \mid P \mid}.$$

Both x^k and P are calculated using the update equation at the prediction step. Equation (3) calculates how close a new observation lies to a predicted position; these values are then combined into the probability of each hypothesis.

After calculating the probability of each hypothesis, we choose the hypothesis j with the maximum probability and also calculate the log-likelihood ratio as follows.

$$\log \Lambda^k = \log \frac{P_i^k}{\sum_{i=1, i \neq j}^{I} P_i^k} \qquad (4)$$

3.3   State Correction

In the correction step, the predicted system state vector for each path will be updated with the Kalman gain and the difference between the assigned observation vector and the predicted vector. The observation vectors are assigned to the targets according to the chosen hypothesis. Equation (5), which is similar to a recursive least square update equation, describes the correction step. In this equation $K = \hat{P}H^T R^{-1}$ is the Kalman gain.

$$\hat{x}^k = \bar{x}^k + K[z^k - H\bar{x}^k] \qquad \text{and} \qquad \hat{P}^k = \bar{P} - \bar{P}H^T(H\bar{P}H^T + R)^{-1}H\bar{P} \quad (5)$$

The so corrected state vector and covariance matrix are then fed back into the prediction equations and the steps are repeated for the next set of samples.

4   Experimentation

To evaluate the privacy risks posed by multi-target tracking, we have asked students on a university campus to carry an off-the-shelf GPS receiver as they go about their daily routine. Here we discuss our preliminary results in applying multi target tracking algorithms to a first batch of data. We also present micro-benchmarks that illustrate how multi-target tracking computes the relative likelihood of an assignment.

Fig. 1. Five GPS paths shown over a satellite image of the area. The paths contain several clusters, where users stayed for an extended time. There are also several areas where different users' paths overlap

The first batch of GPS data comprises five sample tracks of students, each collected over the course of one day. Figure 1 shows their tracks plotted onto aerial imagery. The tracks intersect on campus, but also extend off-campus. It includes a mix of pedestrian and vehicle movements. In short, this data provides us with a sample of students' movement patterns. It is not intended to allow drawing conclusions about user density or 'average' mobility of a larger population.

Unfortunately, two of the paths were rather short, so we decided to run our first experiments only on the three longer ones (depicted in Fig. 2). We also chose two micro-benchmarks: two nearly orthogonal path segments that intersect in space and two parallel segments that first merge and later diverge.   Both cases represent extreme inputs to a two target trajectory-based tracking system. The system should perform best on the orthogonal intersection; the parallel scenario should prove most challenging.

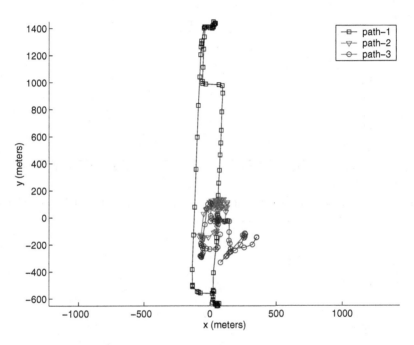

Fig. 2. Three longer paths used for the target tracking experiment

Figures 3 and 4 show the chosen path segments. For the experiment, we removed the labels that identify to which path a given sample belongs. At each step in the tracking process we supply the next two samples and let Reid's algorithm solve the assignment problem. Note that in the actual paths, the two users did not pass this area on the same day, therefore they can be trivially distinguished based on the timestamps. To make this scenario challenging, we have adjusted the timestamps so that the two users simultaneously arrive at the intersection or simultaneously start out on the parallel tracks, respectively.

Reid's MHT algorithm depends on several parameters that affect its performance. We refined the process model described in Sec. 3 by applying an expectation maximiza-tion algorithm [10] that estimates the parameters based on the five location tracks. We implemented both Reid's algorithm and the EM algorithm in MATLAB. To simplify the implementation, we first converted the GPS data into the Universal Transverse Merca-

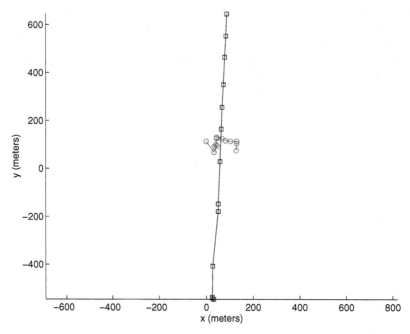

Fig. 3. Two orthogonally intersecting path segments extracted from the GPS data. One user is moving north, the other east

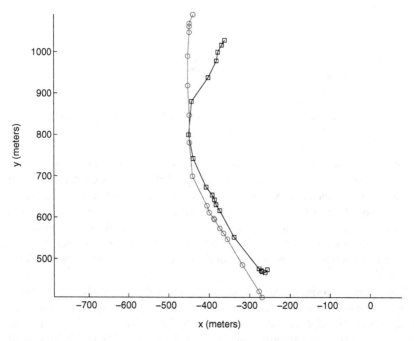

Fig. 4. Two parallel path segments extracted from the GPS data. Both users move north

tor System projection, where (within one zone) a position is described in meters on a cartesian coordinate system.

4.1   Results

Figure 5 describes the result of applying the multi-target tracking algorithm to the three longer paths. The three curves show the paths that the algorithm reconstructed from the anonymous samples. A change in value of a curve means that the algorithm has misassigned samples—three constant curves would mean perfect reconstruction. The algorithm clearly confuses a number of sample points, but many misassignments are only temporary. The first path is correctly tracked until sample 52, the second path has more misassignments, but recovers and is correctly assigned at the end. Only the third path exhibits sufficient track confusion to provide a high level of privacy.

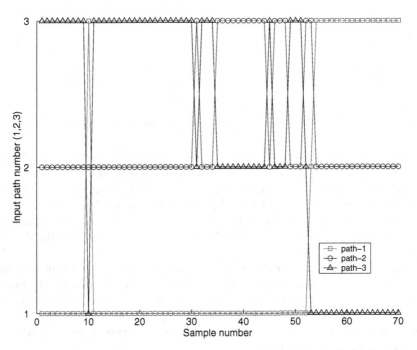

Fig. 5. Disambiguation of paths. The three curves represent the output paths. Each point of a curve shows from which input path the sample was taken. In short, where the curves cross the algorithm misassigned samples

Figure 6 shows the log-likelihood ratio at each step in the MHT process for the orthogonal path segments. The log-likelihood ratio is computed as described in Sec. 3.2. Thus, higher positive values indicate more confidence in the assignment, a value of zero corresponds to equally likely hypotheses, and a negative value to a false assignment.

As shown in the curve with square points, assignment certainty decreases as the two targets approach each other. Their paths intersect at sample index 8, where the log-likelihood ratio actually dips below zero; these particular samples are falsely assigned.

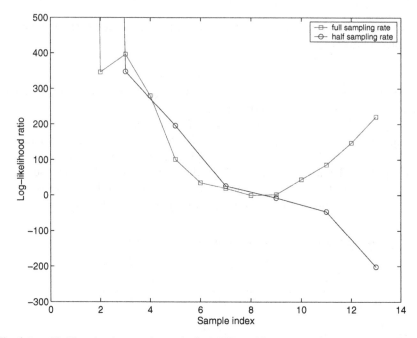

Fig. 6. Log-likelihood ratio at each step in the MHT tracking process for the orthogonal paths

The algorithm recovers, however, with the following sample updates. At sample index 10, after the paths diverged, paths are assigned with high confidence again. This example illustrates how the tracking algorithm disambiguates two intersecting paths. The curve with round points depicts log-likelihood for the same scenario but with only half the sampling rate. We see that reducing the sampling rate results in only small changes in log-likelihood for the first few samples. After the intersection, however, the algorithm now tracks the wrong path.

The curve with round points in Fig. 7 shows the log-likelihood graph for the parallel segments. For these paths, there is not much information that allows the algorithm to distinguish them. The algorithm falsely assigns samples 3–6. Note that the confidence for the fifth sample is comparatively high, even though it is misassigned. This illustrates how an error can propagate. The next point of confusion starts at sample 6, where the log-likelihood again approaches zero.

The curve with square points illustrates the sensitivity of the outcome with regard to slight changes in the movement model. This time we generated the model using only the two path segments rather than the complete five graphs. With this change the association outcome is now reversed. Only the first few points are correctly assigned.

4.2   Discussion

Note that log-likelihood ratios close to zero are neither a necessary nor a sufficient condition for location privacy. It is not sufficient because location privacy depends on how accurate an adversary can estimate a user's position. An adversary may not be able to disambiguate the samples from two users, but if the samples are very close to each other,

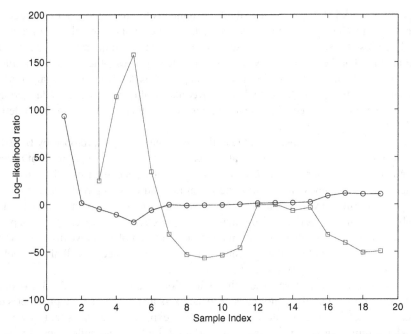

Fig. 7. Log-likelihood ratio at each step in the MHT tracking process for the parallel paths. The curve with square points shows the results with a different movement model. Tracking performance is very sensitive to slight changes in the movement model

the location estimate for both users is still relatively accurate. The parallel paths scenario illustrate this case. The adversary may misassign the samples, but this leads at most to a difference of about 100m. A low log-likelihood ratio is also not a necessary condition because in some cases the adversary will assign samples with high likelihood, but the assignment can still be wrong. This can be observed in Fig. 7, where the log-likelihood falls below -50. If the sample rate was lower, we could observe such low values without first encountering values close to zero.

We can, however, use dropping log-likelihood ratios as an indicator of potential track confusion. Location privacy increases, when the adversaries tracking algorithm confuses paths from at least two users and these paths then significantly diverge.

In our experiments, we have used a linear model with a large white gaussian noise component to model nonlinear user movements. We have seen that this crude model could already provide useful tracking results to an adversary. Tracking results could probably be improved by using nonlinear filters such as Extended Kalman Filtering and colored noise models, where the amount of noise at a given step depends on the previous step.

5   Related Work

The presented results build on prior work in the field of location anonymity. We have analyzed a new class of applications that requires periodic location samples from a larger number of users to infer statistical properties (such as average traffic flow).

In prior work [6], we have described mechanisms to guarantee a defined degree of anonymity in different locations by adjusting the spatio-temporal resolution of location-based queries. These mechanisms assume that location-based queries are generated so infrequently, that they can be viewed as independent queries—the adversary would be unable to link them to the same user. The current paper has described a first analysis aimed at building mechanisms to detect when the frequency of queries becomes dangerously. Another goal of these mechanisms could be to control this frequency so that a defined level of privacy is maintained.

This research is also closely related to the mix zone concept developed by Beresford and Stajano [5, 11]. Mix zones are spatial areas in which users' location is not accessible. When multiple users simultaneously traverse a mix zone, their pseudonyms can be changed and it becomes hard to link the incoming and outgoing path segments to the same user. In this way mix zones can be viewed as segmenting paths. They are more suitable for applications that require quasi-continuous tracking of users during a particular time interval, rather than the less frequent location samples that we discussed in this paper. However, we believe that the multi-target tracking concepts will also be helpful in analyzing unlinkability of paths over mix zones.

Another thread of privacy research for location-aware systems [12, 13, 14] develops privacy policy-based technologies to make users aware of a service provider's data collection practices. It also allows them to easily express preferences that govern under what circumstances private data can be shared. Lederer and colleagues [15] found that the identity of the requester typically is the most significant factor in users' privacy decisions. These mechanisms allow sharing information with trusted parties, while blocking intrusions from untrusted ones. Our location anonymity research is orthogonal to this work. To our knowledge privacy legislation does not mandate data collectors to inform users about *anonymous* data collection. As discussed, however, anonymity is not an absolute property, rather data can afford different degrees of anonymity. Therefore, privacy-policy mechanisms could be used to negotiate an acceptable degree of anonymity between users and service providers.

Serjantov and Danezis [16] as well as Diaz and colleagues [17] have proposed an information theoretic metric for anonymity. The metric was presented in the context of anonymous network communication but appears also applicable to location information. A privacy criterion for periodic samples will likely build on this work.

Privacy-aware data-mining follows a similar objective in allowing inferences about aggregate distributions of users while preserving privacy [18]. It differs in that it does not attempt to maintain anonymity, but rather protect sensitive data about users. For example, one mechanism perturbs sensitive data, such as salary information, by adding a random offset. This hides an individual user's information within an uncertainty interval, while still allowing the reconstruction of the salary distribution for a large user population. These mechanisms also do not address how to perturb time-series data such as location traces.

6   Conclusions

In this paper, we have considered a class of applications that requires a large number of users to reveal periodic location samples. This class is not yet adequately addressed by existing location privacy mechanisms. We have analyzed how multi-target tracking algorithms reconstruct paths from periodic anonymous location samples and proposed to derive a privacy criterion and disclosure control algorithms based on the inherent uncertainty metrics.

From our experiments, we have obtained the following insights. First, while the tracking performance of our implementation was not perfect, it did track the three users for an extended period of time. Most of the confusion between users is only temporary, when two paths cross, and not significant in the long run. Second, reducing the sampling rate with which location samples are published does not have a major effect on the certainty of assignment, unless it coincides with changes in direction or intersecting paths. Third, spoint-wise log-likelihood as a measure of uncertainty is not a good indicator of privacy per se. A path certainty measure that takes into account the uncertainty at previous sample points may be a better alternative. Log-likelihood appears to be a good predictor of potential confusion, though.

We see three important directions for continuing this work. First, we plan to develop an anonymity criterion that signals whether the sampling rate and user density parameters in a given application scenario meet a defined level of anonymity. This criterion should be guided by the performance of more refined versions of the tracking algorithm. In particular, we plan to study the effect of track initiations and of maintaining multiple likely hypotheses over a number of steps.

Second, we are interested in deriving disclosure control algorithms that could dynamically adjust the sampling rate to meet a privacy criterion. As discussed, reducing the sampling rate is most effective when it coincides with unpredictable changes in trajectory. Compared to a static privacy-preserving sampling rate, may provide an overall higher data quality to applications by only reducing the rate when needed. A full solution must also take location-based services' data quality requirements into account. Eventually, it should remain the choice of users and system designers to decide when to trade privacy for reduced service quality.

Eventually, such privacy mechanisms must be compared in light of application's data requirements. Privacy can be trivially improved by reducing the amount of data available, but this may not be adequate for a given application. Once we developed a better understanding of how to define a privacy criterion we also plan to clearly define the data requirements for different applications. The most interesting problem will be to find algorithms that maximize privacy while maintaining the required data quality.

Acknowledgments

We thank Jonathan Bredin and his students for fruitful discussions and for providing us with the GPS traces.

References

1. Jay Warrior, Eric McHenry, and Kenneth McGee. They know where you are. *IEEE Spectrum*, Jul 2003.

2. Louise Barkhuus and Anind Dey. Location-based services for mobile telephony: a study of users' privacy concerns. In *9th Internation Conference on Human-Computer Interaction (INTERACT)*, 2003.

3. Latanya Sweeney. *k*-anonymity: a model for protecting privacy. *International Journal on Uncertainty, Fuzziness and Knowledge-based Systems*, 10(5):557–570, 2002.

4. Latanya Sweeney. Achieving *k*-Anonymity Privacy Protection Using Generalization and Suppression. *International Journal on Uncertainty, Fuzziness and Knowledge-based Systems*, 10(5):571–588, 2002.

5. Alastair Beresford and Frank Stajano. Location privacy in pervasive computing. *IEEE Pervasive Computing*, 2(1):46–55, 2003.

6. Marco Gruteser and Dirk Grunwald. Anonymous usage of location-based services through spatial and temporal cloaking. In *Proceedings of the First International Conference on Mobile Systems, Applications, and Services*, 2003.

7. Rajiv Vyas. Ford device intended to unclog roads. http://www.freep.com/money/autonews/ford27_20040227.htm, Feb 2004.

8. Donald Reid. An algorithm for tracking multiple targets. *IEEE Transactions on Automatic Control*, 24(6):843–854, Dec 1979.

9. Samuel Blackman and Robert Popoli. *Design and Analysis of Modern Tracking Systems*. Artech House, 1999.

10. Todd Moon. The expectation-maximization algorithm. *IEEE Signal Processing Magazine*, 13(6):47–60, Nov 1996.

11. Alastair Beresford and Frank Stajano. Mix zones: User privacy in location-aware services. In *IEEE Workshop on Pervasive Computing and Communication Security (PerSec)*, 2004.

12. Ginger Myles, Adrian Friday, and Nigel Davies. Preserving privacy in environments with location-based applications. *IEEE Pervasive Computing*, 2(1):56–64, 2003.

13. Marc Langheinrich. A privacy awareness system for ubiquitous computing environments. In *4th International Conference on Ubiquitous Computing*, 2002.

14. Sastry Duri, Marco Gruteser, Xuan Liu, Paul Moskowitz, Ronald Perez, Moninder Singh, and Jung-Mu Tang. Framework for security and privacy in automotive telematics. In *2nd ACM International Workshphop on Mobile Commerce*, 2002.

15. Scott Lederer, Jennifer Mankoff, and Anind Dey. Who wants to know what when? privacy preference determinants in ubiquitous computing. In *Extended Abstracts of Conference on Human Factors in Computing Systems (CHI)*, pages 724–725, 2003.

16. Andrei Serjantov and George Danezis. Towards an information theoretic metric for anonymity. In *2nd Workshop on Privacy Enhancing Technologies*, 2002.

17. Claudia Diaz, Stefaan Seys, Joris Claessens, and Bart Preneel. Towards measuring anonymity. In *2nd Workshop on Privacy Enhancing Technologies*, 2002.

18. Rakesh Agrawal and Ramakrishnan Srikant. Privacy-preserving data mining. In *Proc. of the ACM SIGMOD Conference on Management of Data*, pages 439–450. ACM Press, May 2000.

A Theorem Proving Approach to Analysis of Secure Information Flow*

Ádám Darvas[1], Reiner Hähnle[2], and David Sands[2]

[1] Swiss Federal Institute of Technology (ETH), Zurich
Adam.Darvas@inf.ethz.ch
[2] Chalmers University of Technology, Sweden
{reiner, dave}@cs.chalmers.se

Abstract. Most attempts at analysing secure information flow in programs are based on domain-specific logics. Though computationally feasible, these approaches suffer from the need for abstraction and the high cost of building dedicated tools for real programming languages. We recast the information flow problem in a general program logic rather than a problem-specific one. We investigate the feasibility of this approach by showing how a general purpose tool for software verification can be used to perform information flow analyses. We are able to prove security and insecurity of programs including advanced features such as method calls, loops, and object types for the target language JAVA CARD. In addition, we can express declassification of information.

1 Introduction

By understanding the way that information flows from inputs to outputs in a program, one can understand whether a program satisfies a certain confidentiality policy regarding the information that it manipulates. If there is no information flow from confidential inputs to publicly observable outputs—either directly or indirectly via e.g. control flow—then the program may be considered secure.

An appealing property of information flow is that it can be described independently of a particular mechanism for enforcing it. This is useful because in fact the dynamic enforcement of information flow is tricky; information can flow not only directly as in "public.output(secret);" but also indirectly, as in "if (secret==0) public.output(1);" or even (using an arithmetic exception) "tmp = 1/secret; public.output(1);". Denning [7] pioneered an approach to determining whether a program satisfies a given information flow policy using *static analysis*. Since then (in particularly in the last 5-6 years) research in the area of information-flow analysis for programs has flourished. For an excellent overview see [16].

---

* A preliminary short version of this paper appeared in WITS'03, Workshop on Issues in the Theory of Security, April 2003.

D. Hutter and M. Ullmann (Eds.): SPC 2005, LNCS 3450, pp. 193–209, 2005.
© Springer-Verlag Berlin Heidelberg 2005

Most attempts at analysing secure information flow in programs have followed basically the same pattern: information flow is modeled using a domain-specific logic (such as a type system or dataflow analysis framework) with a predefined degree of approximation, and this leads to a fully automated but approximate analysis of information flow. There are two problems stemming from this approach. Firstly, the degree of approximation in the logic is fixed and thus many secure programs will be rejected unless they can be suitably rewritten. Secondly, implementing a domain-specific tool for a real programming language is a substantial undertaking, and thus there are very few real-language tools available [16]. Furthermore, these two problems interact: realistic languages possess features that are omitted in theoretical studies but which can prove increasingly difficult to analyse statically with acceptable precision.

This paper investigates a promising alternative approach based on the use of a general program logic and theorem prover:

– We recast the information flow problem in a *general program logic* rather than a problem-specific one. Program logics based on simple safety and liveness properties (e.g. Hoare logic or weakest precondition calculus) are inadequate for this purpose, since only the most simple information flow properties can be expressed. Our approach is to use dynamic logic, which admits a more elegant and far-reaching characterisation of secure information flow for deterministic programs.
– We investigate the feasibility of the approach by showing how a *general purpose theorem proving tool* for software verification (based on dynamic logic) can be used to perform information flow analyses. So far, our examples are relatively small, but we are able to handle phenomena like partial termination, method calls, loops, and object types. We are also able to prove insecurity of programs and to express declassification of information.

2   Modeling Secure Information Flow in Dynamic Logic

The platform for our experiments is the KeY tool [2], which features an interactive theorem prover for formal verification of JAVA CARD programs.[1]

2.1   A Dynamic Logic for Java Card

In KeY, the target program to be verified and its specification are both modeled in an instance of dynamic logic (DL) [10] called JAVA CARD DL [4]. JAVA CARD DL extends variants of DL used so far for theoretical investigations or verification purposes, because it handles such phenomena as side effects, aliasing, object types, exceptions, finite integer types, as partly explained below. Other programming languages than JAVA CARD could be axiomatized in DL. Once this is done, the KeY tool can then be used on them.

---

[1] Another tool that could have been used is the KIV system [18].

Deduction in JAVA CARD DL is based on symbolic program execution and simple program transformations and is, thus, close to a programmer's understanding of JAVA. It can be seen as a modal logic with a modality $\langle p \rangle$ for every program p, where $\langle p \rangle$ refers to the state (if p terminates) that is reached by running program p.

The *program formula* $\langle p \rangle \, \phi$ expresses that the program p terminates in a state in which ϕ holds. A formula $\phi \rightarrow \langle p \rangle \, \psi$ is valid if for every state s satisfying precondition ϕ a run of the program p starting in s terminates, and in the terminating state the postcondition ψ holds.

Thus, the DL formula $\phi \rightarrow \langle p \rangle \, \psi$ is similar to the total-correctness Hoare triple $\{\phi\} \, p \, \{\psi\}$ or to ϕ implying the weakest precondition of p wrt ψ. But in contrast to Hoare logic and weakest precondition calculus (wpc), the set of formulas of DL is closed under the usual logical operators and first order quantifiers. For example, in Hoare logic and wpc the formulas ϕ and ψ are pure first-order formulas, whereas in DL they can contain programs. In general, program formulas can appear anywhere in DL as subformulas.

In addition, JAVA CARD DL includes the dual operator $[\cdot]$, for which $[p] \, \phi \equiv \neg \langle p \rangle \, \neg \phi$, with the semantics: p either terminates in a state in which ϕ holds or it diverges. In the KeY tool the $[\cdot]$ operator will be supported in the near future.

The programs in JAVA CARD DL formulas are basically executable JAVA CARD code. Each rule of the calculus for JAVA CARD DL specifies how to execute one particular statement, possibly with additional restrictions. When a loop or a recursive method call is encountered, it is necessary to perform induction over a suitable data structure.

In JAVA (like in other object-oriented programming languages), different object variables can refer to the same object. This phenomenon, called aliasing, causes serious difficulties for handling of assignments in a calculus for JAVA CARD DL. For example, whether or not a formula "o1.a = 1" still holds after the (symbolic) execution of the assignment "o2.a = 2;", depends on whether or not o1 and o2 refer to the same object.

Therefore, JAVA assignments cannot be symbolically executed by syntactic substitution. In JAVA CARD DL calculus a different solution is used, based on the notion of (state) *updates*. These updates are of the form $\{loc:=val\}$ and can be put in front of any formula. The semantics of $\{loc:=val\}\phi$ is the same as that of $\langle loc = val; \rangle \, \phi$, but val is a logical term syntactically restricted in such a way that computing its value has no side effects. In addition, loc is either (i) a program variable var, or (ii) a field access obj.attr, or (iii) an array access arr[i]. More complex expressions are not allowed in updates. Such expressions are first decomposed into a sequence of updates when they occur.

In JAVA CARD DL there are three different types of variables: *metavariables*, *program (local) variables*, and *logic variables*.[2] Metavariables, as explained in Section 2.2, are merely placeholders for ground terms. Program variables can

---

[2] The distinction between program and logic variables is forced by side effects in imperative programming languages like JAVA. It is not present in "pure" DL [10].

occur in program parts of a formula as well as outside program parts. Syntactically, they are constants of the logic. Their semantic interpretation varies with the program execution state. Logic variables occur only bound (quantified) and never in programs. Syntactically, they are variables of the logic. Their semantic interpretation is *rigid* in the sense that it refers to one particular program state. This is necessary to refer to values of program variables in different program states within the same formula. Hence, in JAVA CARD DL quantification over program variables like "$\forall x. \langle p\{x\}\rangle \psi\{x\}$" is syntactically illegal.[3]

Updates remedy this problem. Suppose we want to quantify over x of type integer. We declare an integer program variable px, quantify over a logic variable of type integer lx, and use an update to assign the value of lx to px:

$$\langle \text{int px};\rangle \ (\forall lx : int. \{px:=lx\}\langle p\{px\}\rangle \ \psi\{lx, px\}) \tag{1}$$

2.2   Automated Proof Search in KeY

Like other interactive theorem provers for software verification, the proving process in KeY is partially automated by heuristic control of applicable rules. In particular, the KeY theorem prover features a *metavariable* mechanism that makes elimination of universal quantifiers potentially more efficient: without it, whenever a universally quantified formula (that is a positive formula of the form $\forall x.\phi\{x\}$ or a negated existential formula) is encountered, then the standard quantifier elimination rules in first order logic allow to derive, for example, $\phi\{t\}$ from $\forall x.\phi\{x\}$ for any ground term t. This leads to an infinite local search space and, typically, forces user interaction to obtain a term t that advances the proof.

In automated theorem proving (but only in few interactive theorem provers) it is standard practice to use so-called *free variables* or *metavariables* instead. Instead of $\phi\{t\}$ one derives a formula of the form $\phi\{X\}$, where X is a placeholder for a ground term t. The point is that the determination of t can thus be delayed to a later stage in the proof when a useful value for it becomes obvious.[4] This technique is implemented in the KeY prover. With it, many (but not all) user interactions due to quantifier elimination are no longer necessary. Below we will see that in the present application, the metavariable technique is particularly important.

2.3   Secure Information Flow Expressed in Dynamic Logic

We use the greater expressiveness of DL as compared to Hoare logic and wpc to give a very natural logic modeling of secure information flow. Assume without loss of generality that program p contains exactly one low-security variable l and one high-security one h. We want to express that by observing the initial and final values of l, it is impossible to know anything about the initial value

---

[3] The notation $\phi\{x\}$, p{x} emphasizes occurrence of variables in formulas or programs.

[4] To ensure correctness, the skolemization rules that eliminate existential quantifiers must, of course, take into account possible dependency on metavariables present.

of h [6]. In other words:

> "When starting p with arbitrary values 1, then the value r of 1 after executing p, is independent of the choice of h."

This can be directly formulated in standard DL:

$$\forall 1. \exists r. \forall h. \langle p \rangle \, r \doteq 1 \qquad (2)$$

To illustrate our formulation in JAVA CARD DL, assume that all variables are of type integer and (where necessary) program variables and logic variables are prefixed by "p" and "l", respectively. Using (1), we obtain the following JAVA CARD DL version of (2):

$$\langle \texttt{int pl; int ph;} \rangle \, (\forall \mathit{ll:int.} \, \exists \mathit{r:int.} \, \forall \mathit{lh:int.} \, \{\texttt{pl}{:=}\mathit{ll}\}\{\texttt{ph}{:=}\mathit{lh}\}\langle p \rangle \, r \doteq \texttt{pl})$$

For sake of readability we use the simpler DL notation (2) in the rest of the paper, unless the actual JAVA CARD DL formulation is of interest.

The closest approach to ours is by Joshi & Leino [11–Cor. 3] who arrive at a characterisation of secure information flow in Hoare logic that resembles (2). The target language of [11] is a toy language, and nothing was implemented or even mechanized. A crucial limitation of Hoare logic is that quantifiers can only occur *within* an assertion, hence quantifiers that range over program variables or both pre- and postcondition have to be eliminated before one obtains a Hoare triple. In consequence, the existential result variable r in (2) needs to be replaced by the user with a concrete function. Other limitations of Hoare logic that we overcome with dynamic logic are characterization of information leakage by termination behaviour, proving insecurity of programs, and declassification.

In DL we can easily express the additional requirement that no information on the value of h shall be leaked by p's termination behaviour:

$$\forall 1. (\exists h. \langle p \rangle \, true \rightarrow \exists r. \forall h. \langle p \rangle \, r \doteq 1) \qquad (3)$$

In addition to (2) this expresses that, for any choice of 1, if p terminates for some initial value of h, then it terminates for all values.

This formula contains an implicit occurrence of the modality $[\cdot]$. Therefore, with the current version of the prover this formula cannot be used.

3   Interactive Proving of Secure Information Flow

In our experiments, we considered only problems of the form (2) (it is unnecessary to use form (3), because our examples are all terminating, so the antecedent of the implication is true for all values of h).

3.1   Simple Programs

We start demonstrating the feasibility of our approach with some examples taken from papers [11, 16]. Table 1 shows the example programs with the corresponding

Table 1. Simple programs

program	rules applied
l=h;	7
h=l;	11
l=6;	11
l=h; l=6;	12
h=l; l=h;	12

program	rules applied
l=h; l=1-h;	14
if (false) l=h;	16
if (h>=0) l=1; else l=0;	21
if (h==1) l=1; else l=0; l=0;	33

number of rules applied in the KeY system. Note that l, h, and r are single variables in each case.

When evaluating the data one must keep in mind that we used the KeY prover as it comes, we discuss possible performance improvements below in Section 6.

As is usual in the context of a mechanical sequent proof, the proof obligation is implicitly negated, so that $\forall$ quantifiers are treated as existential quantifiers and $\exists$ as universal ones. Therefore, the $\forall$ quantifiers in (2) are simply eliminated by skolemization, while r must be, in principle, instantiated by the user with the result value of l after p did terminate (e.g., 6 in program "l = 6;"). Thanks to the metavariable mechanism, this interaction can mostly be avoided by delaying the instantiation until a point when the heuristics are able to find the required instance automatically (that is, after symbolic execution of p). In fact, none of the proofs on these examples required user interaction and all proofs were obtained within fractions of a second.

If a program is secure, then the DL formula (2) is provable. For insecure programs the proof cannot be completed, and there will be one or more *open goal*. Among our examples there are two insecure programs. In these cases the prover cannot find a proper instantiation for r. Furthermore, if we switch off the metavariable mechanism the prover stops at goals that remain open in an attempt to prove security. Table 2 contains these goals (in this case one for each program) and it is easy to observe that these formulas are indeed unprovable. In fact, the open goals give a direct hint to the source of the security breach.

It is important to note that the number of applied rules (and user interactions) does not increase more than linearly if we take the composition of two programs. For example, to verify security of the program "h = 1; l = 6;", the prover applies 12 rules. By comparison, to prove security of the constituents "h = 1;" and "l = 6;", 11 rule applications are used in each case.

Table 2. Open goals for insecure programs

program	open goal
l=h;	$\exists r.\ \forall h.\ r \doteq h$
if (h>=0) l=1; else l=0;	$\exists r.\ (\forall h.\ (!(h < 0) \to r \doteq 1) \wedge \forall h.\ (h < 0 \to r \doteq 0))$

3.2   Proving Insecurity

To prove that the programs in Table 2 are insecure, the property of insecurity has to be formalized. This can be done by simply taking the negation of formula (2). The syntactic closure property of DL is crucial again here. Negating (2) and straightforward simplification[5] yields:

$$\exists 1. \forall r. \exists h. \langle p \rangle \, r \neq 1 \tag{4}$$

The intuitive meaning of the formula is the following:

> "There is an initial value 1, such that for any possible final value r of 1 after executing p, there exists an initial value h which can prevent 1 from taking that final value r."

Program "1=h;" can be proved insecure in 14 steps without user interaction. The proof on the second program takes 33 steps and requires two user interactions: instantiation on h and running the integrated automatic theorem prover Simplify [8] part of the ESC/Java tool. In the future this type of user interaction will not be needed, since the run of Simplify will be activated automatically by the heuristic control of KeY.

The property of insecurity can be adapted to include termination behaviour, too. In this case (3) has to be negated (as mentioned before, currently the prover cannot handle modality $[\cdot]$, thus formulas of form (5) cannot be proved):

$$\exists 1. (\forall r. \exists h. \langle p \rangle \, r \neq 1 \lor (\exists h. \langle p \rangle \, true \land \exists h. [p] \, false)) \tag{5}$$

The intuitive meaning of the formula is the following:

> "There is an initial value 1 such that either there exists a value h for which p terminates and h interferes with 1 or there exists a pair of h values such that for one value p terminates and for the other it diverges."

3.3   Loops

In this section we report on an experiment with a program containing a while loop. The program would be rejected by a type-based approach as it contains a non-secure statement:

$$\forall 1. \exists r. \forall h. (h > 0 \rightarrow \langle \texttt{while } (h > 0) \; \{h--; \; 1 = h; \} \rangle \, r \doteq 1) \tag{6}$$

The loop contains the insecure statement "$1 = h$;" but the condition of exiting the loop is $h \doteq 0$, thus the final value of 1 is always 0, independently of the initial value of h. The precondition ensures that the body of the loop is executed at least once.

To prove properties of programs containing loops requires in general to perform induction over a suitable *induction variable*. Finding the right induction

---

[5] As now we only consider terminating programs, $\langle \cdot \rangle$ and $[\cdot]$ are interchangeable.

hypothesis is not an easy task, but once it is found, completing the proof is usually a mechanical process; if one runs into problems, this is a hint, that the hypothesis was not correct. Heuristic techniques to find induction hypotheses are available in the literature and will be built into KeY in due time.

After the induction hypothesis is given to the prover, three open goals must be proven: (i) after exiting the loop, the postcondition holds (induction base), (ii) the induction step, (iii) the induction hypothesis implies the original subgoal.

To prove security of (6), the prover took 164 steps; in addition to establishing the induction hypothesis, several user interactions were required of the following kinds: instantiation, unwinding the loop and Simplify.

3.4   Using Object Types

Next we demonstrate that our approach applies to an object-oriented setting in a natural way. The example presented here is taken from [12–Fig. 5.], where an object (specified by its statechart diagram) leaks information of a high variable through one of its operations. The corresponding JAVA implementation is:

```
class Account {
    private int balance;
    public boolean extraService;
    private void writeBalance(int amount) {
        if (amount >= 10000) extraService = true; else extraService = false;
        balance = amount; }
    private int readBalance() {return balance;}
    public boolean readExtra() {return extraService;}
}
```

The *balance* of an Account object can be written by the method `writeBalance` and read by `readBalance`. If the balance is over 10000, variable *extraService* is set to true, otherwise to false. The state of that variable can be read by `readExtra`. The balance of the account and the return value of `readBalance` are secure, whereas the value of `extraService` and the return value of `readExtra` are not.

The program is insecure, since partial information about the high-security variable can be inferred via the observation of a low-security variable. That is, calling `writeBalance` with different parameters can lead to different observations of the return value of `readExtra`.

To prove security and insecurity of this program, we continue to use (2) and (4), respectively. We give the actual JAVA CARD DL formula of security to show how naturally objects are woven into the logic. Where necessary, we use variables with object types in the logic.

$$\langle \text{Account o} = \text{new Account}(); \text{ int amount; boolean result;} \rangle$$
$$\forall lextraService : boolean. \exists r : boolean. \forall lamount : int.$$
$$\{\text{o.extraService:=}lextraService\}\{\text{amount:=}lamount\}$$
$$\langle \text{o.writeBalance(amount); result=o.readExtra();} \rangle r \doteq \text{result}$$

The prover falls into an infinite search for proper instantiation on r, but by disabling the search mechanism we get the following unprovable open goal after 65 rule applications:

$$\exists\, r : boolean.\, (\forall\, lamount : int.\, (!(lamount < 10000) \rightarrow r \doteq \mathsf{TRUE})\ \&$$
$$\forall\, lamount : int.\, (lamount < 10000 \rightarrow r \doteq \mathsf{FALSE}))$$

Insecurity of the program was proved in 120 steps without user interaction.

4   An Alternative Formulation of Secure Information Flow in Dynamic Logic

There is a reformulation of the secure information flow property, which captures it in an even more natural way than (2):

> "Running two instances of p with equal low-security values and arbitrary high-security values, the resulting low-security values are equal too."

This can be rendered in DL as follows:

$$\forall\, 1, 1', h, h'.\, (1 \doteq 1' \rightarrow \langle p\{1, h\};\ p\{1', h'\}\rangle\, 1 \doteq 1') \tag{7}$$

This approach can be used as is only when the two instances of p do not interfere, that is, $p\{1, h\}$ accesses *only* variables 1 and h. Otherwise, the remaining environment must be preserved.

The number of branches in a proof for program p corresponds to the number of symbolic execution paths that must be taken through it. Therefore, in the worst case, the size of proofs for $p; p'$ is quadratic in the size of proofs for p. Theorem 2 below alleviates this problem, but it is future research to find out exactly when and how the increase can be avoided.

Theorem 1. *If p modifies no variables or fields other than 1 and h, then equation (2) and (7) are equivalent.*[6]

It is worth noting that characterization (7) is probably the most suitable if one is restricted to Hoare logic or wpc, because it translates directly into a Hoare triple after elimination of universal quantifiers.

4.1   An Optimization

By exploiting the fact that the two program copies are identical (they just run on different environments) we can significantly decrease the size of the state space with the equivalent formula:

$$\forall\, 1, 1'.\, \exists\, h.\, \forall\, h'.\, (1 \doteq 1' \rightarrow \langle p\{1, h\};\ p\{1', h'\}\rangle\, 1 \doteq 1') \tag{8}$$

Theorem 2. *Equation (7) and (8) are equivalent.*

---

[6] Proofs of Theorem 1 and 2 can be found in the appendix of [1].

The existentially quantified value of h can be arbitrarily chosen and not bound by the actual program p in hand. Thus, when a proof is carried out the user can instantiate it to any value, for example to a value which makes the proof easier. We will see an example of that in Section 4.2.

A further simplification in actual proofs is that precondition "$1 \doteq 1'$" can be rendered in JAVA CARD DL as two updates[7] "$\{pl:=ll\}\{pl':=ll\}$". The first update is needed anyway to enable the quantification over program variable l, as illustrated by (1). Besides making the proofs somewhat shorter, this optimization even eliminates otherwise inevitable manual instantiations in some cases.

Using the same idea as for the first approach, we can extend (8) to include termination behaviour. And by taking the negation of that formula, we get the formulation of insecurity including termination behaviour.

4.2   Examples

In this subsection we show how this approach performs on the example programs from Section 3. On the simple programs in Table 1 the number of applied rules increased, but in most cases not more than linearly. No user interaction was needed. For the two insecure programs we get trivially unprovable goals again and to prove them insecure we negate and simplify (8) to get the formula[8] of insecurity:

$$\exists l, l'. \forall h. \exists h'. (1 \doteq 1' \land \langle p\{l,h\}; \ p\{l',h'\}\rangle 1 \neq 1') \tag{9}$$

The automatic proof on program "$l=h$" takes 18 steps, while the number of 187 applied rules on the second insecure program increased more than threefold compared to the result from the first approach. This is due to the search for a proper instantiation of h' by the prover which leads to a fully automatic proof.

Proving security of the Object Type example introduced in Section 3.4 leads to an unprovable open goal after 191 steps, while insecurity can be proved in 317 steps without user interaction.

The example program containing the while loop is provable in 300 steps with several user interactions of kinds: induction, unwinding the loop, instantiation and Simplify. In the proof we exploit the fact that h can be instantiated to *any* value (conforming the precondition "$h>0$") as pointed out earlier. Thus, h is instantiated with 1, hence, the first loop can be symbolically executed (by unwinding the loop twice) without induction.

Among the example programs, the advantage of (8) compared to (7) is manifested the most strongly by this example. If using (7), none of the loops can be symbolically executed without providing an appropriate induction hypothesis, moreover, two significantly differing hypotheses have to be given by the user. Furthermore, the proof is considerably longer: 497 steps.

---

[7] Prefixing logic and program variables with "l" and "p", respectively.

[8] In JAVA CARD DL the first conjunct can be expressed via updates again.

5   Exceptions and Declassification

In this section we discuss two variations of the secure information flow problem which are handled in a straightforward manner in dynamic logic, but can be problematic in standard typed-based approaches.

The section also motivates the need of the Alternative Approach (7), which may otherwise seem questionable, because it mostly leads to longer proofs as program p has to be symbolically executed twice.

5.1   Exceptions

Exceptions provide the possibility of additional indirect information flows. The presence or absence of an exception may reveal information about secret data, either *directly* through the source of the exception—e.g. $h = 1/h$ reveals whether h is zero or not—or *indirectly* via the context in which the exception is thrown (see the example below).

In the type system setting, the presence of exceptions can lead to rather coarse approximations to the information flow, and lead to complications in the type systems[9] such as ad hoc rules to capture common idioms which would otherwise give unacceptable approximations [15].

As an example of the kind of crude approximation that a type system is required to make, consider an expression such as "if $(h \neq 0)$ h = 1/h;". Avoiding exceptional behaviour of this kind is a natural programming idiom. It is rather easy for our approach to see that no exception can be raised by this program fragment, and hence there is no potential information flow from the conditional test to the exception or its absence. For example, the type rule of [19] requires that the divisor is always of low security clearance to ensure that a divide-by-zero exception can never lead to additional information flows—thus the above program would not be allowed. The *JFlow* [13] and *Flow Caml* [15] systems both contain a more fine grained treatment of exceptions, but are forced to assume that an exception *might* be raised by the above code, thus potentially causing a secure program to be branded as insecure.

Exceptions can, of course, easily lead to genuinely insecure programs. Since JAVA CARD DL fully models the JAVA CARD semantics, the handling of exceptions poses no problem for our analysis. First we show a simple example presented in [13]:

```
y = true;
try {
    if (x) throw new Exception();
    y = false;
} catch(Exception e) {}
```

---

[9] And even errors, such as the error in Meyers' framework uncovered by Pottier and Simonet [14].

Assume x is a confidential and y is a public boolean variable. Then the program is insecure since the code is equivalent to the assignment y = x.

The program can be proved insecure using formulas (4) and (9) without user interaction in 48 and 93 steps, respectively. When trying to prove security of the program with formulas (2) and (7) we get trivially unprovable goals without any user interaction.

When using the **throw** command or performing computations which may raise exceptions, we might want to prove that exceptions are handled in a secure way or that they cannot occur in our program. We illustrate these cases through the simple program "h = 1/h;". Since the value of 1 is not changed the program can only leak information about whether the initial value of h is 0 or not.

This is easily observed when we try to prove security of the program using formula (2). The prover stops at the following open goal[10]:

$$h \doteq 0 \rightarrow \{var0:=obj\_1| : \texttt{ArithmeticException}\}\langle\texttt{throw var0;}\rangle\, r \doteq 1$$

which describes exactly what we expected: if the value of h is 0, then there is an uncaught exception of type `ArithmeticException` (denoted with symbol "| :").

However, by modifying the program or the proof obligation we can prove the program secure. One possibility is to handle the exception in a secure way, for example, by leaving the value of h unchanged if the exception occurs:

```
try { h=1/h; } catch(ArithmeticException e) { }
```

Alternatively, we can add the precondition h ≠ 0, thus avoiding the raise of the exception. This leads directly to a proof that the program "if (h ≠ 0) h = 1/h;" is secure. Both cases are proved (using either approach) without user interaction.

5.2   Declassification

In certain cases programs need to leak some confidential information in order to serve their intended purpose. Obviously we cannot prove security for such programs, but we can establish some "conditional" security which bounds the information leaked from a program. Cohen's early work [6] on information flow in programs introduces a notion of *selective independence* which captures this idea, and this is generalised by e.g. the PER model [17].

For a program which leaks no information about h we observe that the low output does not change as we vary the high input (as encoded fairly directly by formulation (7)). The idea when describing the behaviour of "leaky" programs is to characterize what is leaked and show that if the attacker already has this information then nothing *more* is leaked.

Let us take an example. Suppose that a Swedish national identity number, a ten digit natural number, is considered a secret. The identity number encodes information such as the date of birth and the gender of the owner. Suppose that a program handling identity numbers is permitted to leak the *gender* of the

---

[10] Slightly modified for easier reading.

owner[11]. For such a policy we wish to prove that if the gender is already known then there is no additional information revealed about the personal numbers.

The basic idea is to represent attacker knowledge—in this example the knowledge of gender—as a partition of the state space. In this concrete example the state space is partitioned into two sets, M and F (the personal numbers corresponding to males and females, respectively).

To prove that a program is secure under such a policy, following [6] we can modify (7) to prove security for each partition:

$$\forall 1, 1'. \forall h \in M. \forall h' \in M. (1 \doteq 1' \rightarrow \langle p\{1,h\}; \; p\{1',h'\}\rangle \, 1 \doteq 1') \; \wedge$$
$$\forall 1, 1'. \forall h \in F. \forall h' \in F. (1 \doteq 1' \rightarrow \langle p\{1,h\}; \; p\{1',h'\}\rangle \, 1 \doteq 1')$$

or equivalently

$$\forall 1, 1', h, h'. ((h \in M \wedge h' \in M) \vee (h \in F \wedge h' \in F) \rightarrow$$
$$(1 \doteq 1' \rightarrow \langle p\{1,h\}; \; p\{1',h'\}\rangle \, 1 \doteq 1'))$$

A generalisation of this (which does not require the partition to be finite) is to represent the partition as an equivalence relation.

Such preconditions can be obtained in a mechanized way in some cases. Suppose that the domain D of the high value can be partitioned into a finite number of subdomains: $D = D_1 \uplus D_2 \uplus \cdots \uplus D_n$. Moreover, assume there are formulas $d_i(x)$ for $1 \leq i \leq n$ with exactly one free variable x such that the value of x is in D_i iff $d_i(x)$ holds. Then also $\forall x : D. \; d_1(x) \vee d_2(x) \vee \cdots \vee d_n(x)$ holds.[12] Now, if we add the precondition

$$(d_1(h) \wedge d_1(h')) \vee (d_2(h) \wedge d_2(h')) \vee \cdots \vee (d_n(h) \wedge d_n(h')) \tag{10}$$

to (7), then at most one subdomain for each given pair of h and h' is selected and the security property on that subdomain is checked. But since h and h' are universally quantified the formula checks in fact security of the whole domain of h. Note that we cannot use (8) here, since that would verify only one subdomain.

Let us give two examples on the usage of (10). Suppose we can afford to leak (a) the sign of h or (b) the least significant bit of h. Then we would add the following preconditions:

(a). $((h \geq 0) \wedge (h' \geq 0)) \vee ((h < 0) \wedge (h' < 0))$

(b). $((h \bmod 2 \equiv 0) \wedge (h' \bmod 2 \equiv 0)) \vee ((h \bmod 2 \equiv 1) \wedge (h' \bmod 2 \equiv 1))$.

Obviously, precondition "$h \bmod 2 \doteq h' \bmod 2$" merely is a simplification of (b).

To demonstrate declassification we proved that "if $(h>=0)$ $1=1$; else $1=0$;" does not leak out more information than the sign of h. We merely needed to add precondition (a) to formula (7) and run the prover, yielding a proof in 96 steps

---

[11] The gender is encoded in the second from last digit: if the digit is odd then the owner is male, otherwise female.

[12] As the D_i form a partition of D, this is even true when $\vee$ is replaced by XOR.

without user interaction. Without the additional precondition, the program is insecure, and a proof attempt terminates with the expected open goals.

By means of declassification, the following scenario can be envisaged: if proving security of a program fails, we analyse the open goal(s) to figure out the source of the information leakage, that is, give an upper bound for the leakage. After adding the declassifying precondition there are two possibilities: either the proof can be completed, thus, we know an upper bound on the amount of information leaked. If we can afford this leakage then we have a "relatively" secure program. Otherwise, we have to find a lower upper bound and try the proof with the corresponding precondition; if the proof still cannot be completed, then we underestimated or miscalculated the amount of leakage and have to retry the proof with a stronger or different precondition.

We note that declassification is also expressible with the first approach using the following formulation:

$$\forall \mathtt{l}.\ \exists r.\ \forall \mathtt{h}.\ (d_1(\mathtt{h}) \rightarrow \langle \mathtt{p} \rangle\, r \doteq 1)\ \land \forall \mathtt{l}.\ \exists r.\ \forall \mathtt{h}.\ (d_2(\mathtt{h}) \rightarrow \langle \mathtt{p} \rangle\, r \doteq 1)$$
$$\land \cdots \land \forall \mathtt{l}.\ \exists r.\ \forall \mathtt{h}.\ (d_n(\mathtt{h}) \rightarrow \langle \mathtt{p} \rangle\, r \doteq 1)$$

The drawback is that each subdomain has to be proved secure separately by symbolically executing program $\mathtt{p}$ n times. This can cause substantial overhead.

6   Discussion and Future Work

In this paper we suggested to use an interactive theorem prover for program verification and dynamic logic as a framework for checking secure information flow properties. We showed the feasibility of the approach by applying it to a number of examples taken from the literature. The examples are small, but current security-related papers typically present examples of similar complexity. Even without any tuning of the prover, all examples could be mechanically checked with few very user interactions. The relatively high degree of automation, the support of full JAVA CARD, and the possibility to inspect failed proofs and open goals are major advantages from using a *theorem prover*.

Most approaches to secure information flow are based on static analysis methods using domain-specific logics. These have the advantage of being usually decidable in polynomial time. On the other hand, they must necessarily abstract away from the target program. This becomes problematic when dealing with complex target languages such as JAVA CARD. By taking a theorem proving approach and JAVA CARD DL, which fully models the JAVA CARD semantics, we can prove any property that is provable in first-order logic.

An important advantage of both Hoare logic and dynamic logic is that they are *transparent* w.r.t. the target language, that is, programs are first-class citizen. In contrast to formalisms based on higher-order logic, no encoding of programs and their semantics is required. In addition, verification is based on *symbolic program execution*. Both are extremely important, when a proof requires user interaction, and the human user has to understand the current proof state.

In terms of the way in which we formulated the security condition, the closest approach is that of Joshi & Leino [11], who consider how security can be expressed in various logical forms, leading to a characterisation of security using a Hoare triple. This characterisation is similar to the one used here—with the crucial difference that their formula *contains* a Hoare triple, but it is *not a statement in Hoare logic*, and thus requires (interactive) quantifier elimination before it can be plugged into a verification tool based on Hoare logic. Neither leakage by termination behaviour nor insecurity nor declassification are captured by their formula (although these aspects are discussed elsewhere in the same article). Thus, the greater expressivity of *dynamic logic* has important advantages over Hoare logic in this context. We can provide mechanized, partially automated proofs for JAVA CARD as target language.

The paper presented two approaches to express security in DL. Though the second approach necessarily leads to longer proofs because of the two program copies, it has important advantages. With the use of (8) and instantiating h with any value that conforms present preconditions, the formula does not contain any existential quantifier, thus the metavariable mechanism is not used. This provides a higher degree of automation of proofs by eliminating a manual instantiation. More experience is needed to determine which approach, if any, is the better. Recent work [3] shows that the "single program property" provided by the second approach (7) is applicable to a variety of languages and program logics.

An open question is how this approach would scale up for more complex programs with several high and low variables. Each variable introduces a universal quantifier in both approaches, furthermore in the first approach each low variable introduces an additional existential quantifier. More experiments need to be done to determine how well the automatic proof search mechanism of the prover performs in the presence of several quantifiers.

To reduce the number of variables (and thus the number of quantifiers) the idea of abstract variables as "functions of the underlying program variables" proposed in [11] might be useful.

Automated static analyses have the advantage that they do not require programmer interaction. This is achieved by approximations in terms of accuracy, in favour of good compositionality properties. For example, a simple type system might insist that to prove while(b)p secure one must prove independently that b only depends on the low parts of the state, and that p is secure. Assuming such a rule is sound (it depends on the language and other properties of b) then it amounts to a simple but incomplete way to handle a loop. The KeY system is currently used "as-is". It can and should be further tuned and adapted to security analysis. Many of the benefits of a type-based approach might be obtained by the addition of proof rules akin to the compositional rules offered by such systems. Recently, a compositional proof system tailored to secure information flow was developed [9] that might guide the design of such rules. It allows precise analysis of semantic issues (e.g., characterization of the power of the attacker), but its target language is small and it is not implemented. We performed a first experiment on adding *taclets* which circumvent the need to prove termination of a loop in a case like the above. This was successful and the taclet was simple to add; by proving that the condition and the body of the loop is secure, we can conclude that the loop is secure independently of its termination behaviour. Thus, in such cases there is no need for induction.

The KeY system features additional modalities. As shown above, some of our formulas require the $[\cdot]$ modality. We intend to experiment on such formulas in the near future. Furthermore, modality $[\![\cdot]\!]$ ("throughout", modeled after "future" operators in temporal logic) has been implemented [5]. This makes it possible to specify and verify properties of intermediate states of terminating and non-terminating programs. We intend to experiment with scenarios that involve proving security and insecurity of JAVA CARD applications when a smart card is "ripped out" of the reader or terminal leading to unexpected termination.

Acknowledgements. We thank H. Mantel for valuable discussions and for suggesting the optimization embodied in (8). We thank G. Barthe and T. Rezk for comments. This work was partially supported by SSF and Vinnova.

References

1. Ádám Darvas, R. Hähnle, and D. Sands. A theorem proving approach to analysis of secure information flow. Technical Report 2004-01, Department of Computing Science, Chalmers University of Technology and Göteborg University, 2004.
2. W. Ahrendt, T. Baar, B. Beckert, R. Bubel, M. Giese, R. Hähnle, W. Menzel, W. Mostowski, A. Roth, S. Schlager, and P. H. Schmitt. The KeY tool. *Software and System Modeling*, 2004. Online First issue, to appear in print.
3. G. Barthe, P. R. D'Argenio, and T. Rezk. Secure information flow by self-composition. In *Proc. 17th IEEE Comp. Sec. Founds. Workshop*, 2004.
4. B. Beckert. A dynamic logic for the formal verification of Java Card programs. In *Java on Smart Cards: Programming and Security*, pages 6–24, 2001.
5. B. Beckert and W. Mostowski. A program logic for handling Java Card's transaction mechanism. In *Proc. FASE*, pages 246–260, April 2003.
6. E. S. Cohen. Information transmission in sequential programs. In *Foundations of Secure Computation*, pages 297–335. Academic Press, 1978.
7. D. E. Denning and P. J. Denning. Certification of programs for secure information flow. *Commun. ACM*, 20(7):504–513, July 1977.
8. D. L. Detlefs, G. Nelson, and J. B. Saxe. A theorem prover for program checking. Research report 178, Compaq SRC, 2002.
9. R. Giacobazzi and I. Mastroeni. Proving abstract non-interference. In *Conf. of the European Association for Computer Science Logic*, pages 280–294, 2004.
10. D. Harel, D. Kozen, and J. Tiuryn. *Dynamic Logic*. MIT Press, 2000.
11. R. Joshi and K. R. M. Leino. A semantic approach to secure information flow. *Science of Computer Programming*, 37(1–3):113–138, 2000.
12. J. Jürjens. UMLsec: Extending UML for secure systems development. In *Proc. UML*, pages 412–425, 2002.
13. A. C. Myers. JFlow: Practical mostly-static information flow control. In *Proc. POPL*, pages 228–241, Jan. 1999.
14. F. Pottier and V. Simonet. Information flow inference for ML. In *Proc. POPL*, pages 319–330, Jan. 2002.

15. F. Pottier and V. Simonet. Information flow inference for ML. *ACM Trans. on Progr. Langs. and Systems*, 25(1):117–158, Jan. 2003.
16. A. Sabelfeld and A. C. Myers. Language-based information-flow security. *IEEE J. Selected Areas in Communication*, 21(1), Jan. 2003.
17. A. Sabelfeld and D. Sands. A per model of secure information flow in sequential programs. *Higher-Order and Symbolic Computation*, 14(1):59–91, March 2001.
18. K. Stenzel. Verification of JavaCard programs. Technical report 2001-5, Institut für Informatik, Universität Augsburg, Germany, 2001.
19. D. Volpano and G. Smith. Eliminating covert flows with minimum typings. *Proc. IEEE Comp. Sec. Founds. Workshop*, pages 156–168, June 1997.

An Efficient Access Control Model for Mobile Ad-Hoc Communities

Sye Loong Keoh and Emil Lupu

Department of Computing, Imperial College, 180, Queen's Gate, London SW7 2AZ
{slk, e.c.lupu}@doc.ic.ac.uk

Abstract. Mobile ad-hoc networks support interactions and collaborations among autonomous devices by enabling users to share resources and provide services to each other, whether collaborations are for business or leisure purposes. It is therefore important to ensure that interactions are subject to authentication and access control in order to restrict access to only those resources and services that the user intends to share. Existing access control models that are based on membership certificates incur redundant verifications and therefore require significant computation. They are inefficient because devices have to repeatedly verify the requestor's certificates and check the authorisation policies for each service access request received. In this paper, we present an efficient access control model that combines a membership list with the role-based access control (RBAC) model. Each ad-hoc network has a coordinator that is responsible for maintaining the membership and broadcasting a signed membership list to all participants at regular intervals. The model authorises a service request if the requestor is listed in the membership list and its assigned role is authorised to perform the requested actions. Through experiments, we have observed the efficiency gains obtained through use of this model.

1 Introduction

The advancement of mobile technology has enabled the establishment of ad-hoc networks which can be formed anytime and anywhere without relying on the availability of a fixed network infrastructure. Ad-hoc networks support *interactions* and *collaborations* among autonomous devices to share resources and services. This type of network is particularly useful for military coalitions and disaster relief operations that require rapid establishment of network connectivity, as well as for business meetings or leisure purposes such as resource sharing.

Security is one of the main concerns in the establishment and management of ad-hoc networks in order to protect the device's resources from misuse and control access to its services. The lack of infrastructure support and *a priori* knowledge between devices introduce difficulties for authentication, membership management, and access control. Typically, a user joins an ad-hoc network because it needs to access resources and services that it does not have as well as to provide various services to others. Hence, users must be able to authenticate

D. Hutter and M. Ullmann (Eds.): SPC 2005, LNCS 3450, pp. 210–224, 2005.

each other in order to control access to their resources and services. Without authentication and access control, collaborations are difficult to establish because users typically do not *trust* any *strangers* to access their resources. However, the need for a device to authenticate each service request incurs redundancy in the verification of credentials. For example, whenever a device requests to join a network, all the existing members have to verify its credentials before they grant the admission permission. As a result, there is a need for an efficient access control model that can reduce redundant computations that will result in delays and consume *power* (a precious commodity for mobile devices).

In this paper, we consider an ad-hoc network as a *community* of autonomous devices that interact and collaborate with each other. Each community has a community specification called *doctrine* [7] that governs the admission of participants and defines a set of authorisation policies that specify their respective privileges. Users and services are represented as roles. Thus, roles are used to group users with the same rights and duties, and also act as a placeholder for common type of services. In the community, admission control is undertaken by a *coordinator* that is responsible for periodically broadcasting a membership list to all participants. The proposed access control model enables service providers to use the membership list and the doctrine to determine the requestor's eligibility to join the community and to decide whether permission can be granted to access the services. Through experiments (c.f. section 7), we observed that this model is more efficient than models relying solely on membership certificates.

In section 2, we present some related work, and outline some of the shortcomings of current access control models for mobile ad-hoc networks. Section 3 presents some background information, while section 4 presents an efficient approach to disseminate a community membership list. We introduce our access control model in section 5 and section 6 describes the implementation. This is followed by a description of an experiment setup and results in section 7. We conclude the paper and highlight future work in section 8.

2   Related Work

In infrastructure-based networks such as the Internet, the use of popular Public-key Infrastructure (PKI) standards such as membership certificates provides a scalable solution to address authentication and access control issues. Membership certificates are issued specifically to a particular user, so that the user only needs to present the certificate to the service provider and then authenticate itself in order to access the service. As a result, various studies [8, 16, 13] have attempted to adapt this solution to ad-hoc networking by setting up dedicated certification authorities (CAs) within the ad-hoc network itself. These authorities are responsible for issuing membership certificates to the participants and authentication is performed by checking these certificates. An approach proposed in [8] selects a group leader to handle the admission control in an ad-hoc group and the leader uses its own public key pair to issue membership certificates to the participants. This approach is not flexible because when the group leader leaves, all the certificates need to be renewed and the new group leader must re-issue membership certificates to all the participants. To mitigate this problem, the authors introduced the concept of *delegation*, so that delegated group leaders can also issue membership certificates to admit new users. In addition, these delegated leaders are encouraged to issue redundant certificates to existing group members. Consequently, a member could possibly possess more than one certificate issued by various group leaders in the network. This requires more storage for membership certificates, and more computations are needed to issue redundant certificates.

Other similar approaches that adopt threshold cryptography [16, 13] enable multiple mobile nodes in an ad-hoc network to act as CAs, and use a public-key pair for the entire network. The private-key of the network is split into n shares, where $n \geq 3t + 1$ and these key shares are then distributed to n mobile nodes *out-of-band*. Each of the mobile nodes is required to issue a partial certificate share to every new user who wishes to join the network. Thus, a new user has to gather $t + 1$ certificate shares and combine them to form a valid membership certificate. This approach is proposed in order to prevent the single point of failure. However, when $t + 1$ nodes that have a share of the private-key leave the network, these nodes could jointly issue a valid membership certificate. This issue can be mitigated by using proactive secret sharing [6], where key shares are updated periodically in order to prevent collusion, but this requires a great deal of effort and computations to update all the key shares at regular intervals. Furthermore, the additional message exchanges require significant additional power consumption.

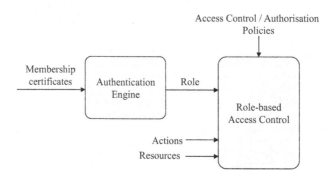

Fig. 1. An access control model that uses the membership certificates in conjunction with RBAC

Figure 1 shows a typical access control model of various approaches that use membership certificates in conjunction with RBAC [12, 3]. For each service request, the requestor must present a valid membership certificate in order to access a service. The authentication engine first authenticates the requestor. Secondly, it checks the membership certificate to determine the participant's role information, and lastly access is granted to perform the requested actions according to the role information and the authorisation policies.

Models based on the PKI standards exhibit three fundamental issues when deployed in mobile ad-hoc networks. First, they wastes devices' computational resources because for every access request, the service providers have to repeatedly authenticate and verify the membership certificates of the requestor, even if the requestor was previously authenticated. Caching methods can be used, but they introduce additional complexities such as determining the caching period as well as deciding which information can be safely cached. Since mobile devices typically have limited computational resources, this model is heavy weight and not efficient. Second, an ad-hoc network is transient in nature; this implies that certificates are valid only within the lifetime of the ad-hoc network. When the network is dissolved, the certificates become useless since they cannot be used in other ad-hoc networks. As a result, the use of certificates in this approach does not justify the effort of going through the certificate issuance process which is both expensive and laborious. Third, the group leaders or the certification authorities in the ad-hoc network have to periodically broadcast a certificate revocation list (CRL) to all participants, so that they know which participant's membership has been revoked. This also incurs additional computational costs because the authenticity of the CRL must be verified and revocation of certificates needs to be checked periodically as well.

Other solutions that use symmetric key cryptography as a shared group secret-key to prove participants' membership [15, 14, 2] are also less flexible. This is because it is not possible to differentiate one participant from another since all of them know the secret-key. This implies that they all must share the same access privileges if the access permission is granted solely based on the possession of a group secret-key.

3   Background

This section provides some background information in association with the proposed access control model.

3.1   The Community Specification, *Doctrine*

In [7], we have proposed a policy-based approach to establish ad-hoc communities. A community specification called *doctrine* defines the participants in terms of roles, the user-role assignment (URA) policies, the policies governing the behaviour of the participants and the overall constraints of the community. Bootstrapping an instance of an ad-hoc community requires a group of participants to agree to use the same doctrine and to designate a coordinator. The participants must also satisfy the URA policies in order to join the community. The authorisation and obligation policies specified in the doctrine define the access privileges and obligations of the respective roles in the community. The URA policies define the constraints on the attribute certificates that a user must possess in order to be assigned to the requested role in the community. These could be the user's role in an organisation, position in a company and membership etc. The doctrine also provides the flexibility to specify additional security requirements such as *separation-of-duty*, *cardinality* and *community establishment* constraints. These constraints define the conditions under which a community can be established as well as the conditions to admit a new user.

Typically, a doctrine is issued by an issuer and expressed in XML. It is signed by the issuer, thus ensuring its integrity, and the signature is encoded using XMLSignature [1].

In [7], we have discussed the evolution and management of communities, with emphasis on the community establishment protocols and the underlying trust assumptions. In essence, each community has a *coordinator* that is responsible for handling the admission requests, thus enforcing the URA policies and community constraints, as well as for periodically broadcasting the membership list to all participants. All participants maintain weak consistency of the membership list with the coordinator. This is efficient because broadcast is inexpensive especially in small ad-hoc communities where devices are in proximity of each other. The use of a coordinator is desirable in order to avoid redundant verifications (otherwise each participant would need to verify that all other participants satisfy the URA policies). However, this does introduce an issue of trust in the coordinator. Typically, communities comprise heterogeneous devices with varying computational capabilities ranging from laptops to PDAs, or low-powered sensors. The coordinator must therefore be chosen amongst the devices with the most processing capabilities, e.g., a laptop or PDA. As all the participants must have fulfilled the URA policies in order to join the community, we assume that they trust each other to act as the coordinator. In addition, participants can expect each other to behave according to the policies of the community, which are specified in the doctrine and known to all participants. Lastly, in order to prevent the single point of failure, a new coordinator can be selected when the current one becomes unavailable.

3.2   The TESLA Authenticated Broadcast

Conventional authenticated broadcast requires an asymmetric approach to generate digital signatures. However, TESLA [9] adds a single message authentication code (MAC) to a message for broadcast and achieves an asymmetric digital signature through clock synchronisation and delayed symmetric key disclosure. It therefore makes authentication less expensive. In TESLA authentication, the sender first chooses a random key K_N and generates a one-way key chain by repeatedly applying a one-way hash function H (such as SHA-1) on K_N in order to generate all other keys: $K_{N-1} = \text{H}[K_N]$, $K_{N-2} = \text{H}[K_{N-1}]$, ... In short, $K_i = \text{H}[K_{i+1}] = H^{N-i}[K_N]$. The receiver can therefore easily compute a key K_j from a key K_i provided that j < i using the equation $K_j = H^{i-j}[K_i]$. However, nobody can compute K_i given K_j because of the one-way property of H. A key is considered authentic provided that when the equation is applied, the computed value matches the previously authenticated key on the chain.

Time is divided into uniform time intervals and a key is assigned to each interval. The generated key chain is used in reverse order for the computation of the message's MAC in each time interval. In addition, the sender pre-determines a key disclosure schedule, δ in which it will disclose the key that was used to compute the MAC. For example, in time interval $(i + \delta)$, the sender reveals the key K_i. The key disclosure delay, δ must be greater than the round-trip time between the sender and receivers [9]. TESLA requires that the sender and the receivers are loosely time synchronised and each node knows an upper bound on the maximum synchronisation error [10]. This is essential for the receiver to ensure that the message received was computed using a key that has not yet been published. Further details on how to establish loose time synchronisation are discussed in [9].

When a receiver receives a message with a MAC, it must first verify that the key K_i used to compute the MAC has not been disclosed. This is necessary because an adversary could have forged the message if it already knows the disclosed key. Therefore, the security condition imposed in TESLA requires the MAC of the received message to be computed using a key that has not yet been revealed. If this is fulfilled, the message is buffered and the receiver waits for the sender to publish the key. Once the key K_i is published, the receiver authenticates the key and then verifies the MACs of the messages that are stored in the buffer.

4   Dissemination of the Membership List

The membership list is maintained by the coordinator and periodically distributed to all the participants in the community. Thus, all participants maintain weak consistency of the membership list with the coordinator. Typically, the list contains the mappings of all participants' public-keys to their corresponding roles in the community and a membership entry in the list is a tuple of ⟨*node address, node id, public-key, role assignments, time of admission, device capability*⟩. However, using asymmetric cryptography to provide authenticity and integrity of the membership list is expensive. In this section, we present a light-weight approach to disseminate the membership list to participants at regular intervals using the TESLA protocol.

4.1   Upon Bootstrapping of the Community

When a group of users have agreed to use a doctrine to bootstrap a community, the user who initiates the community is selected as the coordinator if it has adequate resources and computational capabilities. The coordinator broadcasts a signed ⟨REQUEST⟩ which includes its credentials and public-key as well as the doctrine to be used in order to bootstrap the community. The coordinator must then ensure that all the replying users satisfy the URA policies and that the community constraints are not violated.

As shown in Figure 2, once the community has been bootstrapped, the coordinator generates a set of TESLA parameters, $\langle K_0, \delta, T_{int}, \ell \rangle$ and broadcasts

---

Message 1: *The coordinator, co generates a keychain and TESLA parameters which include the duration of a time interval, T_{int} and the key disclosure schedule, δ. Subsequently, co broadcasts a signed message which contains the TESLA parameters and the membership list to all participants.*

co: $K_n \rightarrow \mathrm{H}[K_n] = K_{n-1} \rightarrow \dots \rightarrow \mathrm{H}[K_1] = K_0$
              $M_{co} = \langle \mathrm{MEMBERSHIP}, co, CID, TS, K_0, T_{int}, \delta, \ell, membership\ list \rangle$
co $\rightarrow$ *: $\langle M_{co}, \mathrm{Sign}(Priv_{co}, \mathrm{H}[M_{co}]) \rangle$

After T_{int} (1 interval)...

Message 2: *After an interval, co computes a MAC for the updated membership list and broadcasts it to all participants. At the same time, it reveals the secret MAC key according to the key disclosure schedule.*

co: $M_{co} = \langle \mathrm{MEMBERSHIP}, co, TS, CID, I_2, membership\ list, K_{1-\delta} \rangle$
co $\rightarrow$ *: $\langle M_{co}, \mathrm{MAC}(K_1, \mathrm{H}[M_{co}]) \rangle$

*TS = timestamp, CID = community id, ℓ = length of keychain

Fig. 2. The protocol to disseminate the TESLA parameters and the initial membership list

them to all the participants. K_0 is the last generated key in the keychain, δ is the key disclosure delay, T_{int} is the duration of a time interval, and ℓ is the length of the keychain. Together with these parameters, the coordinator includes the initial membership list and then signs them using its private-key. Each community has a community id, CID which is a pseudo-random number generated by the coordinator as an identifier for the community instance. The broadcast is also timestamped. Note that, a digital signature is used at this initial bootstrapping phase because all the participants do not know the TESLA parameters for the community. After a time interval, T_{int}, the coordinator broadcasts the membership list using TESLA. From this point onwards, the coordinator broadcasts the membership list at regular time intervals, i.e., the membership list is included in the key disclosure message according to δ. In addition, all participants must loosely synchonise their clocks with the coordinator's using the simple time synchronisation protocol [9].

Once participants have received the initial membership list, they verify it using the coordinator's public-key. At the same time, they store the TESLA parameters. Subsequent membership list updates are cached by the participants. When the corresponding secret-key, K_i (where i is the interval) is disclosed by the coordinator, the participants check the authenticity of the key and subsequently verify the MAC of the membership lists that are stored in their cache. If successful, they update their own local copy of the membership list.

4.2 When a User Joins or Leaves the Community

When a new user requests to join the community, the coordinator has to first check the URA policies and grant admission to the user if the community constraints are not violated. As illustrated in Figure 3, the coordinator sends a ⟨JOIN REPLY⟩ message to the admitted user. The message consists of the TESLA parameters, $\langle K_0, T_1, T_{int}, \delta, \ell \rangle$ and the membership list. T_1 is an additional parameter and denotes the initial time of interval 1. This enables the new user to compute the current interval with respect to the current time in order to determine the authenticity of a secret MAC key. In addition, the admitted user must loosely synchronise its clock with the coordinator.

Message 1: *The coordinator sends the TESLA parameters, the initial time of interval 1, T_1 and the membership list to the newly admitted user, u_0.*

co: $M_{co} = \langle \text{JOIN REPLY}, co, u_0, TS, CID, K_0, T_1, T_{int}, \delta, \ell,$
                   $membership\ list \rangle$
co → u_0: $\langle M_{co}, \text{Sign}(Priv_{co}, \text{H}[M_{co}]) \rangle$

Message 2: *After that, the coordinator broadcasts the membership list to all other participants. The membership list is signed using TESLA.*

co: $M_{co} = \langle \text{MEMBERSHIP}, co, TS, CID, I_i, membership\ list, K_{i-\delta} \rangle$
co → *: $\langle M_{co}, \text{MAC}(K_i, \text{H}[M_{co}]) \rangle$

Fig. 3. The protocol to disseminate the TESLA parameters to a newly admitted user

After that, the coordinator broadcasts the membership list to all participants and signs the membership list using TESLA. When a participant is detected/considered to have left the community, the coordinator has to update the membership list and broadcasts it to all using the same procedures.

4.3 When a New Coordinator Is Selected

It is possible that the coordinator moves out of range or become unavailable. Since all community participants have a copy of the membership list, they can check whether they are eligible to be the new coordinator. Amongst all the eligible participants, only one participant is selected. The choice is really arbitrary, however for implementation purposes, we usually use the participant with a high CPU capability device who is assigned the *lowest node id* in the membership list as the new coordinator (i.e., the oldest member of the community with a sufficiently powerful device). The new coordinator sends a ⟨RECONSTRUCTION REQUEST⟩ message to all participants. Participants would only respond if the new coordinator is listed in the local copy of their membership lists. This is to prevent malicious users from sending *fake* requests in order to take over the admission control in the community. Existing participants can then rejoin the community, and thus the community can be reconstructed.

Soon after the coordinator has gathered sufficient re-join replies and the community constraints have been satisfied, it generates a new key chain and then broadcasts a new set of TESLA parameters to all participants. The protocol is the same as the bootstrapping protocol as shown previously in section 4.1.

5   The Access Control Model

The access control model exploits the local copy of the membership list that each participant possesses in order to optimise the access control mechanism. Therefore, the service providers only need to check the membership list to determine whether the requestor is a valid member of the community, and do not need to repeatedly verify the requestor's credentials. We also use the RBAC model because the doctrine defines the participants in terms of roles. Hence, permissions are assigned to roles rather than individual identities.

As shown in Figure 4, the access control model consists of a *membership management component* and a *policy enforcement component*. Both of these components run on all users' devices. The *membership management component* is responsible for maintaining the membership list that the participant receives periodically from the coordinator, and verifiying the authenticity and integrity of the list received. In addition, it extracts the authorisation policies from the doctrine that the service providers must enforce and forwards them to various enforcement components. The *policy enforcement component* is responsible for enforcing authorisation policies. As shown in Figure 4, all the service requests must be signed by the requestor, they are intercepted and then the policy enforcement component checks whether permissions can be granted by performing the following:

– **Authenticate the requestor** - The policy enforcement component authenticates the requestor by verifying the signature of the service request. Since

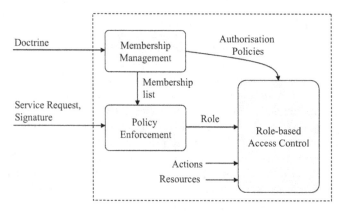

Fig. 4. The proposed access control model that uses the membership list instead of membership certificates

it has access to the membership list, it can obtain the public-key of the requestor in order to verify the signature.
- **Check the requestor's role assignment** - The policy enforcement component determines the role of the requestor by using the membership list.
- **Check permission** - Lastly, based on the role assigned to the requestor and the authorisation policies, a decision is made whether to permit the requested actions or not.

6 Implementation

To implement this model, we have extended the Java security architecture [4], as the default Java security manager and access controller provide a general implementation that can be used to incorporate our access control model.

Figure 5 shows the incorporation of our access control model with the Java security model. Typically, authorisation policies are enforced at the target object. Therefore, when a new community is established using a doctrine, the membership management component extracts the authorisation policies in the doctrine that the participant has to enforce and passes them to the policy enforcement component. Subsequently, the policy enforcement component translates these authorisation policies into Java authorisation policies that can be loaded by the Java security manager.

We have defined a new permission called *ServicePermission* that extends the *java.security.BasicPermission*. The *ServicePermission* represents a permission to access the services, (i.e., invocation of a method on the target object). In addition, the default Java principal-based authorisation only supports the use of X.509 certificates. Therefore, we have extended the *java.security.Principal* to define a new *AdHocPrincipal* that can be used to encapsulate the user's role information in an instance of an ad-hoc community.

Figure 6 shows the translation of an authorisation policy as defined in the doctrine to the corresponding Java authorisation policy. The policy specifies that

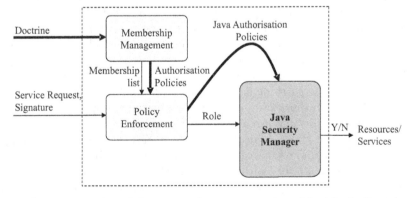

Fig. 5. The incorporation of the proposed access control model with the Java security model

the participants who are assigned to the role *Staff* of the community instance (*CID* = 183674) are granted permission to invoke the method *print* on any target object *Printer*. This policy is enforced by devices which are assigned to the role *Printer* in the community.

```
inst role Staff {
    inst auth+ printAuth {
        Target Printer;
        Action print(); }
}
```

This authorisation policy is being translated into the following Java policy

```
grant Principal AdHocPrincipal "183674-staff" {
    permission ServicePermission "print";
};
```

Fig. 6. This policy defines the rights of participants who are assigned to the role *Staff*. They are authorised to use the print service in the community

In essence, for each access request received, the policy enforcement component determines the requestor's role assignment using the membership list and then it encapsulates the role information in an instance of an *AdHocPrincipal*. Next, it invokes the Java security manager to check whether the requested action is permitted based on the authorisation policies and the role information.

7   Experiment Setup and Results

7.1   Experiments

We developed a proof-of-concept prototype scenario to dynamically establish ad-hoc communities comprising devices for various categories of users such as *Staff, Research Assistants, PhD students, Undergraduate Students*, and intelligent devices such as *Printers*, and *Projectors* in the Department. Users can dynamically bootstrap an ad-hoc community and then use the *print service* and *slide projector service*. These services are implemented using Java RMI invocations in which an authorised participant can invoke the methods *print()* and *project()* on the printer and projector objects.

A doctrine is created to define the roles of the participants as well as their privileges, i.e., the authorisation policies. For example, only *Staff, Research Assistants*, and *PhD students* are authorised to use the *Printer*. This is achieved by first look up the remote object of the *Print Service* and then invoking the *print()* method. The target object, *Printer* checks the eligibility of the requestor and the authorisation policies before it prints the submitted document.

In the experiment, we measured the performance of the policy enforcement component which includes the process of authenticating the requestor, determining its role assignments and invoking the Java security manager to check the authorisation policies. Performance was measured in terms of *transaction rate*, which is a value provided by *perf4J* [5], a tool for metering and monitoring the performance of Java applications. Essentially, *perf4J* measures the average elapsed time it takes to execute the demarked Java code-units, i.e., a transaction. These operations were executed on PII-350Mhz machines with 128Mb of RAM. We compared the performance of three access control models as follows:

- **Model A (a chain of attribute certificates)** — The requestor has to present a set of attribute certificates that are encoded using Simple Public-Key Infrastructure (SPKI)/Simple Distributed Security Infrastructure (SDSI) [11], the policy enforcement component finds a certificate chain and then checks the URA policies in order to determine the role to be assigned to the requestor. Subsequently, authorisation policies are checked based on the assigned role.
- **Model B (the role membership certificate, RMC)** — The coordinator or the group leader is responsible for issuing RMCs to all participants that satisfy the URA policies. An RMC is encoded using SPKI/SDSI as well. When the requestor requests to access a service, it presents the RMC for verifications. The policy enforcement component verifies the RMC before it grants permission to the requestor.
- **Model C (the membership list)** — All participants maintain weak consistency of a membership list with the coordinator. The requestor does not need to present any certificates, the policy enforcement component checks the membership list and the authorisation policies before granting permission to the requestor.

7.2   Results

Figure 7 illustrates the comparison of performance measurements of various access control models. For all models, the elapsed time decreases (i.e., the transaction rate increases) as invocations become more frequent, e.g., when there are 60 service invocations in a time period of 30 minutes (i.e., an invocation every 30 seconds), compared to 10 service invocations. Note that there is a significant performance gap between Model C and other two models; the transaction rate for Model C is at least two times higher for any number of invocations. More specifically, the average transaction rate for Model C is of 19 and 26 when the corresponding number of invocations are 30 and 60. These figures are approximately four times higher than Model B and nine times higher than Model A. In other words, when using the membership list, the *Print Service* can handle up to 25.6 invocations per second as compared to Model B that uses role membership certificates with less than 6.5 transactions per second.

Thus, the proposed model requires significantly less computations than the other two. Model A appears to require the most processing time because it has to perform complex operations to evaluate the certificate chain, while Model B also requires the execution of public-key cryptography which is expensive.

We have also measured the overhead incurred when verifying the authenticity of the membership list received at regular intervals. The average transaction rate

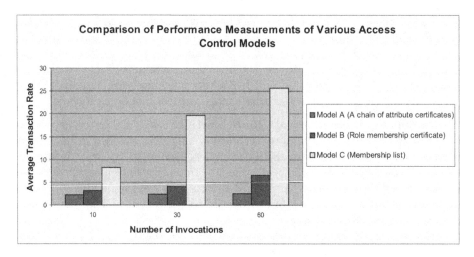

Fig. 7. Performance measurements of the access controller for various access control models

Table 1. The size of the membership messages, $|ML|$ = size of the membership list

Message Content	size
⟨MEMBERSHIP⟩ with TESLA parameters	2.133kB + $|ML|$
⟨MEMBERSHIP⟩ with a secret key	1.417kB + $|ML|$

to verify a TESLA key is ≈ 66.06, while the rate to authenticate the MAC of the membership list is approximately 56.63. A variant of Model C which uses digital signatures instead of TESLA can be used to provide authenticity of the membership list. In this alternative model, we observed that the average transaction rate for verifying digital signatures is ≈ 46.10. This indicates that for a powerful machine e.g., PII-350 Mhz, the use of digital signatures does not have major impact on the performance as it is slightly heavier than the use of TESLA.

In addition, as shown in Table 1, we have measured the approximate sizes of the ⟨MEMBERSHIP⟩ messages to convey TESLA parameters and to reveal a 128-bit secret-key.

8   Conclusion and Future Work

This paper has presented an access control model that requires significantly less computations than the other models, and is therefore more efficient. Although there is a small amount of overhead incurred by the periodic broadcast of membership list using TESLA, this overhead is not significant because TESLA uses symmetric-key cryptography and broadcast in wireless networks is inexpensive. In all other computations, our access control model does not involve additional cryptographic operations except for verifying the signature of the service requests. However, this verification is required in all models encountered. This indicates that the overhead imposed by the periodic broadcast of the community membership list is justifiable for small to medium-size communities as the performance gains in terms of computation are significant by comparison with models where service providers have to re-verify requestor's credentials or certificates for each access request. In the latter models, we have also not taken into account the required computations to verify the certificate revocation lists (CRLs).

However, a consequence of the use of TESLA is that only weak consistency between the membership of the community as perceived by different participants, can be guaranteed. Slight inconsistencies of the membership list among the participants are inevitable because when a user joins or leaves the community at time t_i of interval j, the coordinator needs to broadcast the updated membership list to all participants, but the membership list will only be authenticated and therefore valid after $\lambda = (\delta * T_{int}) + (ET_j - t_i)$, where δ is the key disclosure schedule, T_{int} is the duration of a time interval and ET_j is the end time of interval j. This means that the participants have to wait untill the secret-key used to sign the membership list is published by the coordinator in order to update their local membership list. As a result, for the time period λ, the membership lists of the coordinator and the newly admitted user are in sync, while the other participants still hold the previously authenticated membership list. This can be mitigated by minimising δ, as this also minimises the time period of having inconsistent membership lists, thereby shortening the waiting time for which the newly admitted user can start interacting with other participants. However, this implies that the membership list is broadcast more frequently thereby increasing the resources (computation and transmission power) required. An alternative approach to avoid this drawback is to use digital signatures to sign the membership list. However, a reasonably powerful device is required to perform digital signature verifications, while constrained devices might not be capable of continuously executing this operation.

One advantage of using the doctrine to express the underlying security policies is that all participants are aware of the admission criteria and their respective privileges in an ad-hoc community. Hence, this builds *trust* among the participants and ensures that the behaviour of the coordinator and the other participants can be monitored. Consequently, immediate actions can be taken if the coordinator is found to have misbehaved. However, we are still investigating the use of the presented model in conjunction with a monitoring framework that is able to detect policy violations.

Finally, the approach to broadcast a membership list is suitable for relatively small to medium mobile ad-hoc networks that typically interconnect devices in the vicinity of each other. The use of a membership list is two-fold, first it serves as an input to the policy enforcement component to determine the eligibility of the requestor before authorising its actions. Second, it can be used as the CRLs of the community. On this basis, the proposed access control model is efficient and effective although only weak consistency of the membership list can be maintained.

Acknowledgements

We gratefully acknowledge financial support from the EPSRC for AEDUS research grant GR/R95715/01 and from the EU FP6 TrustCOM Project No. 01945. In addition, we are indebted for many comments and suggestions to our colleagues Dr. Naranker Dulay and Prof. Morris Sloman.

References

1. M. Bartel, J. Boyer, B. Fox, B. LaMacchia, and E. Simon. XML-Signature Syntax and Processing, 2002.
2. J. Bray and C. Sturman. *Bluetooth Connect Without Cables*. Prentice Hall PTR, 2000.
3. D. Ferraiolo and R. Kuhn. Role-Based Access Controls. In *Proceedings of the 15th National Computer Security Conference*, pages 554 – 563. NIST, 1992.
4. L. Gong. *Inside Java 2 Platform Security Architecture, API Design and Implementation*. Addison-Wesley, 1999.
5. J. Hebert. The Perf4J API, 2002.
6. A. Herzberg, S. Jarecki, H. Krawczyk, and M. Yung. Proactive Secret Sharing Or: How to Cope with Perpetual Leakage. In *Proceedings of the 15th Annual International Cryptology Conference on Advances in Cryptology*, pages 339–352. Springer-Verlag, 1995.
7. S.L. Keoh, E. Lupu, and M. Sloman. *PEACE* : A Policy-based Establishment of Ad-hoc Communities. In *Proceedings of the 20th Annual Computer Security Applications Conference (ACSAC), Tucson, Arizona, USA*. IEEE Computer Society, December 2004.
8. S. Mäki, T. Aura, and M. Hietalahti. Robust Membership Management for Ad-hoc Groups. In *Proceedings of the 5th Nordic Workshop on Secure IT Systems (NORSEC 2000), Reykjavik, Iceland*, 2000.
9. A. Perrig, R. Canetti, J.D. Tygar, and D. Song. The Tesla Broadcast Authentication Protocol. *RSA Cryptobytes*, 2002.
10. A. Perrig, R. Szewczyk, V. Wen, D. E. Culler, and J. D. Tygar. SPINS: Security Protocols for Sensor Networks. In *Mobile Computing and Networking*, pages 189–199, 2001.
11. R.L. Rivest and B. Lampson. SDSI – A Simple Distributed Security Infrastructure. Presented at CRYPTO'96 Rumpsession, 1996.
12. R.S. Sandhu and E.J. Coyne. Role-Based Access Control Models. *IEEE Computer*, 29(8):38–47, 1996.
13. N. Saxena, G. Tsudik, and J.H. Yi. Admission Control in Peer-to-Peer: Design and Performance Evaluation. In *Proceedings of the First ACM Workshop on Security of Ad-hoc and Sensor Networks (SASN), Fairfax, Virginia, USA.*, October 2003.
14. F. Stajano. The Resurrecting Duckling – What Next? In *Proceedings of the 8th International Workshop on Security Protocols*, LCNS. Springer-Verlag, 2000.
15. F. Stajano and R.J. Anderson. The Resurrecting Duckling: Security Issues for Ad-hoc Wireless Networks. In *Proceedings of the 7th International Workshop on Security Protocols*, LCNS. Springer-Verlag, 1999.
16. L. Zhou and Z. J. Haas. Securing Ad-Hoc Networks. *IEEE Network Magazine*, 13(6), November/December 1999.

TrustAC: Trust-Based Access Control for Pervasive Devices*

Florina Almenárez, Andrés Marín, Celeste Campo, and R. Carlos García

Dept. Telematic Engineering, Carlos III University of Madrid
Avda. Universidad 30, 28911 Leganés (Madrid), Spain
{florina, amarin, celeste, cgr}@it.uc3m.es
http://www.it.uc3m.es/pervasive

Abstract. Alice first meets Bob in an entertainment shop, then, they
wish to share multimedia content, but Do they know what are trustworthy users? How do they share such information in a secure way? How do
they establish the permissions? Pervasive computing environments ori-
ginate this kind of scenario, users with their personal devices interacting
without need of wires, by forming ad-hoc networks. Such devices considered pervasive are having increasingly faster processors, larger memories
and wider communication capabilities, which allows certain autonomy
for collaborating and sharing resources. So, they require a suitable access
control in order to avoid unauthorised access, or disclosure/modification
of relevant information; in general, to protect the data that are usually
confidential and the resources. This paper presents a distributed solution
for access control, making use of the autonomy and cooperation capability of the devices, since in open dynamic environments is very difficult
to depend on central server. The access control is based on a pervasive
trust management model from which trust degrees are dynamically obtained. We present the TrustAC reference and functional model, as well
as a prototype implementation using XACML-compliant policies.

1   Introduction

Pervasive devices provide a user with the ability for receiving and gathering
information from anywhere, at anytime. They interact with other surrounding
devices offering services or sharing resources, that is, peer-to-peer applications,
for instance, a user with its personal digital agenda (PDA) arrives to the airport, the PDA interacts with information points, hotspots, automatic check-in
machine, etc., but How do we know that the available services are authentic?
How do we authorise the access to the services? How do we protect our device
from malicious users? Nowadays, pervasive devices can act as secure client, but
they cannot act as secure peers; therefore, they require a flexible mechanism
for access control to the services, so that the resources are protected. Theft or

---

* Thanks to UBISEC (IST STREP 506926) and EVERYWARE (MCyT N°2003-
08995-C02-01) projects.

D. Hutter and M. Ullmann (Eds.): SPC 2005, LNCS 3450, pp. 225–238, 2005.

loss of data stored on personal devices is the most significant threat. The access control is a security issue that grants specific access rights to the resources (information, services, network interfaces, and database, among other); it often includes authentication, for instance, in a PDA, when the user is authenticated by introducing a PIN code, this has full access.

Several access control schemes have been devised for multilevel secure military applications as Mandatory Access Control (MAC), for operating systems as Discretionary Access Control (DAC), and for enterprise environments as Role-Based Access Control (RBAC). On the other hand, some authorization infrastructures have been defined for Internet as X.509 Privilege Management Infrastructure (PMI) defined by ITU, Simple Public Key Infrastructure/Simple Distributed Security Infrastructure (SPKI/SDSI), Keynote and for Web Services as Secure Assertion Markup Language (SAML). Such access control systems and authorization infrastructures are reviewed in the next section.

Making an analysis of them, we could conclude that they present some drawbacks to be applied in dynamic open spaces where users are often unknown, ad-hoc interactions and pervasive devices having constrained capabilities, since they require negotiating on access control policies between autonomous domains, an administrator to manage the system in the presence of frequent changes, and sometimes definition of complex policies that are not interoperable each other. The infrastructures' security depend on a trusted third server (SOA, AAs, or in general, credential issuer authorities). Thus, we define an access control scheme based on trust called TrustAC, which is based on our pervasive trust management (PTM) model.

Our access control decisions are based on trust because in our scenarios (open and dynamic environments) the users are peers, there are no roles, pre-configured access control lists (ACLs), or previously deployed infrastructures. Likewise, the trust is subjective and changeable, each user stores his/her own trust values, without he/she depends on third parties to guarantee his/her security; therefore, at anytime we know the user's trustworthiness to grant or deny him/her the access to our resources. Each user is autonomous to establish his/her trust thresholds for granting access. This is supported by the underlying trust management model, PTM, which offers us trust values in a dynamic and automatic way, minimizing the user intervention. On the other hand, the use of numeric values allows establishing categories to control the access, instead of managing by individuals. The trust values can be used in several domains, by allowing the interoperability among them unlike roles or explicit permissions.

Section 2 reviews previous work in access control. PTM is briefly explained in the section 3. Then, section 4 introduces our new system for access control, TrustAC. In section 5, we present TrustAC specification including the reference and functional model. Next, section 6 briefly describes the new standard eXtensible Access Control Markup Language (XACML) since this standard are being used to implement TrustAC policies. In section 7, we give details of our first TrustAC prototype implementation by using the Sun's XACML implementation. Finally, we summarise and mention our future research directions in section 8.

2   Previous Work in Access Control

This section briefly explains the several access control schemes (MAC, DAC and RBAC), as well as the authorization infrastructures that have been defined (PMI, SPKI/SDSI, Keynote, and SAML).

- In MAC systems [1], every target receives a security label, which includes a classification, and every subject receives a clearance, which includes a classification list. The classification list specifies which type of classified target the subject is allowed to access. A typical hierarchical classification scheme is unmarked, unclassified, restricted, confidential, secret and top secret. A typical security policy designed to stop information leakage is 'read down and write up'. This specifies that a subject can read targets with a lower classification than his or her clearance and can write to targets with a higher classification.
- In DAC systems [1], the administrator can give users access rights to resources which hold these rights as Access Control Lists (ACLs). It is the most popular and well-known model.
- Role-based Control Access (RBAC) systems [2] define a number of roles to control the access. These roles typically represent organisational roles such as secretary, manager, employee, etc. In the authorization policy, each role is given a set of permissions, i.e. the ability to perform certain actions on certain targets. Each user is then assigned to one or more roles. When accessing a target, a user presents his or her role, and the target reads the policy to see if this role is permitted to perform this action.
- X.509 PMI complements Public Key Infrastructure (PKI) for authorization purposes [3]. It is the set of hardware, software, people, policies and procedures needed to create, manage, store, distribute and revoke Attribute Certificates (ACs) that are the primary data structure. Trust depends on the Source of Authority (SOA) which allocates privileges and access rights to trusted holders (end users or subordinate Attribute Authorities, AAs). X.509 PMI supports MAC by allowing subjects to be given a clearance AC, DAC by holding the access rights within the privilege attributes of AC issued to users, and RBAC by defining role-specification ACs that hold the permissions granted to each role, and role-assignment ACs that assign various roles to the users.
- SPKI/SDSI is composed by two mechanisms: Authorization management and control based on distributed delegation (SPKI) [4],[5] and a distributed local name system (SDSI) [6]. SPKI/SDSI introduces the concept of authorization certificate[7]. In the certificate the permissions are assigned to a public key, since all the principals (people, organization, software agent, etc.) are public keys, so that it allows authentication. Then, such public keys are mapped to a local name instead of global names. Local names are defined by two elements: the word "name" and the name identifier, for instance, A can define the B's name in its name space as A: (name B). In addition, there are extended names, which comprise one o more identifiers. Each principal can act like certification authority; therefore, a CA in SPKI/SDSI can

issue two certificate kinds, *name certificates* (formed by a four-element tuple) and *authorization certificates* (formed by a five-element tuple). A name certificate binds a local name to a public key, whose elements are: issuer (public key or hash), local name, subject (public key or composite name), and validity (initial and final date); this is equivalent to the tuple C = $(K; A; S; V)$. An authorization certificate grants an authorization to a principal, which includes: issuer, subject, label (authorization), delegation bit, and validity; this is equivalent to the tuple $C=(K; S; T; d; V)$. In SPKI/SDSI, the access control policies are represented by access control lists (ACLs) that are stored by the principal controlling the resource. Finally, SPKI/SDSI also includes certificate revocation lists (CRLs), which are made by the issuer.

– KeyNote is an approach for specifying and interpreting security policies, credentials ("assertions") y trust relations [8]. The framework includes actions, principals, policies, credentials and a verifier. Policies, trust relations, and credentials are defined in an own language. There is a special class of principal identified as POLICY, which is considered the trust root. This principal is authorised for performing any action and acting like a SOA (in PMI) or root CA (in PKI). Assertions are always positive, that is, they do not consider denying specific actions.

– Secure Assertion Markup Language (SAML) is a framework for exchanging authentication and authorization information adopted by OASIS in November 2002. SAML provides single sign-on (SSO), authorization services and distributed transactions [9]. It uses XML schema-based assertions for expressing the information; likewise, it defines a XML schema for defining a request/response protocol used to exchange assertions. There are three assertion kinds: authentication (affirm that the user has been authenticated), attribute (affirm that the user is associated with certain attribute and values), and authorization decision (response for an access request). These assertions are issued by SAML authorities, which can be authentication authority, attribute authorities and policy decision points (PDPs) in accordance with the assertions.

3   Pervasive Trust Management (PTM) Model

TrustAC defines access control policies based on trust degrees obtained from PTM [10]. Our model assumes devices with certain autonomy to manage its own security similar to Pretty Good Privacy (PGP) [11]. These devices act on behalf of a user, that is, a physical body such as persons, organizations, etc. If there are established trust relationships among users these would be used; but a device can also create its own trust relationships in ad-hoc mode. So, each user handles a protected list of trustworthy and untrustworthy users, the trust degree associated, behaviour's information, the public key and the public key's validity. It is important to store information about untrustworthy users because distrust is different from not to have any trust.

Trust relationships are expressed as a continuous function ranging from 0 to 1, being these values the extreme cases of complete distrust and complete trust respectively; in addition, we include intermediate states between the extremes, for instance, 0.5 would be used as ignorance value. We rely on fuzzy logic because it enables us more granularity than boolean logic. These relationships fulfil certain properties, such as: reflexive, non-symmetrical, conditionally transitive, and dynamic.

The trust relationships can be established in *direct* or *indirect* way. A direct trust relationship is given by previous knowledge of the user's nature or being unknown, we assign an initial trust degree according to certain rules. The indirect trust relationships are given by recommendations from other trusted third parties (TTPs). Recommendations are distributed using a pervasive recommendation protocol (PRP) among close users or using public key certificates. The trust degree is obtained making an average of all the recommendations weighted by the recommender's trust degree. We use the weighted average because is very simple, allows to distinguish among the sources, and obtains results that correspond well with intuitive human judgement.

Once the trust degree is obtained, this degree forms our *belief* similar to the Jøsang's model [12]. The believes are described as a set of fuzzy propositions, which express the ownership degree of a user to the set of trustworthy entities through a quantitative adverb, for example, *A believes that B is very trustworthy*; in this way, we create certain ranks. Nevertheless, the belief can change according to the user's behaviour along the time providing feedback about user's performance during the interaction. The interactions are *evidences* of the behaviour, which is measured taking into account the actions performed. Actions are classified in positive (right actions) and negative. However, we assume that all negative actions are not the same, for this reason we distinguish between wrong actions (bad actions that do not cause any damage or cause mild damages) and malicious actions (attacks). To calculate the value of the actions (V_a), each action has an associated weight applying fuzzy logic. Such weight is rewarded or penalized according to the past behaviour (both positive and negative) and the security level (m).

Thus, when a new action is performed, the trust degree is recalculated, increasing or decreasing it in accordance with the actual behaviour multiplied by a strictness factor. So, trust degrees are automatically calculated, minimizing human intervention.

These trust degrees are used for creating ranks or categories that are assigned the permissions, similar to RBAC. So, TrustAC also simplifies the access control management for large number of users because it allocates permissions to trust degrees rather than individuals, and there are generally fewer trust degrees than users. The permissions are defined through policies. Additionally, PTM allows dynamically to change a user from a category to another without explicit configuration.

4   Trust-Based Access Control

As mentioned above, Trust-Based Access Control (TrustAC) is a new management system of access control, which is based on trust degrees in order to protect resources. Trust degrees are automatically generated from our PTM model as well as the mapping between users and their trust degree, reducing the need of a centralized and manual administration. The use of numeric values allows to create categories and facilitates the mapping between different domains. Unlike to RBAC, it is not necessary an administrator for mapping roles on inter-domain relationships, creation of roles, assigning of users to those roles, creation of ACLs for each resource, or maintenance of information updated, etc.

TrustAC overcomes the limitations presented by RBAC in open and dynamic environments, since RBAC works well in close environments, with a definition of roles clearly established and an administrator for management; but, in open dynamic environments and peer-to-peer interactions, we cannot assume:

- the existence of roles predefined and the relations between them,
- a valid interpretation of roles accross all domains,
- that the user sets statically the association "user-role" when it is required,
- that the user updates the relationships when the conditions change,
- that the user updates the policies when the roles change,
- and, that the user always remains in the same environment and under the same conditions.

TrustAC is focused on open dynamic environments where there is neither a previously defined organizational hierarchy nor specific roles for each user. These environments are characterised by ad-hoc networks where interactions between unknown users and heterogeneous devices are frequent; therefore, we cannot have pre-configured ACLs. It can be also used in any device, for instance, pervasive devices with computation, communication and storage capabilities because these devices have a very restricted access control mechanism. In addition, it minimizes user intervention to manage the system. On the other hand, TrustAC takes into account the environment conditions (context) to define the access control policies, being very important for mobile users. It is dynamic along the time, since the trust evolves according to the user's behaviour. Finally, it guarantees the interoperability among several domains, by using fuzzy numeric values.

5   Trust-Based Access Control Specification

TrustAC specification is based on RBAC specification but we use trust degrees instead of roles as being the main difference. The specification includes a *Reference Model* defining sets of basic TrustAC elements and relationships among them, and a *Functional Model* defining the features required of the system.

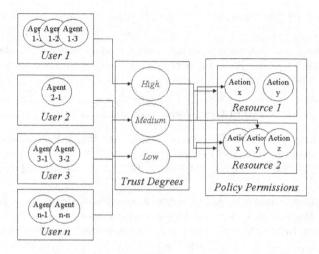

Fig. 1. TrustAC Reference Model

5.1   TrustAC Reference Model

The reference model includes two components: TrustAC elements and Hierarchical Trust Degree (HTD). TrustAC elements define a collection of elements, element sets, and relations in order to achieve a trust-based access control system. HTD is defined in terms of sets and subsets ordering mathematically the trust value range.

Elements. TrustAC includes sets of six basic data elements called *users(U)*, *agents(Au)*, *trust degree(TD)*, *resources(R)*, *actions(A)*, and *permissions(P)*.

A *user* is defined as a human being. Although the concept of a user can be extended to include organizations, departments, etc. An *agent* is a user process (program) executing on behalf of users within a machine, it can be an autonomous agent. A *trust degree* is a degree that represents the trustworthiness of the user; the trust degree granularity could be defined by the user, although it supports a default division. A *resource* is an entity that contains or receives information, for a system implementing TrustAC, the resources can be information containers such as files or directories in an operating system, and/or columns, rows, tables within a database management system; or can be system resources such as printers, disk space, ports, memory and CPU cycles. An *action* is an executable image of a program, which upon invocation executes some function for the agent, for example, within a file system, actions might include read, write, and execute; within a database management system, actions might include append, update, insert, delete; within a printer, actions might include print, manage printer, manage document. A *permission* is an approval to perform an action on one or more protected resources.

The relation between users and trust degrees (User Assignment, UA) is one-to-many relationship, that is, a user can be assigned to one trust degree, and a trust degree can be assigned to one or more users. UA is assigned automatically from PTM (section 3). The assignment of permissions to trust degrees (Permission Assignment, PA) provides great flexibility and granularity. These permissions are expressed through access control policies. In these policies the constraints on authorization, action execution, resources, and context can be defined. Thus, an agent can execute an action only if the action is authorized for the trust degree in which the agent belongs one (owner's trust degree). We summarize the above in the following formal description:

1. **Elements**: U, Au, TD, R, A, and P are users, user agents, trust degree, resources, actions and permissions.
2. **User's Trust Degree**: $UA \subseteq U \times TD$, a one-to-many relationship mapping a user to a trust degree.
3. **Assigned users to trust degree**: $assigned\_users(td) = \{u \in U \,|\, (u, td) \in UA\}$, the mapping of trust degree td onto a set of users.
4. **Agent belonging**: $U \times Au$, a one-to-many relationship mapping user processes to a user. An agent belongs to a single user and a user can have many agents. Agents initiate actions on resources.
5. **Permissions**: $P = 2^{(A \times R)}$, the set of permissions.
6. **Assigned permissions to trust degree**: $assigned\_permissions(td) = \{p \in P \,|\, (p, td) \in PA\}$, the mapping of trust degree td onto a set of permissions, $PA \subseteq P \times TD$, a many-to-many mapping permissions to trust degree assignment relationship.
7. **Actions associated with permissions**: $(p: P) \rightarrow ac \subseteq A$, the permission to action mapping, which gives the set of actions associated with permission p.
8. **Resources associated with permissions**: $(p: P) \rightarrow re \subseteq R$, the permission to resource mapping, which gives the set of resources associated with permission p.

Finally, there is an inheritance relation among trust degrees. Each trust degree inherits (contains) implicitly all the permissions from lower trust degrees, but these permissions could have different constraints. It is described formally:

– $HTD \subseteq TD \times TD$ is an inheritance relation $(\Rightarrow)$, $td1 \Rightarrow td2$ "privileges of trust degree 1 inherits privileges of trust degree 2"
   $\rightarrow assigned\_permissions(td2) \subseteq assigned\_permissions(td1)$.

5.2   TrustAC Functional Model

In this section we describe the functions that are required for creation and maintenance of our model in order to ensure enforcement of access control policies to the resources, as well as supporting system and review functions.

Administrative Functions (AFs)

– Creation and maintenance of element sets. A and R are predefined by the underlying system for which TrustAC is deployed. For example, a travel broker system may have predefined actions for accessing information, booking, updating, deletion, buying. The responsible of the system can create its own trust categories (although, these are defined by the TrustAC specification). The users are added to the system automatically in accordance with PTM, however the responsible of the system could add users manually. Administrative functions for U are *AddUser* and *DeleteUSer*, and for TD are *AddTrustDegree*, *UpdateTrustDegree* and *DeleteTrustdegree*.

- Creation and maintenance of relations (UA, PA). Functions to create and delete instances of UA relations (users and their trust degree) are generated automatically by PTM. For PA, the responsible of the system adds the required functions, such as *GrantPermission* and *RevokePermission*. These functions implement the descriptions 3, 6, 7, and 8 in section 5.1. The permissions are described as access control policies.

Supporting System Functions (SSFs). These functions are required for regulating the user's agent access to a service/resource. SSFs can be implemented as two components [1]: Policy Enforcement Point (PEP) that is a policy decision enforcer and Policy Decision Point (PDP) which is the making-decision.

PDP is responsible for processing and managing of all requests related to the access to the resources. PEP performs control and management routines and interacts with the PDP for decisions. PDP takes decisions regarding the information delivered by PEP and evaluating the access control policies. Once the decisions are taken, PDP gives them to the PEP.

Review Functions (RFs). When UA and PA instances have been created, it should be possible to view the contents of those relations from both the user and trust degree perspectives. For example, from the *PA* relationship, the responsible of the system should have the facility to view all the users assigned to a specific trust degree and the permissions associated with the same. These functions are defined as optional/advance functions. Examples of these functions are:

- *Agent_user(Au: agents)* = the user associated with agent Au
- *Assigned_users(td: trust degree)* = users with the trust degree td
- *Assigned_permissions(td: trust degree)* = permissions associated with the trust degree td
- *Actions_OnResource(r: resource)* = actions permitted on the resource r

6   eXtensible Access Control Markup Language (XACML)

XACML (eXtensible Access Control Markup Language) is an OASIS Standard that describes a language for defining access control policies and a request/response language both encoded in XML. The policy language is used to

---

[1] These components represent the architecture proposed by the IETF Policy-based Management Framework [13].

describe general access control requirements, and has standard extension points for defining functions, data types, combining logic, etc. The request/response language lets you form a query to ask whether or not a given action should be allowed, and interpret the result[14].

The typical setup is that someone wants to take some action on a resource. Then, the user performs a request to whatever actually protects that resource, which is called a Policy Enforcement Point (PEP). PEP receives it and forms an understandable request for Policy Decision Point (PDP) based on the requester's attribute, the resource in question, the action, and other information pertaining to the request (environment). The PEP will then send this request to PDP, which looks at the request, find some policy that applies to the request, and come up with an answer about whether access should be granted. The answer contains a decision (permit, deny, indeterminate or not applicable), some status information (for instance, why evaluation failed), and optionally one or more obligations (things that PEP is obligated to do before granting or denying access). It response is sent back to PEP, which can then allow or deny access to the requester.

A *Policy* has a *Target*, a *Rule-combining algorithm id*, a set of *Rules* and *Obligations*. A *Target* consists of *Subjects* (users), *Resources*, and *Actions* that must be met to apply to a given request. The *Rules* consist of a *Target*, an effect ("permit" or "deny"), and conditions which are the core logic. Such conditions can be restrictions about identities, roles, categories, or contextual information.

The *Request* consists of *Subjects, Resources, Actions* and *Environment* which have characteristics called *Attributes*. They are compared to attribute values in a policy to make the access decisions through two mechanisms: *AttributeDesignator* and *AttributeSelector*. An *AttributeDesignator* lets the policy specify attributes with a given name and type, and optionally an issuer as well. PDP looks for that value in the request or in any other location like an LDAP service, database, etc. *AttributeSelectors* enables a policy to look for attribute values through an XPath query.

Sun's XACML Implementation [15] is an access control policy evaluation engine written entirely in the Java programming language (J2SE). Using this implementation, we can build and customize PDPs, PEPs, or any related pieces that fit into the XACML framework.

7   TrustAC Implementation

TrustAC have been implemented as a XACML Profile by using the Sun's XACML API. We have chosen the XACML standard by its advantages such as: It uses a standard language (XML) which facilitates the interoperability between authorization systems, it can be used in any environment, it is distributed since a policy can be kept in arbitrary locations, and it is powerful as supporting a wide variety of data types, functions, and rules.

Although we have mentioned a distributed architecture, where each device manages its own security, so far for testing reasons, using the definitions in section 5.1, our test scenario consists of a server that protects R in a smart room, and mobile users (U) want use the services offered by the devices in that room, for instance, a multimedia projector, a printer, a PC, etc. (see Fig. 2). U can be both known and unknown. According to the trust model, our server obtains information about users and assigns trust degrees (UA). The user information is stored in a local repository, a MySQL database for PC and text file for pervasive devices. The users will access to the resources and perform A in accordance with the P established in the XACML-compliant policy documents, which contains conditions based on trust degrees and contextual information. So far, TrustAC has not been integrated with the operating system; therefore, we made a simple interface to request the service, then, the answer is shown on the screen.

In this scenario, the PDA, the PC (or server) and the laptop contain both PEP and PDP modules. Nevertheless, each client device contains a PEP module. Thus, two PDAs could communicate each other allowing access control. PEP and PDP are modules that can be located of different ways according to the scenario, simply identifying who (device) controls the resources and who are the clients.

When there are servers controlling the access to other services, we could combine trust degrees with roles, for instance, in home environments or organizations where there are roles well defined, if the access control is performed by a gateway (central server), then it could use roles mixed with trust degree, mainly for temporary users (visitors) like friends, external workers, etc., since only trust degrees would not be enough. In this point, it is very important to clarify that TrustAC is designed for autonomous and constrained devices, which interacts in open dynamic spaces, therefore, such devices require a protection mechanism that be simple and efficient for minimizing as much as possible the manual management.

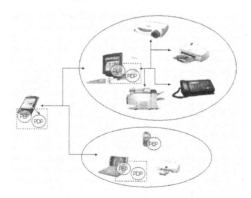

Fig. 2. Access Control Scenario

We have built our own PDP and PEP modules for implementing XACML-based TrustAC in two distinct ways either the PEP or the PDP searches for the trust degree associated to the user. First, the search is made by the PEP before making the request, after that the PEP will form the request with the user's trust degree, the resource and the action. The PDP contains policies based on the trust degree and context information as *SubjectAttributeDesignator* and *EnvironmentAttributeDesignator*. With this implementation way, changes in the Sun XACML implementation are not required.

We have also developed a new class that extends a XACML class called (*AttributeFinder*) for searching the trust degree (in our repository) which is a *SubjectAttributeDesignator*. Then, PEP sends the request to PDP with the user's identifier, the resource and the action. PDP contains policies whose rules are conditioned by the trust degree and specifying the actions permitted and denied. With these rules, PDP evaluates whether the condition is true. This implementation is more adequate than the first because it can be integrated easily in the XACML implementation as being more standard since the attributes used in the request are not changed.

7.1   XACML-Based TrustAC Policies

Sun XACML implementation 1.1 contains a sample class that shows how to build and generate a simple XACML Policy (*SamplePolicyBuilder*), but it does not provide a graphic tool (GUI) for generating these policies. So, we are developing a graphic tool oriented to final users (see Fig. 3) by using Java, called *Policy-Creator*. This tool helps users to build their own XACML policy documents in a friendly and easy way.

Fig. 3. PolicyCreator GUI

The policies are generated according to the second implementation mentioned above. Such policies establish the P. The rules are conditioned by the degrees of trust together with other conditions, for example, related to the environment, for instance the time as is shown in the Fig. 3. This information is put on the *constraints* field. Some functions used for the conditions are given through mathematics operators, for instance, conditions for the time can be expressed as: *string-one-and-only* (=), *:time-less-than-or-equal* (≤), *time-greater-than-or-equal* (≥). Another predefined functions can be inserted from the menu. Finally, obligations can be added in the *obligations* field.

The policy documents can be edited and customized by the user at will. Our aim is to develop a generic and flexible tool in order to be used for any profile such as TrustAC, RBAC, ACL, etc. Therefore, we need to extend this prototype implementation. Besides, different policy documents referencing each other must be considered.

8   Conclusion

We have presented TrustAC as a solution for access control in pervasive devices within open dynamic spaces. Our objective is to automate management tasks as much as possible in order to reduce the need of a centralized and manual administration. Nowadays, the only disadvantage to implement TrustAC is the lack of a standard distributed trust model that allows us to get trust values for each user. In this paper, we have used the results on our previous work on PTM, for trust computation and to generate the access control policies. TrustAC like RBAC simplifies the access control management for large number of users. In addition, TrustAC does not require any previously deployed infrastructure, it can be implemented in any device with computation, communication and storage capabilities, it takes into account important aspects for mobile users such as the context, and different domains can interoperate easily.

An initial implementation has been developed by using the new standard XACML, besides a graphic tool for helping to generate policy documents. The main advantage of XACML is to enable the interoperability between several applications and the reuse of the policies. In addition, we have a prototype implementation on Personal Java for a Pocket PC, but we are improving this implementation, by using an XML parser smaller, for instance, kxml. In addition, we are going to integrate our solution with the operating system in order to can be used by every application.

We are thinking to use an architecture more complex with PEPs, PDPs and policy repositories distributed and that can be supported by any device. Our goal is that in open dynamic spaces the security can be managed by own users as providing them required tools for that.

Acknowledgment

This work is being developed within the Pervasive Computing Laboratory Group (PerLab) of the Carlos III University of Madrid. The authors would like to thank Seth Proctor from Sun Microsystems for his support.

References

1. Barkley, J.: Security in Open System. Technical report, National Institute of Standards and Technology (NIST) (1994)
2. Ferraiolo, D., Cugini, J., Jun, D.: Role based access control (RBAC). National Institute of Standards and Technology (NIST). http://csrc.nist.gov/rbac/ (1992)
3. Farrell, S., Housley, R.: An internet attribute certificate profile for authorization. (IETF RFC 3281). http://www.ietf.org/rfc/rfc3281.txt (2002)
4. Ellison, C.: SPKI Requirements. Technical Report RFC 2692, IETF Network Working Group (1999)
5. Ellison, C., Frantz, B., Lampson, B., Rivest, R., Thomas, B., Ylonen, T.: SPKI Certificate theory. Technical Report RFC 2693, IETF Network Working Group (1999)
6. Rivest, R., Lampson, B.: SDSI - a simple distributed security infrastructure. Presented at CRYPTO'96 Rumpsession (1996)
7. Ellison, C.: SPKI/SDSI certificates. http://world.std.com/ cme/html/spki.html (2004)
8. Blaze, M., Feigenbaum, J., Ioannidis, J., Keromytis, A.D.: The KeyNote trust management system. Internet Request for Comment RFC 2704, Internet Engineering Task Force (IETF) (1999)
9. OASIS: Security Assertion Markup Language (SAML). http://www.saml.org, http://www.oasis-open.org/committees/security (2002)
10. Almenßrez, F., Marfn, A., Campo, C., Garcfa, C.: PTM: A Pervasive Trust Management Model for Dynamic Open Environments. In: First Workshop on Pervasive Security, Privacy and Trust PSPT'04 in conjunction with Mobiquitous 2004. (2004)
11. Zimmermann, P.: The Official PGP User's Guide. MIT Press, Cambridge, MA, USA (1995)
12. Jøsang, A.: An algebra for assessing trust in certification chains. In: Network and Distributed Systems Security (NDSS'99) Symposium, The Internet Society. (1999)
13. Yavatkar, R., Pendarakis, D., Guerin, R.: A framework for policy-based admission control. Internet Request for Comment RFC 2753, Internet Engineering Task Force (IETF) (2000)
14. S.Godik, (ed.), T.M.: extensible access control markup language (XACML). OASIS eXtensible Access Control Markup Language TC (2003)
15. Proctor, S.: Sun's XACML implementation. Sun Microsystems Laboratories. http://sunxacml.sourceforge.net/ (2003)
16. Anderson, A.: XACML profile for role based access control (RBAC), version 2.0. http://www.oasis-open.org/committees/download.php/6806/wd-xacml-rbac-profile-02.1.pdf (2004)
17. Ferraiolo, D., Cugini, J., Kuhn, R.: Role based access control (RBAC): Features and motivations. In: Annual Computer Security Applications Conference, IEEE Computer Society Press (1995)
18. Curphey, M., Endler, D., Hau, W., Taylor, S., Smith, T., Russell, A., McKenna, G., Parke, R., McLaughlin, K.: A guide to building secure web applications. Technical report, The Open Web Application Security Project (2002)

Author Index

Lecture Notes in Computer Science

For information about Vols. 1–3346

please contact your bookseller or Springer